"HAZARDOUS WORK"

An account of the decorations and commendations awarded to members of the Home Guard in recognition of acts of gallantry performed on duty 1940-1944.

by

Lieutenant-Colonel J. D. SAINSBURY, T.D.

1985

First published in 1985 by Hart Books, Welwyn
©Copyright J. D. Sainsbury 1985

British Library Cataloguing in Publication Data
Sainsbury, John David

"Hazardous Work": an account of the decorations and commendations
awarded to members of the Home Guard in recognition of acts of gallantry
performed on duty 1940-1944.
1. Great Britain. *Army, Home Guard*—Medals, badges, decorations, etc.
2. World War, 1939-1945—Great Britain
I. Title

940.54'6   D760.H6

ISBN 0 948527 00 5

Printed in England by
Staples Printers Rochester Limited
at The Stanhope Press.

CONTENTS

To all those who served King and Country in the Home Guard and whose gallantry, devotion to duty and self sacrifice received no official recognition. Those whose awards are recorded here are their worthy representatives.

PREFACE AND ACKNOWLEDGEMENTS

This book springs from a chance encounter with the name of Volunteer Glynn Jones, M.M. in a card index at the Ministry of Defence. A Home Guard Military Medal seemed worth following up, as indeed it was, for it led to well over a hundred other awards to the Home Guard and indicated, at a time when the television serial "Dad's Army" was at the height of its popularity, that were was more to the Home Guard than endless comedy, however important the good times were to those who still remember them. It would hardly occur to those of us observing the Home Guard with forty years of hindsight (and a good deal of ignorance) that they ever engaged in "hazardous work"—as the citations for their awards described it. Yet it is amply clear that they did, and that a more objective record of their devotion to duty, sacrifice and achievement is long overdue—not just a record of honours and awards but a proper account of their contribution to the common cause. In the absence of such a history I can only hope that this spotlight on those who were decorated for gallantry while on duty will serve partly to redress the balance. It is my own observation that recipients of decorations are the first to minimise their own achievements and point to others whose bravery was recognised by their comrades but never by the honours system. There were without doubt hundreds of other instances of gallantry on duty with the Home Guard, most of which are now forgotten for ever—hence the dedication opposite.

Research for this account has extended over many years and would have been impossible without the patience and willing co-operation of the individuals and organisations listed below:

Central Chancery of the Orders of Knighthood
Ceremonial Branch, Management and Personnel Office
Ministry of Defence—Military Secretary's Department,
    Army Medal Office and Central Library
Public Record Office
Imperial War Museum—Department of Printed Books and Department of
    Photographs
Guildhall Library, City of London
Bank of England—Staff and Reference Libraries
The Controller of Her Majesty's Stationery Office, by whose kind per-
    mission appear extracts from papers in the Public Record Office
Major P. E. Abbott, Major H. H. Barnsley, Mrs E. R. Gardner, L.V.O.,
O.B.E., Major D. V. Henderson, G.M., Miss J. Large, D. B. Nash, Esq.,
Major R. D. Owen, C. Potts, Esq., M.B.E., Lt.-Col. A. J. Robertson,
Brigadier J. S. Ryder, Major J. M. A. Tamplin, T.D.

I would also like to extend my thanks to the librarians and staff of the many Local Authority libraries with which I have corresponded; to the members of the and Medals Research Society who replied to my appeal for help in the Society's Journal; and to Melanie Crick who typed the manuscript.

The opinions expressed occasionally in this work are my own. The errors and omissions, which I hope will prove to be few, are also mine. The likelihood of a second edition in which corrections can be made is very remote but through the good offices of the Editor of the Journal of the Orders and Medals Research Society I shall hope to keep at least a proportion of readers informed if new information comes to light or it proves necessary to amend the present text.

Digswell   J. D. SAINSBURY
Welwyn,
Hertfordshire
June 1985

BIBLIOGRAPHY

Home Guard—General
GRAVES, C. *The Home Guard of Britain* London, Hutchinson and Co. Ltd., 1943
LONGMATE, N. R. *The Real Dad's Army—The Story of the Home Guard* London, Arrow Books Ltd., 1974
Ministry of Information *The Home Guard of Britain* London, [? H.M.S.O.] n.d. [1943] (Imperial War Museum)
Regulations for the Home Guard London, War Office, 1942
Home Guard List London, War Office, 1941-1944
THOMAS, C. *Cloth Insignia of the L.D.V. and the Home Guard* Military Historical Society Bulletin, Volume XIX, Nos. 72 and 73—May and August 1968 and Volume XXXV, No. 138—November 1984
Home Guard Information Circulars (Nos 1-57) London, War Office, 1941-44

Home Guard—Unit histories referred to in the text and in the list of awards
BARCLAY, E. D. *The History of the 45th Warwickshire (Birmingham) Battalion, Home Guard* Birmingham, James Cond, n.d. [1945]
FINCH, P. *Warmen Courageous—The Story of the Essex Home Guard* Southend, J. H. Burrows and Sons Ltd., 1952
HAYMAN, P. M. C. *A Short History of the Local Defence Volunteers and Home Guard in the County of Gloucester* Cheltenham, n.d. [1948]
LIDSTONE, G. H. (Ed.) *On Guard—A History of the 10th (Torbay) Battalion, Devonshire Home Guard* Torquay, Battalion Publication Committee (printed Torquay Times), 1945
MACKAY, E. A. *The History of the Wiltshire Home Guard* Wiltshire Territorial Army Association, 1946
WILTSHER, H. J. *To The Ever Faithful—Being the History of the 1st (Loyal City of Exeter) Battalion, Devon Home Guard 1940-1945* Exeter, n.d. [?1946]
Record of the Birmingham City Transport Home Guard May 1940—December 1944 Birmingham, Buckler and Webb, n.d. [1945]
The 29th Warwickshire (Birmingham) Battalion, Home Guard May 1940—December 1945
Seven Battalions—The Story of London Transport's Home Guard 1940—1946 London, L.P.T.B., 1947

Honours and Awards
ABBOTT, P. E. and TAMPLIN, J. M. A. *British Gallantry Awards* London, Nimrod Dix and Co., 1981

HENDERSON, D. V. *Dragons can be defeated—A complete Record of the George Medal's Progress from 1940 to 1983* London, Spink and Son Ltd., 1984

SAINSBURY, J. D. *"For Gallantry in the Performance of Military Duty"* London, Samson Books Ltd., 1978

Committee on the Grant of Honours, Decorations and Medals *White Papers—Cmd.6833 and Cmd.7035* London, H.M.S.O., 1946 and 1947

Campaign Stars and Commemorative Medals Instituted for the 1939-45 War (W.O. Code No 1911) London, War Office, 1953

Pamphlet on Military Honours and Awards (W. O. Code No 10414) London, War Office, 1953

Statutes of the Most Excellent Order of the British Empire [London, Central Chancery of the Orders of Knighthood] 1957

PART ONE

HISTORICAL BACKGROUND TO THE LOCAL DEFENCE VOLUNTEERS AND THE HOME GUARD

Formation of the Local Defence Volunteers, May 1940

The Home Guard was, in effect, raised overnight. After only three days of discussion and planning at the War Office and at G.H.Q. Home Forces, the Secretary of State for War broadcast an appeal for volunteers on the evening of 14th May 1940. Even as the broadcast continued the first volunteers arrived at their local police stations to enroll and for the next two days harassed desk sergeants recorded names. Lords-Lieutenant of counties were confirmed in their age-old responsibilities for raising forces in emergency by a telegram from the Secretary of State and Area Commanders of Home Forces were charged with bringing in the detailed arrangements. The principles followed seem to have been similar throughout England, Scotland and Wales. (For the special position of Northern Ireland see page 3). Counties were divided into areas of suitable size known initially as 'zones'. Zone commanders' appointments were approved by Army Commanders-in-Chief and a delegated process of selection and appointment of battalion, company and platoon commanders ensued. By the end of May 400,000 men had been enrolled and the organisation was taking shape. The title of the force in these early days followed that used in the Secretary of State's broadcast—"Local Defence Volunteers". Reduced to the initial letters 'L.D.V.' the title was hastily printed under local arrangements on arm bands, known officially as 'brassards', and these constituted the only uniform of the force until the promised denim overalls and khaki field service caps arrived, sometimes many weeks after formation.

Title changed to Home Guard; command and discipline; ranks

Constitutionally the force existed under the Defence (Local Defence Volunteers) Regulations passed on 17th May 1940. On 31st July 1940 a further regulation, instigated by the Prime Minister, changed the title to "Home Guard". Although for the first nine months of its existence the Home Guard was recognised as part of the Armed Forces of the Crown, no arrangements were made for the commissioning of officers or for conferring and delegating powers of command and discipline. As a result no appointment in the Home Guard was legally recognised as higher than private in the Regular forces (with implications as far as awards for gallantry and distinguished service are concerned—see pages 7 to 10). The agreed appointments and badges of rank were published in A.C.I. 924 of August 1940, as shown on page 2.

1

Home Guard Appointment	*Equivalent Army Rank*
Zone Commander	Brigadier/Colonel
Group Commander	Colonel
Battalion Commander	Lieutenant-Colonel
Company Commander	Major
Platoon Commander	Captain/Lieutenant/2nd Lieutenant
Section Commander	Sergeant
Squad Commander	Corporal/Lance-Corporal
Volunteer	Private

It was not long before it was realised that the system of 'appointed' ranks was unsatisfactory and on 6th November 1940 it was announced in the House of Commons that steps were being taken to place the Home Guard on a similar footing to the Regular forces, i.e. with officers holding the King's Commission and with warrant- and non-commissioned officers. Despite this early recognition of the need for change, it was not until 12th February 1941 that the Home Guard Officers' Commissions Order was passed, with retrospective effect to 1st February 1941. Commissions in the Home Guard were notified in Command Home Guard Orders rather than in the *London Gazette*. The *Home Guard List,* published at intervals between September 1941 and October 1944, shows, in a format similar to the *Army List,* the seniority of Home Guard officers and their allocation to battalions, together with zone/sector staffs, etc. From February 1941 officers and men were known by orthodox army ranks with the exception of privates, who were styled 'volunteer'. This honourable title was dropped in favour of 'private' in the spring of 1942 when powers were taken to direct enrolment into the Home Guard and the force lost its exclusively volunteer character.

Administrative support from T.A. Associations

From the earliest days zone organisers had the support of their county Territorial Army Associations in administrative matters and the Associations gradually increased their involvement, without, of course, being concerned with matters of command or training. The Associations were ideally fitted for this task, given their experience in providing similar services for the Territorial Army since its inception in 1908 and for the Volunteer Force (the successors to the Volunteer Training Corps and the Great War equivalent of the Home Guard) between 1916 and 1919. Relations with counties were further cemented early in August 1940 when Home Guard battalions were affiliated to their local Territorial battalions and authorised to wear their cap badges. (The multiplicity of cap badges within the London Regiment, T.A. was overcome by instructing all City of London Home Guard battalions to wear the badge of the Royal Fusiliers and the County of London battalions that of the King's Royal Rifle Corps.) The armlets issued in the early months were withdrawn when printed "Home Guard" shoulder titles were issued. These were worn in conjunction with a standard rectangular printed flash giving the city or county abbreviation and another showing the battalion number. (For a full list of the abbreviated designations see bibliography-*Thomas.*)

The Ulster Home Guard

While the Home Guard in England, Scotland and Wales were able to rely on county Territorial Army Associations for a range of essential administrative services, any similar force raised in Northern Ireland would not have been able to do so, for the Territorial Army did not extend to the Province. It was thus necessary to identify another organisation to provide equivalent services and it was judged that this could best be done by the Ulster Special Constabulary. Some ten days after the Defence (Local Defence Volunteers) Regulations took effect in the rest of the United Kingdom a Northern Ireland Ministry of Home Affairs Order authorised the establishment of the Local Defence Volunteers Section of the Ulster Special Constabulary. The status of the Ulster Local Defence Volunteers, which did not adopt the title "Home Guard" until early 1942, was thus technically that of policemen, rather than members of the Armed Forces. All training was carried out by the Army, however, and the force was, as elsewhere in the United Kingdom, fully integrated in defence plans and would have come under military command on call-out. Accomodation and administrative support for the force were provided through the Ministry of Home Affairs, which was also responsible for quartermaster services.

Strengths and ceilings; early operational role

The overall strength of the Home Guard increased throughout the early months to a figure of about 1,700,000 before the end of 1940, a force three times the size originally envisaged. A peak of 1,793,000 was reached in March 1943. Units were rigorously subject to manpower ceilings and the total strength changed little from its peak to stand-down in late 1944. The back-bone of the force was what came to be known as the 'General Service' battalion. This Home Guard equivalent to the infantry battalion was generally around 1000 strong—sometimes considerably more—and was principally armed with rifles and section light automatic weapons. As supplies became available heavier weapons were issued (notably the Northover grenade projector, the 29-mm spigot mortar and the medium machine gun). These were generally grouped in heavy weapons platoons in an organisation akin to that of the infantry battalion's support company. Signals and medical platoons were an important feature of the Home Guard company, rather than battalion, reflecting the often wide-spread areas of battalion responsibility.

The operational role of the Home Guard was the subject of a great deal of argument, official and unofficial, throughout its existence. The higher military authorities, mainly the War Office and G.H.Q. Home Forces, were determined that it should remain a static, local force. In the early months, marked as they were by lack of arms and training, patrolling and minor static guards were as much as could reasonably be expected from the force, which could barely be said to have been incorporated in defence plans. During 1941 the situation changed as better organisation, training and arms began to make themselves felt. Home Guard battalions were included in the overall static defence scheme, which was based on 'defended localities', each incorporating one or two 'keeps' (smaller, heavily defended areas). Superimposed upon the static defence were mobile formations, exclusively Regular, who would provide containing and counter-

3

attack forces once the main thrusts of any invasion had been identified. The key function of locating and identifying enemy movements fell largely upon the Home Guard because of their widespread coverage of the country and continued to be written into their operation orders as these evolved during subsequent years. The static role of the Home Guard was confirmed, too, as the war progressed. The Home Guard was never allotted (indeed it is doubtful if it ever sought) a truely 'mobile' role, for this would have depended upon armour, artillery and transport. Mobility in the Home Guard was provided largely by bicycles, with civilian cars, vans and lorries transporting or towing the heavy weapons. But this mobility was restricted to authorised mobile reserve companies intended for purely local reinforcement. The Home Guard also provided the 'cover' for the Auxiliary Units formed in coastal areas as an embryo resistance movement.

Relationship with the Civil Defence Services

At an early stage it was recognised that the Home Guard could be of great value in assisting the Civil Defence authorities in the aftermath of air raids. As experience of the 'Blitz' grew, units, even without orders, arranged to man their headquarters overnight and placed themselves at the disposal of local Civil Defence controllers. These informal arrangements were quickly codified and formed part of operational instructions. They were published, though some time after the main weight of the enemy bombing attack, in *Home Guard Regulations, 1942* as follows:

"The principle tasks on which the Home Guard is likely to be employed are:

(a) *Before invasion*

   i-ii.   . . .

   iii.   Assistance to Civil Defence Authorities, both during normal times in routine duties and during and after heavy raiding. (All such assistance will be carried out as an operational duty and members of the Home Guard will act under their own commanders.)

(b) *During invasion*

   i-viii. . . ."

The Home Guard's role in support of the Civil Defence authorities continued, even though the threat of large scale enemy bombing had been almost eliminated by the spring of 1944. It was as well, however, that the force was not released from the commitment, for with the beginning of the flying bomb attacks Home Guard units in the south-east of England were once more turning their hand to rescue work and to the guarding of damaged premises until the over-stretched police could spare manpower.

4

Special units formed within the major public services

Shortly after the formation of the Home Guard it became apparent that on 'call-out' (i.e. in the event of invasion) there would be a conflict between the Home Guard duties and the civilian responsibilities of employees of the major public undertakings, particularly the railways and the Post Office. The conflict was resolved by forming units based on the regional organisation of e.g. the railway companies, the Post Office and the London Passenger Transport Board. These units were assigned mobilisation roles which reflected their vital part in nationwide communications and allowed for differing call-out dates and for them to continue in uniform the manning of railways and the maintenance of telephone communications after invasion.

Factory units

In the early days factory units were considered to have a prime role in defence of their own factories but this was quite quickly abandoned in favour of integration within sector defence schemes. Units raised in Ministry of Aircraft Production factories which incorporated their own airfields were an exception to this general rule and the strength, equipment and efficiency of these units grew to such an extent that they were able in mid-1942 to take over the whole of the ground defence of these airfields and much of the close defence of the factories against air attack. (Lease-lend Lewis and Marlin guns had been issued for anti-aircraft use at these factories in the autumn of 1940.)

Coast defence; anti-aircraft defence; motor transport

Specialised units, as opposed to specialist platoons or teams within units, were generally confined to coast and anti-aircraft artillery and transport. Coast defence, traditionally a role for volunteer forces, was undertaken by Home Guard sub-units attached to Regular coast defence installations. The first Home Guard anti-aircraft battery was raised in April 1942 and by mid-1944 a useful number of Regular anti-aircraft units had handed their responsibilities over to Home Guard batteries and troops, who manned 3.7-in and 4.5-in guns, rocket projectors and a variety of lighter weapons. The Regular units thus released joined the field army assembling for the invasion of Europe.

The formation of Home Guard motor transport companies was authorised in September 1942 and they were raised in the succeeding months, often on a nucleus of existing transport platoons in general service battalions. They relied entirely on civilian lorries earmarked for requistion in emergency, as did the small number of transport units based on civilian bus undertakings. Bomb disposal was not officially a Home Guard responsibility until September 1942, when existing civilian bomb disposal teams in factories were incorporated as Home Guard auxiliary bomb disposal units.

Adjustments to the operational role

During 1943 the threat of invasion was assessed as 'remote' and the operational role of the Home Guard, with the exception of the anti-aircraft units, came under scrutiny, even criticism. It was felt by some that personnel would be better employed in agriculture and industrial production rather than in training for an event that would never happen. The War Office instructed that members of the Home Guard should spend as much time as possible in agriculture or war production but the threat of raids, as opposed to a full-scale invasion, had not entirely disappeared and, as the Allied landings in Normandy approached, there was even more reason to expect that the enemy would land commando or parachute troops to disrupt the preparations. Two steps were accordingly taken to make more use of the Home Guard. First, in the autumn of 1943, some inland districts were ordered to find general service companies for a new role—that of reinforcement of coastal areas under attack or threat of attack. Secondly, and again to counteract the decreasing numbers of Regular troops available for routine guards as the Normandy landings approached, arrangements were made for the Home Guard to undertake full-time duty, both on the coast and guarding the routes to the embarkation ports. Since there was no "actual or apprehended invasion" of the United Kingdom, the Home Guard could not be mustered for these important duties. However, by a combination of full-time volunteers and part-time shifts much useful work was done "securing the back of the front" (as one official report described the task).

Stand-down; disbandment

With the Allied forces firmly ashore and fighting their way across Europe, and with the Luftwaffe less and less able to mount even 'nuisance' raids against the United Kingdom, the grounds for keeping the Home Guard fully in being had greatly diminished. In addition to rescue work following flying bomb attacks, Home Guard light anti-aircraft units provided relief gun detachments in the 'Diver' defences along the south coast as the last of the many operational tasks the force undertook. 'Stand-Down' was ordered from 1st November 1944 and final parades were held on Sunday 3rd December 1944. Administrative cadres then dealt with all the problems of disbanding units which, especially in the early days, had existed with the minimum of paper work. The disposal of ammunition and explosives, some homemade, was not without hazard (see pages 42 and 46 for two incidents that occurred prior to Stand-Down) and there were no doubt all the usual difficulties with equipment that had 'walked'. Nevertheless disbandment was possible once "the present emergency" for which members had enrolled was over, and took effect from 31st December 1945.

A definitive history of the Home Guard has yet to be written. Meanwhile, readers interested in a deeper study than is possible here should refer to *Graves* and *Longmate* (see Bibliography) and to local unit histories as appropriate. Regretably Home Guard histories are not included in White's *Bibliography of Regimental Histories of the British Army* but the Imperial War Museum has a large collection and the local studies departments of county libraries will invariably be able to help.

PART TWO

THE AWARD OF DECORATIONS AND COMMENDATIONS TO MEMBERS OF THE HOME GUARD—POLICY AND PRACTICE

Early consideration of decorations for the Home Guard

The likelihood that it would be necessary to be able to award gallantry decorations to members of the Home Guard was recognised soon after formation but all the emphasis was on gallantry in action—in repelling the anticipated invasion. During September 1940 the matter came under consideration by the Committee on the Grant of Honours, Decorations and Medals in Time of War. Their initial view, prompted by some discussion in sub-committee and doubtless 'in the corridors', was that there would be no difficulty in awarding the Victoria Cross and the Empire Gallantry Medal (though the latter was not, in fact, a decoration for gallantry in action) to all ranks of the Home Guard, or the Distinguished Conduct Medal and the Military Medal to those whose appointments equated to warrant officers, non-commissioned officers and private soldiers in the Regular Army. The Distinguished Service Order and the Military Cross could not, however, be awarded to Home Guard personnel of officer status because the Royal Warrants governing these two decorations specified that they were to be awarded to commissioned officers (D.S.O.) or commissioned and warrant officers (M.C.). In neither case were these provisions fulfilled in the Home Guard.

By late October 1940 it was clear that the difficulty in awarding decorations to Home Guard 'officers' would probably be overtaken by the grant of commissions—a procedure which was already some way advanced because of difficulties over powers of command. Accordingly the Committee's final paper was not circulated and no submission was made to the King. It is of interest to record here however, that, had it not been decided to commission Home Guard officers, the Committee would have recommended very little change in the Royal Warrant for the Military Medal, which had already been awarded to one member of the Home Guard (Volunteer G. Jones, 3rd Monmouthshire Bn., *L. G. 19.ix.1940*). In the case of the Victoria Cross, Distinguished Service Order, Military Cross, Distinguished Conduct Medal and Empire Gallantry Medal the Committee would have recommended that the Royal Warrant should be altered in each case "to include specific reference to the Home Guard ranks eligible". With the original problem—that of gallantry decorations for Home Guard officers—solved by commissioning, a new problem arose as a result of widespread enemy air attack (see below) and the question of amendments to the Royal Warrants covering decorations for gallantry in action was shelved for some time, but not entirely forgotten. Amending Warrants were published for the Victoria Cross (A.W. dated 31st December 1942—"Persons of any rank in the ... Military ... Forces ..., including the Home Guard"); the Distinguished Service Order (A.W. dated 8th March 1943—"a commission ... in the ... Military ... Forces, including the Home Guard ..."); and the Military Cross

7

(A.W. dated 14th April 1943—"a Major, . . ., a Commissioned Officer of a lower grade, or a Warrant Officer, in any of our Military Forces, including our Home Guard . . ."). No such amendments were made in the Royal Warrants for the Distinguished Conduct Medal and the Military Medal, the existing phraseology ". . . of our Military Forces . . ." being deemed sufficient to cover 'other ranks' of the Home Guard.

The need to recognise non-combatant gallantry; awards available; the George Cross and the George Medal

As things turned out, the most urgent requirement was not to be able to recognise gallantry in action but gallantry arising from enemy air raids—a problem which was not unique to the Home Guard and was attracting the personal attention of the Prime Minister and the King throughout the late summer of 1940. (For a full account see *Henderson.*) The Honours system was in fact ill-equipped to deal with large scale non-combatant gallantry. (It had been in rather the same situation vis-à-vis gallantry in action in 1914-15 and new decorations, including, for Land Forces, the Military Cross and the Military Medal, were instituted in consequence.) In 1940-41 the existing range of civilian, or non-combatant, gallantry awards was almost entirely set aside and a new series of awards was brought into use. This was able to recognise four degrees of gallantry in the same way that gallantry in action could be recognised by the Victoria Cross (at the highest level), the Distinguished Service Order or the Distinguished Conduct Medal, the Military Cross or the Military Medal, or a Mention in Despatches. (These examples cover Land Forces; similar levels were recognised by, in some cases, different decorations in the Royal Navy and Royal Air Force.) Two entirely new decorations for civilian or non-combatant gallantry were instituted in September 1940—the George Cross, to recognise gallantry at the highest level, and ranking second only to the Victoria Cross, and the George Medal. After the institution of these two awards appointments in the Order of the British Empire and awards of the British Empire Medal (depending on the service rank or civilian status of the recipient) were confirmed as the third level of award and a new fourth level, comparable to the active service Mention in Despatches and known as the King's Commendation for Brave Conduct, was introduced. There were thus two clear, four-stage hierarchies of award for gallantry in action and non-combatant gallantry, with some differences within the levels, depending upon the rank or status of the recipient, as follows:

Gallantry in action (Army)	*Civilian or non-combatant gallantry*
Victoria Cross[1]	George Cross[1]
Distinguished Service Order/	George Medal[1]
Distinguished Conduct Medal[2]	
Military Cross/	Appointment as O.B.E. or M.B.E./
Military Medal[2]	Award of British Empire Medal[2]
Mention in Despatches[1]	King's Commendation for
	Brave Conduct[1]

[1] Awarded regardless of rank/status
[2] Depending upon rank/status

8

The Royal Warrants for the George Cross and the George Medal, both dated 24th September 1940, specified that these two decorations were for award to "Persons of any rank in the ... Military ... Forces ..., including the Home Guard, ...". There was, therefore, from that date, no difficulty in recognising the higher levels of gallantry displayed by Home Guard personnel, whether during air raids or in other non-combatant situations.

The Order of the British Empire

Appointments in the Order of the British Empire had been made in some numbers during the Great War "for an act of gallantry not in the face of the enemy", such appointments recognising gallantry below the standard required for awards of the Albert Medal in Gold and the Albert Medal. They had continued, as necessary, between the wars and it was these appointments which were now confirmed by the Committee in third place below the George Cross and the George Medal. The Statutes of the Order were specific, however, that appointments to the Military Division were restricted to "... all commissioned and warrant officers subject to the Army ... Act ...". Consequently no such appointments were made until after the introduction of Home Guard commissions, though one—the appointment of Company Commander A. W. Richards, M.M. as O.B.E. (see page 53)—relates to an incident which took place some months before the Home Guard Officers' Commissions Order took effect. It is possible to speculate that, had Home Guard commissions not been introduced, Home Guard 'officers' could have been appointed to the Civil Division of the Order (as were officers of the Royal Observer Corps). Alternatively the Statutes could have been altered to permit the appointment of "officials"—the term used in the original statutes to cover members of the women's services of the Great War who were of officer status but who did not hold commissions.

The British Empire Medal

In addition to the Albert Medals, two awards were available during the Great War to recognise non-combatant gallantry on the part of non-commissioned officers and men. They were the Meritorious Service Medal, under an alteration to the Royal Warrant permitting award for "gallant conduct in the performance of military duty otherwise than in action" (for details see *Sainsbury*), and the Medal of the Order of the British Empire, which had been instituted with the Order in 1917. This medal was not widely used as a gallantry award for the armed forces but it was used *inter alia* to recognise the bravery and devotion to duty of Royal Engineers personnel engaged in rescue work following air raids on London during the Great War. Use of the Meritorious Service Medal as a gallantry decoration was discontinued in 1928, largely as a result of a revision of the Statutes of the Order of the British Empire in 1922 which abolished the original Medal of the Order and instituted two new Medals. One, the Medal of the Order of the British Empire for Gallantry, usually known as the Empire Gallantry Medal (E.G.M.), was reserved for instances of outstanding gallantry and was abolished on the institution of the George Cross in 1940. The main purpose of the other, the Medal of the Order of the British Empire for Meritorious Service, known as the British Empire Medal (B.E.M.), was to recognise "meritorious service" as a half-yearly Honours List award. It was also used to recognise gallantry of a lower standard than that required for the Empire Gallantry Medal and its use as a gallantry award ranking below the George Cross and the George Medal was now confirmed by the Committee (see above). Both Civil and Military Divisions of the Medal were awarded extensively throughout the Second World War to recognise non-combatant gallantry. Award of the British Empire Medal (Military Division) was restricted to "persons subordinate to those who are eligible for the Military Division of the various classes of the Order". Since warrant officers were eligible for appointment as Members of the Order, the Medal applied to non-commissioned officers and servicemen and women. There does not appear to have been any difficulty in obtaining agreement that non-commissioned officers and men of the Home Guard were eligible for award of the British Empire Medal (Military Division) either in recognition of gallantry or as an Honours List award. In 1974 appointments in the Order of the British Empire and awards of the British Empire Medal "for Gallantry" ceased with the institution of the Queen's Gallantry Medal which is awarded regardless of the rank or status of the recipient for acts of gallantry of a standard below that necessary for the George Cross and the George Medal.

Mentions and Commendations

A 'mention' in a despatch from a commander-in-chief in the field is perhaps the oldest form of recognition of "gallant and distinguished services", both in action and in administrative posts. During the Great War the procedure for awarding Mentions in Despatches was simplified and integrated with the award of other honours and decorations. At the end of the war it was announced that those who had been mentioned would receive a certificate and would be entitled to wear an emblem (multiple oak leaves in bronze) on the ribbon of the Victory Medal. The Mention in Despatches was thus firmly established as the lowest level in the hierarchy of active service awards and continued as such between the wars. A new emblem (a single bronze oak leaf) was authorised to be worn on the ribbon of the appropriate campaign medal. Mentions in Despatches were included in the periodic lists of recommendations for honours and awards submitted by commanders-in-chief during the Second World War and the single oak leaf emblem was authorised to be worn on the ribbon of the 1939-45 War Medal. At the opening of the Second World War there was no civilian equivalent to the Armed Forces' mention in despatches but the need for one was swiftly realised, initially as a means of recognising gallantry arising from enemy attacks on merchant shipping, then as a result of air raids. The names of Merchant Navy personnel first appeared in the *London Gazette* of 15th December 1939 "as having received an expression of commendation for their good services", while members of the Civil Defence Services were first "brought to notice for good service in connection with Civil Defence" in the *London Gazette* of 30th September 1940. It is clear from the citations for civilian decorations for gallantry notified at the same time that these "good services" involved gallant conduct rather than just hard work. Before long the idea was extended to cover, for example, rescues from crashed aircraft and fires in munitions factories. The blanket description "King's Commendation for Brave Conduct" was adopted later in the war and the fourth level of civilian gallantry award thus established

10

continues to this day (as the Queen's Commendation). Civilian King's Commendations awarded during the Second World War are denoted by a certificate and by an emblem (multiple laurel leaves in silver) which is worn on the ribbon of the Defence Medal, providing the recipient has qualified for the medal by service with one of the authorised organisations. Recipients who do not hold the Defence Medal wear the emblem directly on the coat in the position in which medal ribbons would be worn.

Since the Armed Forces were using essentially civilian awards to recognise non-combatant gallantry it is not surprising that they should have adopted the King's Commendation to provide the fourth (and lowest) level of recognition. Lists of personnel commended for brave conduct were published periodically in the *London Gazette* under the aegis of all three service ministries. An Armed Forces King's Commendation is denoted by a certificate almost identical to that for a Mention in Despatches and by the same bronze oak leaf emblem worn on the ribbon of the 1939-45 War Medal. It must be noted that service in the Home Guard alone did not qualify for the 1939-45 War Medal. The oak leaf emblem denoting commendation of a member of the Home Guard is therefore worn directly on the coat unless the recipient subsequently qualified for the medal by service in the Armed Forces or another approved body (e.g. the Merchant Navy). It is not correct for the Armed Forces oak leaf emblem to be worn on the ribbon of the Defence Medal.

Commanders-in-Chiefs' Certificates

A *de facto* fifth level of award was established during the Second World War by extension of the procedure under which Armed Forces personnel were "brought to notice" in Commanders-in-Chiefs' Orders. From late 1941/early 1942 officers and men who were cited in Command Orders received a certificate, as well as having the fact endorsed on their record of service. Such certificates were originally "for Gallantry" and recognised actions which, while displaying bravery, were thought not to merit an award from the Sovereign. Later, certificates "for Good Services" were introduced and extensively awarded in half-yearly lists. Members of the Home Guard were eligible for awards of certificates both for gallantry and for good services by the G.O.C.-in-C. of the Command in which their unit was located. These awards were notified in Command Home Guard Orders, which were separate from, and complimentary to, Command Orders (see also page 2). (Some details of the system of award of Commanders-in-Chiefs' Certificates can be found in the London County Council Records—H.G.57.)

Special position of the Ulster Home Guard

The legal status of the Ulster Home Guard, whose officers were not commissioned and none of whose members were technically members of the armed forces, meant that, while there was no difficulty vis-à-vis the George Cross and the George Medal, the force did not qualify for the Military Division of the Order of the British Empire or the British Empire Medal. As a result both Honours List awards and those for gallantry were in the Civil Division and are relatively more difficult to trace in the *London Gazette*. Only one award for gallantry on duty has so far come to light—the British Empire Medal awarded to Platoon Sergeant W. B. Anderson (*L.G. 4.ii.1944*). It is interesting, though hardly profitable, to

11

speculate on the awards for which the Ulster Home Guard would have qualified had they had the opportunity of displaying gallantry in action against the enemy.

Posthumous awards

The practice as the British honours system has developed has been to avoid making posthumous awards of decorations except in instances of the highest gallantry. This practice has recently been changed (see *Abbott and Tamplin* for details) but throughout the Second World War the George Cross alone among the decorations available for non-combatant gallantry in the Home Guard could be awarded to an officer or man who lost his life as a result of his heroism. The technicalities which prevented awards of decorations to deceased personnel did not apply in the case of Mentions in Despatches and it had always been the practice to include in a despatch the names of officers and men who had been killed in action or died of wounds. This practice was carried over to the analagous King's Commendation for Brave Conduct, with the result that only two awards (the George Cross and the King's Commendation) were available to recognise the gallantry of those who died.

The Honours Lists

The announcement of awards to Home Guard personnel in the Half-Yearly Lists began in July 1941 (King's Birthday Honours—*L.G. 1.vii.1941*), the first list after the promulgation of the Home Guard Officers' Commissions Order, which, as shown above, was the key to the appointment of Home Guard officers to the Military Division of the Order of the British Empire and the award of the British Empire Medal to 'other ranks'. Thereafter, officers and men appeared regularly in the New Year and King's Birthday Lists up to and including the King's Birthday of 1944. A final list of awards was published as the so-called Stand-Down Honours List (*L.G. 15.xii.1944*).

It was not, in general, the intention of the Half-Yearly Lists to recognise gallantry on a specific occasion, but there is some evidence that awards which were primarily, some perhaps exclusively, in recognition of gallantry may have 'escaped' into these lists. Unlike similar awards during the Great War, there was no annotation of the *London Gazette* announcement and it is thus not possible to list the recipients. Occasionally reference is made to the circumstances in unit histories. For example, Lieutenant H. T. Coneybeer of 6th Gloucestershire (South Gloucester) Battalion is said in *Hayman* to have been appointed M.B.E. for his part in the defence of Parnell's aircraft factory against enemy air-attack on 7th March 1941. The lapse of time between the attack and the announcement of the award in the *London Gazette* of 11th June 1942 does leave some room for doubt and it may be that his recommendation was written in much more general terms. It is similarly suggested (in *Wiltsher*) that the appointment as M.B.E. of Lieutenant H. J. Ferguson of 1st Devon (Loyal City of Exeter) Battalion was in recognition of his gallant conduct when battalion headquarters was bombed on 4th-5th May 1942. In this case lapse of time is unreliable as a guide. Ferguson's M.B.E. was announced in the King's Birthday Honours of 1943 (*L.G. 2.vi.1943*) while Corporal Kitson's King's Commendation for bravery on the same occasion was not announced until nearly three months later, a total of seventeen months after the incident (*L.G. 28.ix.1943*).

The earliest awards; precedents not followed

Having established how the systems of active service and non-combatant gallantry awards were developed to accommodate the Home Guard it is now necessary to examine the extent to which use was made of the new arrangements. It is interesting too, to draw attention to some of the anomalies which seem to have arisen.

As has been pointed out earlier, the most pressing need, apparent in the late summer of 1940, was to recognise gallantry during and after enemy air raids. Throughout the Second World War service in the ground defence of the United Kingdom did not constitute 'operational' service, in contrast to the aerial defence conducted by Royal Air Force Fighter Command, or naval action in coastal waters, both of which did. It was accordingly quite unusual for members of the Land Forces to be awarded decorations for gallantry "in action against the enemy" and it was technically not possible for Mentions in Despatches to be awarded. Nevertheless the first award to the Home Guard was a Military Medal (to Volunteer G. Jones, 3rd Monmouthshire Battalion), gazetted as early as 19th September 1940. This award was for gallantry during, rather than after, an air raid. It seems likely that it resulted from the need for some immediate signal that the authorities were prepared to recognise Home Guard gallantry. As has been shown briefly above (see *Abbott and Tamplin* for amplification), the Royal Warrant for the Military Medal was capable of wide interpretation. There was very little difficulty in demonstrating that other ranks of the Home Guard were eligible and at the time it was perhaps the only award that could have been made. A recommendation for anything else would have to have been kept 'on ice' pending the outcome of the Committee's deliberations (see pages 7-10).

The award is in several respects unique. It is certainly the only decoration for gallantry in action awarded to a member of the Home Guard. (It was actually gazetted "in recognition of gallant conduct in action with the enemy".) It set a precedent which the authorities chose not to follow—for all subsequent awards for gallantry during or after air raids were 'civilian'—and one cannot help feeling that they might have regretted an early, hasty decision. Comparison with awards to the Regular Forces in the United Kingdom (including the Royal Air Force) is not conclusive. The Military Medal was awarded to Corporal J. M. G. Robbins, W.A.A.F. (*L.G. 20.xii.1940*) for bravery in circumstances very similar to those of Volunteer Jones's award. On balance, it does look as if a decision to award the British Empire Medal rather than the Military Medal was made, probably late in 1940, but no record of this decision has been traced. It is clear, though, that the matter of decorations for the Home Guard had undergone further discussion, for the following appeared in *The Times* of 1st January 1941:

> "It is officially announced that the King has given approval in principle for the grant of certain awards in the Home Guard early in the New Year. As soon as the reorganisation of the force has reached a sufficiently advanced stage the announcement will be made."

Assuming that this statement covered gallantry, and not just Honours List awards, it forecast the move away from the Military Medal and towards the civilian awards, the first list of which (one George Medal and nine British Empire

Medals) was published in the *London Gazette* of 22nd January 1941. Meanwhile another unique award, comparable to Jones's Military Medal, remained to be announced.

The classification of the award, to Volunteer P. D. Willeringhaus of 6th Battalion, 'P' Zone, London, as a Mention in Despatches is all the more unusual for the publication in the same *London Gazette* (21st January 1941) of the name of the first Home Guard to receive a King's Commendation for Brave Conduct (Volunteer J. Greenman, Upper Thames Patrol). Yet there seems no doubt about the intention to award a Mention in Despatches. The *London Gazette* announcement reads:

> "The King has been graciously pleased to approve that the following be Mentioned for gallantry during enemy action:
> 6094871 Lance-Sergeant J. R. Cowell, Dorset Regiment
> Volunteer P. D. Willeringhaus, Home Guard"

and creates two extremely rare awards—Mentions in Despatches to members of the Land Forces in the United Kingdom during the Second World War—possibly the only ones. As in the case of Volunteer Jones's Military Medal the precedent was not followed. It seems probable that there was, with the best of intentions, a series of mistakes. It would be interesting to know whether these mistakes culminated in the issue of a Mention in Despatches certificate or whether, with five years' hindsight and experience, the authorities decided that the circumstances required a King's Commendation certificate.

The key qualification—"on duty"

From February 1941 onwards the intricacies of the system were better understood. It was clearly laid down (by War Office letter of 22nd February 1941) that when members of the Home Guard were recommended through military channels for honours and awards the recommendation had to be accompanied by a certificate to the effect that:

> "(a) The member was on Home Guard duty at the time that the act for which he is recommended was performed; and
> (b) He is a properly enrolled member of the force."

It is not clear whether "duty" was defined as early as February 1941. A definition is given in *Regulations for the Home Guard, 1942* and, interestingly, excludes the journey to and from the "place of assembly". Since a number of awards were made to members of the Home Guard who took part in air raid rescue work on the way to their place of duty it seems that a more pragmatic definition was in use at the height of the 'Blitz'. Official records show that some Home Guard personnel were extracted from early group recommendations that had been submitted through civilian channels and steps were taken before awards were decided upon to obtain G.O.C.s' views on whether a 'duty' (and hence military) award would be appropriate. In one case civilian awards were actually cancelled and higher military awards substituted. (Sergeant W. Davies and Private G. E. Rees, both of 15th Glamorganshire Battalion, received British Empire Medals instead of their earlier civilian King's Commendations.)

An examination of the honours and awards listed in unit reports in *Graves* shows that in very many cases reporting units misinterpreted the questionnaire and included awards made in recognition of gallantry in a civilian, rather than a Home Guard, capacity (i.e. recipients had not been, or been considered to be, 'on duty' at the time of the action for which they were decorated). For example, the George Medal reported by 7th Bedfordshire Battalion as awarded to Captain J. C. Cunningham, D.S.O. was gazetted amongst civilian awards for services during and after air raids (*L.G. 3.i.1941*), as was Volunteer Gant's George Medal 'claimed' by 28th Kent (Southern Railway) Battalion (*L.G. 7.ii.1941*).

Whereas it seems impossible that a recommendation through military channels which was not accompanied by the 'on duty' endorsement would have succeeded, the same may not be true of recommendations through civilian channels for personnel who were in fact on duty. It is possible that some of these recommendations slipped through the screening process. Particular doubt attaches to the incident at Torquay gas works on 4th September 1942, as a result of which two George Medals and one M.B.E. (Civil Division) were awarded to members of 10th Devonshire (Torbay) Battalion (*L.G. 4.i.1943*). The circumstances are fully described in *Lidstone* and clearly suggest that the recipients were on duty. The *London Gazette* gives no such impression. It is quite likely that there were other similar cases, even possible that those responsible for some recommendations selected the channel through which they felt they were most likely to 'score' and wrote the recommendation accordingly. Correspondence resulting in the eventual appointment of Lieutenant G. D. Eccles, 48th County of London (L.C.C.) Battalion as M.B.E. (Mil.) is preserved in the London County Council Records at H.G.-57. Eccles was a doctor at a London County Council hospital and it was only after prolonged argument that it was decided that the correct channel for his recommendation was the military one.

Bomb disposal

Awards to members of the Home Guard who took part in bomb disposal operations presented no difficulty, provided only that the 'on duty' requirements were met. It had already been agreed that bomb disposal personnel of the Regular Forces working in the United Kingdom would be considered for awards in the 'civilian' categories (G.C., G.M., O.B.E./M.B.E./B.E.M., King's Commendation) and the Home Guard would automatically have been covered by this decision, although at the height of this activity they were not officially tasked with bomb disposal (see page 5). Similarly, gallantry in preventing loss of life on grenade ranges, appropriate recognition of which had caused a great deal of argument in the Great War (see *Sainsbury*), was now readily regarded as qualifying for the civilian awards.

Action against the enemy

With hindsight it can be said that the only field of Home Guard activity in which there was any continuing difficulty about the appropriate awards was that in which they actually were "in action against the enemy"—the low level air defence of 'vulnerable points'. By any reasonable assessment, taking on a Heinkel with a Lewis gun from a factory roof in daylight was action against the enemy. The aircraft could, and did, hit back—with machine gun fire as well as bombs. A classic Military Medal awarded to Gunner Sidney Francis, who continued to engage enemy aircraft though wounded (*L.G. 26.xi.1942; Times 28.xi.1942*), demonstrates that anti-aircraft action in the United Kingdom qualified for recognition as "bravery in the field". Similar awards of the Military Medal were made much earlier (*L.G. 20.xii.1940*) to members of the Royal Air Force—Corporal B. Jackman, who was severely wounded manning a twin Lewis gun, and Aircraftsman Class 2 A. D. Rowe who manned a Hispano cannon, both in action against enemy aircraft. Awards to the Home Guard for anti-aircraft action are confined to the lowest level discussed earlier (i.e. Mention in Despatches or King's Commendation) and all five awards were in fact King's Commendations (four members of 3rd Kesteven Battalion and Corporal J. Griffin, 1st Warwickshire Battalion). Their citations leave no doubt that the circumstances of their awards were similar to those of Gunner Francis, and Corporal Jackman and Aircraftsman Rowe. However, given that the scale of their gallantry was not sufficient to merit the Military Medal (i.e. the third level), it was not possible to award the 'in action' fourth level—a Mention in Despatches—for the reasons discussed earlier. Accordingly a King's Commendation was the only choice open. It must be added that some members of the Merchant Navy received King's Commendations for action in defence of their ships. It is not clear whether any members of the Regular Forces in the United Kingdom (including the Royal Air Force) received similar awards, but it would not be surprising if they had done so.

The Defence Medal

The Defence Medal was among the eight stars and two medals instituted to recognise service in the Second World War, details of which were published in Army Order 108 of 1945 and in two White Papers and a War Office pamphlet (see Bibliography). The qualifying period for the Defence Medal for military personnel, including the Home Guard, was three years' non-operational service in the United Kingdom. A special award of the Medal was made to personnel whose service was terminated before three years by death or wounds due to enemy action whilst on duty, or who were awarded an honour, decoration or King's Commendation. Accordingly, all officers and men listed in Part Four qualified for the Defence Medal. The Medal was not issued automatically, however, and award depended upon a claim, either by a unit on behalf of an individual or by the individual in person.

PART THREE

SOURCES; VERIFICATION OF AWARDS; CITATIONS; INVESTITURE

With the exception of the one British Empire Medal (Civil Division), all the awards included in the list which follows were announced in War Office Supplements to the *London Gazette* and the date of publication is shown. It was most unusual for the citations for awards to the Army (including the Home Guard) to be published in the *London Gazette* during the Second World War, those for the Victoria Cross excepted, and in none of the cases covered in this account did the citation accompany the *London Gazette* announcement. Apart from the Military Medal and Mention in Despatches (see pages 13 and 14) each list of awards was introduced by the very simple statement:

> "The King has been graciously pleased to approve the award of ....to the undermentioned in recognition of conspicuous gallantry in carrying out hazardous work in a very brave manner"
> or
> "The King has approved the publication of the names of the undermentioned as having been commended for brave conduct"

There were minor differences but none affected the general tenor of the statement. Despite the absence of citations, the *London Gazette* must be regarded as the underlying authority for each award.

At the time the London Gazette announcement was made it seems to have been normal procedure for a War Office press release to be made available, though details of the circumstances of some awards, notably those for bomb disposal, were omitted from press releases on security grounds. Press releases, none of which have yet been traced in their original form, appear only to have covered decorations, not King's Commendations. These press releases are the closest that most Home Guard awards come to a 'citation'—a statement of the circumstances of award, based on the original recommendation—intended for publication or to be read out at the investiture or presentation ceremony. In all cases where a press release relating to an award in this account has been traced the citation is deemed to have been published and is shown in inverted commas and without any brackets. The source (or sources) are quoted. *The Times* has been searched and is always quoted if a press release appeared. It has not been possible to search all the local newspapers that may have carried reports of the award of decorations to members of the Home Guard but wherever such reports have been traced they too are quoted.

A further important source for the citations for Home Guard awards is the series of *Home Guard Information Circulars* but these only began publishing citations in March 1944. (The series is available in the Public Record Office and in the Ministry of Defence Library.)

Details of some awards, usually the full recommendation, appear in the papers relating to the Committee on the Grant of Civilian Gallantry Awards to the Armed Forces, some of which are included in Air 2 at the Public Record Office. A search has revealed relevant material in Air 2/6262, 8908, 9001, 9289, 9504 and 9537, all of which have been quoted. The difficulty of conducting a thorough search is such that more papers may yet come to light. As these papers are now open to the public the citations extracted from them are deemed to have been published, albeit long after the event, and are shown in inverted commas and without brackets. Extracts from material now in the keeping of the Public Record Office appear by permission of the Controller of Her Majesty's Stationery Office.

Some further references to decorations awarded to members of the Home Guard appear in *Graves* and in various unit histories. These have been quoted as appropriate. Where the circumstances of award are widely known or have been described in e.g., a unit history, but without the precise form of a citation, they are shown without brackets, but without inverted commas, since they are not a direct quotation from an official record or press release.

Two important sources which are not generally available to the public have been used to fill the (quite large) gap which exists between publicly available citations and a full record. These are:

  i. Records of recommendations for the British Empire Medal and higher awards, usually on Army Form W 3211, held in the Ministry of Defence; and

  ii. Similar records, but for all levels of award, usually in the form of papers put before the Civilian Gallantry Awards Scrutiny Committee, at present held in the Cabinet Office but awaiting transfer to the Public Record Office.

Recommendations extracted from these two sources have been edited to a certain extent to form citations. They are given in inverted commas but in all cases enclosed in square brackets.

The scarcity of citations for Land Forces awards for the Second World War is partly explained by Twenty-First Army Group General Routine Order 99/1503 dated 10th August 1945. This order states that the extra clerical work involved prevents the issue of citations by the War Office but confirms that there is no objection to units which hold copies of recommendations presenting one to the recipient after the award has been approved by the King. Without doubt the problems of "extra clerical work" extended to other formations besides Twenty-First Army Group, and the change to peace-time conditions offered no opportunity for the War Office (later the Ministry of Defence) to catch up on the back-log of unissued Second World War citations. Happily, in the age of the photocopier it is no longer difficult for recipients of decorations, or their next-of-kin, to obtain a copy of the relevant recommendation, providing that it is on file in the Ministry of Defence (which does not apply in all cases). Recommendations resulting in Mentions in Despatches or Commendations have not been retained. The Ministry have no plans at present to transfer their recommendation files to the Public Record Office.

Almost all awards of British Empire Medals and above were presented to the recipients at investitures the dates of which are shown after the appropriate citation or recommendation in the List of Awards. These were usually several months after the *London Gazette* announcement and often as long as two years after the act of gallantry itself. The dates may help those interested in tracing photographs of individual recipients in, e.g. local newspapers. It is probable that recipients attended early investitures in civilian clothes, although announced by their Home Guard rank and receiving, where appropriate, awards in the Military Division of the Order of the British Empire and the British Empire Medal (see *Graves,* page 127).

ANALYSIS OF AWARDS

	Air Raids	Accidents during Grenade Practice	Bomb Disposal	Rescues from Crashed Aircraft	Action against the Enemy	Other	Total
George Cross	1	1					2
George Medal	10	1	2				13
O.B.E. (Mil.)	1						1
M.B.E. (Mil.)	2	8		1		1[1]	12
B.E.M. (Mil.)	32	6	3	5		2[2][3]	48
B.E.M. (Civ.)		1					1
Military Medal	1						1
Mention in Despatches	1						1
King's Commendation	37	8	5	2	5	1[4]	58
	85	25	10	8	5	4	137

(1) Fire in an ammunition store
(2) Action against armed escaped p.o.w.
(3) Action following the explosion of defective ammunition
(4) Rescue following the mining of a ship

PART FOUR

LIST OF AWARDS BY UNITS

The list which follows is intended to include all awards of the status of King's Commendation for Brave Conduct or above which were made to the Home Guard, including its Permanent Staff, in recognition of acts of gallantry performed while on duty, the recommendations for which were processed through military channels. It has been compiled by searching the *London Gazette*. The results of the search have been compared with records of awards given in the Ministry of Information booklet, in *Graves* and in certain county and unit histories (see Bibliography), and with an unpublished record held in the Ministry of Defence. It is believed that the list of awards to officers and men serving on Home Guard commissions/engagements is complete and correct, following published corrections. However, in a very small number of cases it has not proved possible to trace the exact details of the units to which recipients of awards belonged. It is not possible to be similarly confident that all awards to the Permanent Staff have been traced, since they cannot be distinguished in the available records from their Regular colleagues serving elsewhere. At the time of publication only two awards to permanent staff instructors have been traced—both of these through unit histories—and the possibility that there were others cannot be discounted.

It would have been appropriate to include awards of the Life Saving Medal of the Order of St. John of Jerusalem and the Medals of the Royal Humane Society. However, a search of the records of the Order and the Society indicates that no such awards were made in recognition of gallantry on Home Guard duty.

An explanation of the conventions observed in the list to indicate the degree of publication and the source of individual citations will be found on pages 17-18. The date of investiture is shown after any references to sources.

21

5th BEDFORDSHIRE BATTALION

British Empire Medal

Private J. M. SHELTON
(L. G. 19.xi.1943)

"On Friday, 9th July 1943 Antonio Amedeo, an Italian prisoner of war, escaped from a working party by killing a guard with a hedging hook. He took possession of the guard's service rifle and ten rounds of ammunition.

Armed parties of soldiers, Home Guards and police carried out a search of the district from shortly after the escape until the early afternoon of 10th July but the escaped man was not found.

At about 6 p.m. on 10th July the escaped man entered a house occupied by Private Shelton and his family and helped himself to a meal. During this time the occupiers were also having a meal and the escaped prisoner, having finished his, passed into the passage of the house with a rifle in his hands and came face to face with Private Shelton, who had entered the passage from another room. The escaped prisoner immediately fired at Private Shelton and narrowly missed him. He then raced upstairs. Private Shelton instantly went up another staircase and worked his way along the landing until he located the escaped prisoner in his sister's bedroom, in a position from which the Italian could cover anyone coming up the main staircase. In spite of this Private Shelton entered the room and, with his service rifle, shot the Italian through the chest.

Private Shelton was confronted with a situation where there was no time to ask for orders from his superior in the Home Guard. He showed marked initiative, personal courage and presence of mind, backed by sound training and thus gave an outstanding example of the way a Home Guard should behave in a situation of this kind." *(H.G.I.C. No 41-15.xii.1943) (Inv. 17.x.1944)*

Section Leader A. H. G. BRUNGES, 2nd Birmingham Battalion who with Patrol Leader C. W. L. TOZER (*see next page*) rescued more than fifteen people trapped in an air raid shelter which had been hit by a bomb and was beginning to flood—26th October 1940.
Both were awarded the George Medal.

22

Patrol Leader C. W. L. TOZER, 2nd Birmingham Battalion, who joined Section Leader A. H. G. Brunges *(see previous page)* in rescuing more than fifteen people trapped in an air raid shelter—26th October 1940.
Both were awarded the George Medal.

2nd BIRMINGHAM BATTALION
[later 22nd WARWICKSHIRE (BIRMINGHAM) BATTALION]

George Medal

Section Leader A. H. G. BRUNGES
Patrol Leader C. W. L. TOZER
(L.G. 30.ix.1941)

"On the 26th October 1940 a bomb explosion caused the destruction of a public shelter. Section Leader Brunges and Patrol Leader Tozer showed the utmost bravery and devotion to duty in going to the assistance of a considerable number of persons who were trapped in the debris. The work of rescue seemed hopeless as the basement was filling rapidly with water. Loose beams had to be removed where possible but this was highly dangerous owing to the possibility of huge blocks of concrete from the floor above becoming dislodged. Section Leader Brunges and Patrol Leader Tozer took the risk of moving these beams without a moment's thought for their own safety. The debris they removed with their hands, mostly under water and in kneeling or half lying positions.

Heavy bombs were falling in the vicinity, but work was carried on until between fifteen and twenty persons had been extricated, about half of them still being alive. It was not until it was impossible to discover any further victims that Section Leader Brunges and Patrol Leader Tozer gave up their work of rescue." *(The Times 1.x.1941) (Invs. 29.ix.1942)*

5th BIRMINGHAM BATTALION
[later 25th WARWICKSHIRE (BIRMINGHAM) BATTALION]

King's Commendation for Brave Conduct

Sergeant P. H. BERMINGHAM
(L.G. 13.i.1942)

["This n.c.o. showed great courage and devotion to duty on the night of 9th/10th April 1941. During an enemy air attack the factory which he was guarding was hit by high explosive bombs and caught fire. Although the raid was still in progress he played a prominent part in the evacuation of 400 work people from the building. In spite of the fact that the building was by this time ablaze and beginning to collapse, he broke his way through to the armoury and recovered and brought to safety all the arms and ammunition of his Home Guard unit."]

6th BIRMINGHAM (FACTORIES) BATTALION

[later 26th WARWICKSHIRE (BIRMINGHAM) BATTALION]

George Medal

Volunteer A. W. BAILEY
(L.G. 11.ii.1941)

"On the night of 19th November 1940 Volunteer Bailey was due to report for duty with B.S.A. Guns Ltd Home Guard at 9.30 p.m. Hearing bombs, however, he arrived at about 7.00 p.m. and remained on duty helping to deal with incendiary bombs. At about 9.00 p.m. he reached the unit headquarters where he met an officer who called for volunteers to rescue people trapped under the debris of a building that had suffered direct hits by bombs. He first helped to rescue a Home Guard and later, with another Home Guard, got out two workmen from the same place. He then went to the other side of the debris and helped out a man and then a girl. He then tried to crawl into the building through a hole but was obstructed by some concrete. On attempting to knock a hole through the concrete he found that a girder prevented further progress. An oxy-acetylene cutter was used to cut through the girder and a girl and four men were released one at a time. A fierce fire was burning inside and was being fought from outside but Bailey held up a piece of concrete with his raised arms for some time and was saturated with oil and water. He finally collapsed near the entrance to the hole and was taken home in an ambulance."
(Birmingham Gazette 12.ii.1941; The Times 12.ii.1941) (Inv. 18. vii.1941)

Platoon Commander T. SIMPSON

(L.G. 27.v.1941)

"On the night of 11th December 1940 Platoon Commander Simpson actively assisted in rescuing several persons who were trapped beneath debris when an A.R.P. depot was hit. He had to crawl through debris with men supporting props and there was great danger of other parts of the building collapsing on him. He managed to saw through steel pipes and removed debris which was lying across trapped persons. He showed conspicuous gallantry and devotion to duty." *(The Times 28.v.1941) (Inv. 10.iii.1942)*

Volunteer A. W. BAILEY, 6th Birmingham Battalion. Instrumental in rescuing the survivors trapped under the debris of a building destroyed during an air raid on B.S.A. Guns Ltd.—19th November 1940.
Awarded the George Medal.

Platoon Commander T. SIMPSON, 6th Birmingham Battalion, who showed conspicuous gallantry while helping rescue people trapped beneath the wreckage of an A.R.P. depot at ·Tysely, Birmingham—11th December 1940.
Awarded the George Medal.

British Empire Medal

Sub-section Leader J. H. BEATTIE
(L.G. 11.ii.1941)

"Sub-section Leader Beattie assisted in the rescue of nine people from the flaming debris of a building. On several occasions he crawled into a hole in the debris and made contact with trapped survivors. He held up lumps of concrete to prevent them falling into the hole and he was saturated with oil and water. After some hours work he was completely exhausted and was evacuated by the medical authorities." *(The Times 12.ii.1941) (Inv. 22.iii.1941)*

Volunteer W. SARAGINE
(L.G. 11.ii.1941)

"Volunteer Saragine, a Home Guard despatch rider, was continuously on the road visiting damaged places and various fire fighting stations during an air raid on Birmingham. The anti-aircraft barrage was severe and high explosive and incendiary bombs were dropping continuously. On at least one occasion he passed within a few feet of a delayed action bomb." *(The Times 12.ii.1941) (Inv. 22.iii.1941)*

Section Leader J. TOPHAM
(L.G. 11.ii.1941)

"When members of the Home Guard were trapped under the debris of an air raid shelter which had been hit by a bomb Section Leader Topham and other volunteers entered the shelter and brought out four men, one of whom was dead and three injured. Topham then went to a building which had been struck by high explosive and incendiary bombs and assisted in saving five people. Later he returned to the hole where he had been working and played a hose on the blazing debris. His action resulted in four more survivors being evacuated. In all he was material in rescuing nine people." *(The Times 12.ii.1941) (Inv. 22.iii.1941)*

King's Commendation for Brave Conduct

Volunteer F. KNIGHT
(L.G. 11.ii.1941)

["For devotion to duty on the occasion of the bombing of the New Building, B.S.A., Small Heath, Birmingham on the night of 19th/20th November 1940.

He was conspicuous in his endeavours to rescue the wounded and worked continuously for several hours, until exhausted. Being of small stature he crawled into various holes under the debris on several occasions to locate the position of people trapped there. He was to a very great extent successful in these efforts and it was partly on the information he gave that successful evacuation of several people took place."]

Volunteer G. J. TREEN
Volunteer G. WILSON

(L.G. 11.ii.1941)

["For devotion to duty and great zeal on the occasion of the bombing of the New Building, B.S.A., Small Heath, Birmingham on the night of 19th/20th November 1940.

Both these men made several trips from the casualty centre to fetch blankets and comforts for the injured from the guard room. The anti-aircraft barrage was very severe at the time and bombs were falling but these men showed intense willingness to serve although neither was in possession of a steel helmet.

These men are very young and it is all the more to their credit that they showed absolutely no fear during the whole of this very severe bombardment."]

Notes: The 6th Birmingham Battalion could reasonably have claimed to be 'the most decorated battalion'. Six of their awards—those to Volunteer Bailey, Section Leaders Beatie and Topham, and Volunteers Knight, Treen and Wilson are attributable to gallantry within the factory premises of B.S.A. Guns Ltd. at Small Heath, Birmingham on the night of 19th/20th November 1940. Bailey was only eighteen years old and Treen and Wilson were both seventeen. For their gallantry in the same incident the following members of the factory staff also received awards: A. F. Stevens—George Medal; A. W. Goodwith and A. R. E. Harris—British Empire Medal (Civil Division); and S. S. Ashburner, E. Hoof and E. Williams—King's Commendations *(L.G. 17.i.1941).*

Platoon Commander Simpson was joined in his rescue efforts at the A.R.P. Depot, King's Road, Tysely, Birmingham by Deputy Superintendent W. T. Bates of the A.R.P. Casualty Service. Bates was also awarded the George Medal *(L.G. 21.iii.1941).* It is possible that civilian King's Commendations also arose from this incident.

Platoon Commander R. HAIGH, 9th Birmingham Battalion. Climbed 200 feet to the top of a gasholder during an air raid to extinguish a fire and prevent the escape of gas—22nd November 1940.
Awarded the George Medal.

9th BIRMINGHAM (PUBLIC UTILITIES) BATTALION
[later 29th WARWICKSHIRE (BIRMINGHAM) BATTALION]

George Medal

Platoon Commander R. HAIGH
(L.G. 11.ii.1941)

"At about eight p.m. on 22nd November 1940 a number of incendiary bombs fell on the Wagon Repair Shops and on Washwood Heath Gas Works. Haigh was P 19 Company Duty Officer and after one or two small fires in P 19 area had received attention, he proceeded, with Volunteer S. A. Tyler, to the Gas Works. They found two fires in the coal stack and extinguished them. Two smoke screen containers had been ignited and were burning with considerable flame. These, in the absence of equipment for dealing with oil fires, were extinguished with some difficulty. There was a plume of flame in the crown of one gasholder; at the time the crown on the gasholder was some 200 feet high. Haigh, taking the initiative and with three other men, ascended to the crown of the holder carrying sacks, and after considerable effort extinguished the fire and partially stopped the escape of gas with bags and clay. Another aperture in the crown of the holder, through which gas was escaping but not burning, was dealt with in the same way. No protective equipment was carried. The raid was still in progress, with bombs dropping in the vicinity, and the flame from the holder must have provided a continuous beacon. The action taken by Haigh and the other three men not only promptly removed the beacon, but also saved a considerable quantity of gas from escaping." *(The Times 12.ii.1941) (Inv. 18.vii.1941)*

King's Commendation for Brave Conduct

Volunteer S. A. TYLER
(L.G. 11.ii.1941)

For bravery and devotion to duty during an air raid at Washwood Heath Gas Works, Birmingham on 22nd November 1940.

> *Notes:* Two further awards of the George Medal and five King's Commendations in recognition of services at Washwood Heath Gas Works on 22nd November 1940 were announced in a list of awards "for services in Civil Defence" *(L.G. 31.i.1941).* The two men who climbed on to the gasholder with Haigh and Tyler were A. Bowles and G. T. Phillips, who both received King's Commendations.
>
> The incident is described, with portrait photographs, in the battalion history (see Bibliography).

Section Commander G. W. INWOOD, 10th Birmingham Battalion, who lost his life rescuing air raid victims trapped in a gas filled cellar—16th October 1940.
Posthumously awarded the George Cross

10th BIRMINGHAM (PUBLIC UTILITIES) BATTALION [later 30th WARWICKSHIRE (BIRMINGHAM) BATTALION]

George Cross (Posthumous)

Section Commander G. W. INWOOD
(L.G. 27.v.1941)

"Immediately following an intense air raid on the night of 15th/16th October 1940, Section Commander Inwood was called upon by the police to assist in rescue duty in Bishop Street, Birmingham.

Taking charge of a party of six volunteers, he found that several people were imprisoned in a gas-filled cellar. A small hole was made and Section Commander Inwood was lowered into the cavity. With great bravery he succeeded in bringing up two males alive. Although nearly exhausted, he entered the cavern a third time and was overcome by fumes. He was dragged out by one of his comrades, but despite the attention of a doctor and nurse, it was impossible to revive him.

He showed the highest form of cool courage and self-sacrifice for others." *(The Times 28.v.1941)*

> *Note:* Section Commander Inwood died on 16th October 1940 and is buried in Yardley Cemetery, Birmingham. His widow received his George Cross at an investiture on 10th October 1941.

British Empire Medal

Volunteer L. I. TIDBALL

(L.G. 27.v.1941)

["Following an intense air raid on 15th/16th October 1940, the police called on a battalion of the Birmingham Home Guard to assist in rescue duty. Volunteer Tidball was a member of a party of six volunteers under a section commander. They found several people imprisoned in a gas-filled cellar. A small hole was made and the section commander, with great bravery, was lowered into the cavity and rescued two males alive. He entered a third time but was overcome by fumes and was dragged to the surface by Volunteer Tidball, who was also overcome by fumes, but later recovered in hospital. It was impossible to revive the section commander.

Volunteer Tidball showed the utmost gallantry and devotion to duty in the face of great personal danger."] *(Inv. 29.vii.1941)*

12th BIRMINGHAM (PUBLIC UTILITIES) BATTALION [later 32nd WARWICKSHIRE (BIRMINGHAM) BATTALION]

King's Commendation for Brave Conduct

Sergeant G. H. ROWE

(L.G. 11.iii.1943)

["Sergeant Rowe was assisting in the supervision of live grenade throwing practice by a squad under instruction at Pheasey Farm Grenade Range, Birmingham on 29th November 1942.

One man failed to clear the top of the parapet with his throw and the grenade rolled back into the bay. He attempted to pick it up again but Sergeant Rowe, realising the danger of its immediate detonation, pushed the man away and literally carried him away from the throwing bay to safety.

Later a second man dropped his grenade after extracting the pin. In a moment of panic he attempted to climb out of the bay. Again Sergeant Rowe saved the situation by forcing the man away, pushing him to the ground and flinging himself on top of him. On this occasion fragments of the bursting grenade cut Sergeant Rowe's greatcoat.

These prompt actions, which he took without consideration for his personal safety although fully aware of the danger, undoubtedly averted serious, if not fatal, accidents. Sergeant Rowe's behaviour was exemplary."]

> *Notes:* A description of these two incidents which differs in some details appeared in the *Birmingham Gazette* of 23rd March 1943.
>
> 32nd Warwickshire Battalion was formed entirely from the employees of Birmingham Corporation Transport. Sergeant Rowe was a member of P 34 Unit, D Company, based at Selly Oak Garage. He was later awarded the British Empire Medal (Military Division). *(L.G. 8.vi.1944—Birthday Honours)*

F7 (AUSTIN AERO ENGINE CO LTD) COMPANY, BIRMINGHAM ZONE
[later part of 43rd WARWICKSHIRE (BIRMINGHAM) BATTALION]

George Medal

Platoon Commander R. E. Cooke
(L.G. 11.iii.1941)

"On 28th October 1940 a 550-lb bomb with delayed action fuse was located at the factory of Messrs. Burman Ltd., Hyland Road, Birmingham and the clock was found to be still ticking. The bomb had been down for approximately 45 hours and from experience an explosion was considered so imminent as to justify withdrawal of the working party. An attempt to remove the fuse failed and the officers concerned, together with Cooke, who was present the whole time, withdrew to consider the matter.

In view of the importance of the factory it was decided to attack the fuse a second time using a heavy crowbar. Three people were necessary and Cooke volunteered to make up the party. This time the fuse was partially removed but the ticking clock and the detonators still remained intact. It was then decided to flood the pit in an endeavour to stop the clock and Cooke's assistance again proved invaluable in what turned out to be a successful operation. The bomb was safely removed." *(P.R.O.—Air 2/9504) (Inv. 29.vii.1941)*

Note: 2nd Lieutenant R. H. Lee, 9th Bomb Disposal Company, Royal Engineers received the George Medal *(L.G. 22.i.1941)* for his part in the same incident.

Platoon Commander R. E. Cooke, Austin Aero Engine Ltd. Company, who assisted in rendering safe a 550-lb. delayed action bomb at a Birmingham factory—28th October 1940. Awarded the George Medal.

31

25th BIRMINGHAM BATTALION
[later 45th WARWICKSHIRE (BIRMINGHAM) BATTALION]

King's Commendation for Brave Conduct

Volunteer T. McINTYRE
(L.G. 2.xii.1941)

"On the night of 9th April 1941, during a heavy air raid, Volunteer McIntyre was a member of the guard from F 90 Unit at Messrs. Newey and Taylor's factory, Brearley Street, Birmingham. The works of E. Elliott Ltd. in Summer Lane received a direct hit from a high explosive bomb and the guard acted with great promptitude and efficiency, manning a trailer pump for one and a half hours and keeping the fire under control until the arrival of the Auxiliary Fire Service. During this incident great heroism was shown by Volunteer McIntyre, who, at very great risk to himself from falling masonry, rescued a number of people who were trapped." *(Barclay)*

POST OFFICE HOME GUARD UNIT, BIRMINGHAM
[later part of 47th WARWICKSHIRE (BIRMINGHAM) (G.P.O.) BATTALION]

British Empire Medal

Section Leader F. WRIGHT
(L.G. 22.i.1941)

["In the early hours of 27th August 1940 Section Leader Wright was on voluntary duty at Telephone House, Birmingham in charge of the Home Guard detachment when a prolonged enemy air attack developed with particular intensity on the central area of the city. A number of incendiary bombs fell on and around Telephone House and started serious fires in the surrounding properties, most of which were completely destroyed.

During and following the attack Section Leader Wright took a leading part in the measures adopted to protect Telephone House and personally assisted in extinguishing incendiary bombs. He also organised and led an attempt to suppress the fires in adjacent properties pending the arrival of the City Fire Brigade. In addition, he took the initiative in successfully rescuing a number of Post Office motor vans from a nearby garage which was threatened by fire from an adjacent building.

For a period of over two hours Section Leader Wright displayed courage, initiative and resource of a high order and his actions were a material contribution in saving Telephone House and Post Office property from serious damage. By his conduct throughout the incident he inspired a fine co-operative spirit in his colleagues."] *(Inv. 5.v.1942)*

King's Commendation for Brave Conduct

Volunteer L. HARTLAND
Volunteer F. J. PEACOCK

(L.G. 27.v.1941)

["On the night of 22nd/23rd November 1940 during an intense enemy air attack on Birmingham the guard room of the G.P.O. Home Guard battalion at the Post Office depot received a direct hit from a high explosive bomb. One of the guard was killed outright and another had his leg blown off.

Two other members of the guard, Volunteers Hartland and Peacock, rendered first aid to the injured man and left him in charge of a first aid party. They then went in search of a doctor. At this time the bombing was intensive and the streets were being machine-gunned. They found a doctor at a shelter about a quarter of a mile from the depot and Peacock guided him to the First Aid Post while Hartland went to the nearest First Aid Station about half a mile away to bring an ambulance.

Both Hartland and Peacock are eighteen years old".]

1st CARMARTHENSHIRE (CARMARTHEN) BATTALION

Member of the Order of the British Empire

Lieutenant J. R. RICHARDS

(L.G. 18.xi.1941)

"On 16th July 1941, at Ystrad Bombing Range, Carmarthen, an accident occurred under the following circumstances.

A volunteer of the Home Guard, after receiving theoretical instruction, was practising the throwing of a live Mills bomb. After he had removed the retaining pin, the bomb slipped from his hand and rolled some little distance away. The bombing instructor, Lieutenant Richards, an old soldier whose right arm was shot off in the Great War, ran to the bomb—the fuse of which by that time would have been burning for three or more seconds, picked up the bomb and threw it to a place of safety. One volunteer was injured, but had not Lieutenant Richards acted quickly with great presence of mind, many casualties would have been incurred." *(P.R.O.—Air 2/6262) (Inv. 28.vii.1942)*

2nd COVENTRY BATTALION
[later 12th WARWICKSHIRE (COVENTRY) BATTALION]

King's Commendation for Brave Conduct

Volunteer W. A. LEWIS
(L.G. 27.v.1941)

["Volunteer Lewis, who was on duty at company headquarters in Coventry during the night of 14th/15th November 1940, commandeered a double-decker bus, the only available transport, and without previous experience of driving a vehicle of this type conveyed casualties to hospital throughout the period of the raid—1900 hours to 0600 hours. He drove the bus continuously to whatever part of the city was being most heavily bombed and collected casualties, helping to extricate, load and unload the injured.

When enemy action had finished he had to be ordered to leave the driver's seat on account of exhaustion. He is 19 years old."]

6th COVENTRY BATTALION
[later 16th WARWICKSHIRE (COVENTRY) BATTALION]

King's Commendation for Brave Conduct

Volunteer C. J. RHODES
(L.G. 2.xii.1941)

["On 8th April 1941 Volunteer Rhodes reported at Daimler Home Guard headquarters for duty during enemy action.

While incendiary bombs were dropping on the works he assisted in emptying the guard room of ammunition and firearms. He then took up roof fire watching duties and afterwards proceeded to ascertain damage caused by a high explosive bomb that had dropped outside the works gates. As he was returning another high explosive bomb dropped outside the gates and brought several houses down. Volunteer Rhodes assisted in first aid treatment to several injured people.

On returning again to the works he met two firemen carrying an injured colleague from the works to the nearest place of safety. He assisted in carrying this man but while he was doing so another bomb fell, killing one of the firemen, seriously injuring the other, injuring the patient further and injuring Rhodes severely."]

7th COVENTRY BATTALION
[later 17th WARWICKSHIRE (COVENTRY) BATTALION]

King's Commendation for Brave Conduct

Platoon Commander A. L. LYON
(L.G. 8.vii.1941)

For bravery and devotion to duty during an air raid on Coventry on the night of 14th/15th November 1940, when he led a party that recovered valuable equipment from a fiercely burning building. His exemplary courage inspired confidence in his men.

8th COVENTRY BATTALION
[later 18th WARWICKSHIRE (COVENTRY) BATTALION]

British Empire Medal

Volunteer R. C. GRIFFIN
(L.G. 22.i.1941)

"On the night of 14th/15th November 1940 Volunteer Griffin was on duty in a roof-top observation post at Sir Alfred Herbert's machine tool factory in Coventry. A very heavy air raid developed but Volunteer Griffin remained at his post, constantly reporting to the control room below, for five hours while high explosive and incendiary bombs rained down.

After the complete destruction of a building some thirty yards from his post Volunteer Griffin was ordered to come down and report to the control room. There he immediately volunteered for further duty and was sent to fetch the works rescue squad from a street three-quarters of a mile away at a time when high explosive bombs were falling thickly in the area. Having brought back the rescue squad Griffin was sent to find a doctor to attend a badly wounded man. This entailed covering a considerable distance under conditions of great danger. Having found the doctor Griffin remained on duty until 9.00 a.m." *(The Alfred Herbert News Vol.15, No.1—Jan.-Feb. 1941)*

Section Commander W. LAKE
(L.G. 29.iv.1941)

"Section Commander Lake is a member of a works unit and on the night of 14th/15th November 1940 he was in charge of a strong point. He assisted in extinguishing numerous incendiary bombs and later at the request of the local fire brigade he cycled into the city centre through intense bombardment to seek assistance from the city brigade. He reported back to his post on foot as his cycle had been damaged. He then assisted in putting out more incendiary bombs and continued on duty until 10.00 a.m., when he left his post on hearing that his home was badly damaged and his wife and family seriously injured." *(The Times 30.iv.1941) (Inv. 24.ix.1942)*

UNIDENTIFIED WARWICKSHIRE (COVENTRY) BATTALION

King's Commendation for Brave Conduct

Volunteer J. A. YEOMANS
(L.G. 27.v.1941)

["Volunteer Yeomans, who is a member of Messrs. Webster and Bennett Ltd. Works Unit, volunteered for duty at the commencement of the raid on the night of 14th/15th November 1940. He did good work in extinguishing incendiary bombs and while returning from dealing with one which fell on neighbouring property he was severely wounded by a high explosive bomb. As a result of this injury one leg had to be amputated at the knee.

On previous raids Volunteer Yeomans has always shown courage and he has been prominent in volunteering for extra duties when raids occurred."]

1st DEVONSHIRE (LOYAL CITY OF EXETER) BATTALION

King's Commendation for Brave Conduct

Corporal A. H. HOPKINS
(L.G. 28.ix.1943)

For bravery and devotion to duty when Battalion Headquarters received a direct hit during an air raid on Exeter 4th/5th May 1942. *(Wiltsher)*

> *Note: Wiltsher* also states that Lieutenant H. J. Ferguson was appointed a Member of the Order of the British Empire in recognition of his services during the same incident. The appointment was announced in the Birthday Honours List of 1943 *(L.G: 2.vi.1943)* and is outside the scope of this account (see page 12).

7th DEVONSHIRE (OKEHAMPTON) BATTALION

George Medal

Lieutenant H. W. ROXBURGH
(L.G. 10.iii.1944)

"On 6th June 1943 at Hele Bridge Rifle Range, Hatherleigh, this officer made a faulty throw with a No.36 grenade, which fell close to the pit. Thinking that the lives of others might be endangered, he immediately picked up the grenade, which exploded in his hand. As a result he lost his right hand and left arm." *(H.G.I.C. No.48—24.v.1944/P.R.O.—Air 2/9001) (Inv. 24.x.1944)*

17th DEVONSHIRE (DEVONPORT) BATTALION

British Empire Medal

Sergeant H. A. SEARLE
(L.G. 28.ix.1943; amended 19.xi.1943)

"During the three nights 21st, 22nd and 23rd April 1941 Sergeant Searle did outstanding work as a runner after all telephone communication was out of action during air raids on Devonport. He maintained communication for the Passive Defence Officer and during one night carried messages for distances totalling ten miles in the Dockyard, under extremely heavy bombing.

On another occasion it was reported that a submarine's moorings had been destroyed by bombs and that this submarine was adrift and a danger to navigation. It was essential to get tugs away to secure this ship and Sergeant Searle got through to the tugs with the message and enabled the necessary action be be taken." *(H.G.I.C. No.43—1.iii.1944) (Inv. 2.iii.1945)*

21st DEVONSHIRE (POST OFFICE) BATTALION

British Empire Medal

Volunteer A. E. JANE
(L.G. 2.xii.1941)

["During the very heavy enemy air attack on Plymouth on the 20th March 1941 Volunteer Jane was on Home Guard duty at the front entrance to a telephone exchange when numerous incendiary and high explosive bombs were dropped. Premises adjoining the telephone exchange were set on fire. Realising that the armoury was in danger, Volunteer Jane, assisted by other members of the Home Guard, saved 40 rifles and over 4,000 rounds of ammunition. Shortly afterwards a lorry which was in the yard caught fire; the lorry contained some rifles and ammunition. Volunteer Jane immediately seized a fire extinguisher and put out the flames. He then returned to his post when a high explosive bomb dropped in the approach to the telephone exchange, injuring two members of the guard. Volunteer Jane assisted in carrying the injured into the building and rendered valuable first aid to both of the injured men, but one of them died shortly afterwards.

Volunteer Jane again returned to the front of the building and assisted in putting out fires which had broken out in lorries, and subsequently helped to move the lorries to a safer position. His cool bearing and utter disregard of personal danger were a source of inspiration to his comrades, and his knowledge of first aid was most valuable at a time when outside medical assistance was impossible to obtain."] *(Inv. 13.x.1942)*

Platoon Commander A. R. BALLANTYNE, 2nd Dumbartonshire Battalion, who displayed "conspicuous courage, energy and determination" in fighting fires during air raids on Clydebank—13th/14th and 14th/15th March 1941.
Awarded the George Medal.

2nd DUMBARTONSHIRE BATTALION

George Medal

Platoon Commander A. R. BALLANTYNE
(L.G. 8.vii.1941)

"On the night of 13th/14th March 1941, while on Home Guard duty in Singer's factory, Clydebank, during an intense air raid, Platoon Commander Ballantyne took command of all available Home Guards. Large quantities of incendiary and high explosive bombs were falling and he organised the fire-fighting with an utter disregard for his own safety. He then found a timber yard ablaze and personally assisted the Works Firemaster to carry hoses into the heart of the fire. Later, the Shipping Department took fire and he entered the building at great risk to himself and fought the fire. At 5.00 a.m. on 14th March, when the building containing the rifles, automatic weapons and ammunition of the Home Guard caught fire, he succeeded in saving all the weapons and practically all the ammunition. The factory was the focal point of this exceptionally heavy raid which was repeated on the following night.

During both periods, in spite of extreme fatigue, he displayed conspicuous courage, energy and determination in the face of great danger and was an inspiring example to his men." *(The Times 9.7.1941) (Inv. 8.xii.1942)*

38

British Empire Medal

Patrol Leader J. STEWART

(L.G. 30.ix.1941)

["On the night of the 13th/14th March 1941 Patrol Leader Stewart was on telephone duty at Douglas Street, Clydebank, maintaining communication under heavy bombardment when windows and doors were blown in all round him. On being relieved from this duty he joined a Home Guard rescue party detailed for work in Napier Street, Clydebank, where his energy and courage set a fine example to all in circumstances of great difficulty and danger. At great risk to himself he rescued three people from burning debris in the face of collapsing buildings and encroaching fire."] *(Inv. 3.iii.1942)*

King's Commendation for Brave Conduct

Sergeant R. DUNCAN

(L.G. 30.ix.1941)

For bravery and devotion to duty during and after air raids on Clydebank 13th/14th and 14th/15th March 1941.

Volunteer J. LATIMER

(L.G. 30.ix.1941)

["On the night of 13th/14th March 1941 in the vicinity of the Drill Hall, Douglas Street and in John Knox Street, Clydebank, Volunteer Latimer gave notable service in rescuing people injured and trapped in collapsed buildings. High explosive bombs continued to fall close at hand and his fine example and disregard for his personal safety gave encouragement to all those engaged in rescue work on these houses."]

Sergeant R. McKENZIE

(L.G. 30.ix.1941)

["On the night of 13th/14th March 1941 Sergeant McKenzie took command of a rescue party in Napier Street, Clydebank, where many people were trapped in burning debris. By his personal example and leadership he encouraged his men and was the means of saving the lives of a number of the victims. Heavy bombing of the immediate area was in progress at the time and the work of rescue was carried out in the face of considerable danger."]

Note: For some further details of the part played by 2nd Dumbartonshire Battalion, and notably A and C Companies of the Battalion, see *Graves* pages 204-5 and 340-1.

1st DUMFRIESSHIRE BATTALION

British Empire Medal

3178648 Company Sergeant-Major E. SMITH, K.O.S.B.
(L.G. 16.x.1942)

["On 3rd June 1942 C.S.M. Smith was supervising live grenade practice by members of the 1st Dumfries Battalion, Home Guard, to which he was attached. During the practice a grenade hit the top of the parapet and fell back into the priming bay. He closed the lids of the fuse and grenade boxes and kicked the grenade round a corner into the passage. The grenade exploded almost immediately, severely wounding C.S.M. Smith, whose action undoubtedly averted very serious consequences and probably saved the life of the soldier who was present in the bay. Had C.S.M. Smith not contrived to kick the grenade round the corner there would have been a grave chance of it coming to rest and exploding with very serious consequences at the entrance to the shelter, which contained forty men. His courageous conduct is enhanced by the fact that he was aware that the grenade was fitted with a four second fuse. He is now making a good recovery from his wounds."]

13th DURHAM (SEAHAM) BATTALION

King's Commendation for Brave Conduct

Sergeant R. L. TAYLOR
(L.G. 25.v.1943)

["On 7th February 1943 during live grenade throwing practice at a disused quarry at North Moor, County Durham, a member of Sergeant Taylor's company drew the safety pin from a No.36 grenade with seven second fuse and allowed the grenade to drop to the ground. The grenade began to roll down a slope towards the remainder of the company, who were watching the proceedings.

With great courage and presence of mind Sergeant Taylor, who was acting as instructor at the practice, dived for the grenade and threw it to a place of safety just before it exploded, thus undoubtedly averting a number of casualties."]

1st ESSEX BATTALION

Member of the Order of the British Empire

2nd Lieutenant S. J. WHITE
(L.G. 2.xii.1941)

"On 18th May 1941 a platoon of the Home Guard was ordered to attend at Thorpe Hall Golf Links for practice with live hand grenades. A member of the platoon who had had experience in the last war was instructed to throw one of the grenades. He pulled the pin and, instead of throwing the grenade, dropped it and ran away. Second-Lieutenant White, who was nearby, immediately and calmly picked up the smoking grenade and threw it clear of others who were in attendance, thereby displaying a fine demonstration of personal disregard of his own safety for the sake of others. The grenade exploded immediately after Second-Lieutenant White had thrown it away." *(P.R.O.—Air 2/6262/Finch) (Inv. 23.iii.1943)*

3rd ESSEX BATTALION

British Empire Medal

Private J. E. BASS
(L.G. 5.v.1944)

"During an air raid incendiary bombs were dropped on railway property. Private Bass at once reported for duty and on arrival at the scene he observed fires burning. The area was full of smoke and sparks. A number of wagons were loaded with filled canisters for generating smoke screens.

As Private Bass realised that the fire would spread to a number of other wagons unless those that were burning were segregated, he went to the engine house and raised steam in an engine that was warm. He then located the local railway inspector who happened to be on duty and asked him if he could take the engine out and deal with the burning trucks. This permission was given and Private Bass, single-handed, took the engine by a necessarily circuitous route which involved dealing with eight sets of points. With assistance he then segregated the burning wagons. In carrying out the operation Private Bass displayed cool courage, initiative and devotion to duty." *(H.G.I.C. No.51—28.vi.1944/Finch) (Inv. 2.ii.1945)*

King's Commendation for Brave Conduct

2nd Lieutenant P. F. BENNETT
(L.G. 7.vii.1944)

For bravery and devotion to duty when a railway goods yard was hit during an air raid and wagons containing ammunition were set on fire.

Note: Private Bass, 2nd Lieutenant Bennett and T/224765 Driver H. G. Atkins, R.A.S.C. were all involved in the same incident, as is made clear by H.G.I.C.s Nos. 51 and 55. Driver Atkins also received a King's Commendation.

7th ESSEX BATTALION

Member of the Order of the British Empire

Captain W. L. WAINWRIGHT
(L.G. 15.ix.1944)

"On 8th May 1944 Captain Wainwright, who is 76 years of age, displayed bravery, initiative and fortitude when a small house containing explosives caught fire a short distance away from his garden. The wooden sides of the building quickly caught fire. Realizing that he could not prevent the fire from spreading, Captain Wainwright entered the building and, at great risk, was successful in carrying out a considerable quantity of explosives. Whilst he was doing this the roof of the building collapsed causing Captain Wainwright to sustain serious burns about the face, neck, hands and arms. After having had his burns dressed, however, he insisted on returning to the scene and gave all the assistance he possibly could until it was found that nothing further could be done to save the building." *(The Times 16.ix.1944/Finch) (Inv. 3.vii.1945)*

1st FIFESHIRE BATTALION

Member of the Order of the British Empire

Lieutenant T. F. WILSON
(L.G. 10.xi.1944)

"At Newburgh on 23rd April 1944 during live grenade practice a four-second No.36 grenade failed to clear the cover and rolled back behind the thrower. Lieutenant Wilson, seeing that the man who had thrown the grenade might not be able to get to cover in time ran over to try and move the grenade, but it exploded, causing serious injuries to this officer, but leaving unhurt the man for whom he felt himself responsible." *(Dunfermline Press 18.xi.1944) (Inv. 22.vi.1945)*

1st GLAMORGANSHIRE (ABERDARE) BATTALION

Member of the Order of the British Empire

Major S. L. C. BOUGHTON, M.C.
(L.G. 17.ii.1942)

"On 14th September 1941 at Cwmbach, Aberdare, Major Boughton was in charge of the throwing bay at a live bombing practice when a volunteer about to throw a grenade accidentally released the handle after withdrawing the safety pin. The volunteer was instructed by Major Boughton to get rid of the grenade but in his confusion he threw it into the priming bay among three volunteers and three instructors. Major Boughton at once called to the men to get out. He then jumped into the priming bay, seized the grenade and threw it over the parapet, where it exploded immediately in the air. As a result only one man was wounded and then only slightly, whereas, but for Major Boughton's prompt action, which was carried out at great risk to himself, at least six men would have been seriously wounded or possibly killed." *(P.R.O.—Air 2/8908) (Inv. 14.iv.1942)*

9th GLAMORGANSHIRE (MERTHYR) BATTALION

Member of the Order of the British Empire

Lieutenant T. H. THOMAS

(L.G. 11.i.1944)

"Lieutenant Thomas acted with great presence of mind whilst he was supervising a practice with live grenades on the 5th September 1943. A member of the Home Guard, after withdrawing the safety pin preparatory to throwing a grenade, dropped the live grenade between his feet. Lieutenant Thomas made an attempt to pick it up and throw it out of the throwing bay, but as the man was between him and the grenade, he pushed the man away to cover, kicked the grenade into cover of the throwing bay, and stamped it into the earth. As a result of this officer's prompt and courageous action, the only result of the accident was that the man received a slight flesh wound in the foot. Lieutenant Thomas has always shown great conscientiousness and presence of mind in the performance of his duties and has also shown great keenness in detecting unexploded mortar bombs on a number of occasions." *(H.G.I.C. No.44—8.iii.1944)*

12th GLAMORGANSHIRE (SWANSEA) BATTALION

King's Commendation for Brave Conduct

Volunteer P. E. R. HANSEN

(L.G. 26.viii.1941)

["Volunteer Hansen showed great initiative and personal bravery in dealing with incendiary bombs in Swansea on the night of 17th/18th January 1941. In the absence of a ladder he climbed a drainpipe to the high roof of a fire station and threw incendiary bombs down to the street below. By so doing he saved an extensive conflagration in a vital part of the town which was all the time under enemy parachute flares and into which high explosive bombs were constantly dropping.

Further, on the night of 17th/18th January he entered a blazing furniture shop and assisted in the removal of a car and cans of petrol. Several fires were raging close to the affected area during these two actions.

His courage and leadership have been of inestimable value and he has been the subject of mention for continual personal bravery during further attacks on Swansea on 19th, 20th and 21st February."]

15th GLAMORGANSHIRE (GOWER) BATTALION

British Empire Medal

Sergeant W. DAVIES
Private G. E. REES

(L.G. 4.ii.1944)

["On 11th December 1942 a report was received indicating that Royal Air Force personnel were in danger off Burry Holmes. Sergeant Davies instructed Private Rees to accompany him and they went to the point indicated where they saw five men clinging to the rocks in the sea some distance from the mainland. These five men had been there for three days in a rubber dinghy without food and were totally exhausted.

In extremely dangerous conditions, at high spring tide, and in a raging storm Sergeant Davies and Private Rees plunged into the open sea to render assistance. Sergeant Davies and Private Rees reached the five men, rendered them first aid and remained with them for two hours until the tide had receded sufficiently for them to be helped to the mainland. But for such assistance all five men would unquestionably have lost their lives as they were in imminent danger of being washed away in the storm.

The actions of these two men called for the greatest bravery and determination and resulted in the saving of the lives of the five Royal Air Force personnel.''] *(Invs. 16.ii.1945)*

> *Note:* Sergeant Davies and Private Rees originally received a civilian King's Commendation for Brave Conduct "when rescuing from the sea the crew of a crashed aircraft" *(L.G. 30.vii.1943)*. This was cancelled with the announcement of the award of the British Empire Medal.

UNIDENTIFIED GLAMORGANSHIRE (CARDIFF) BATTALION

King's Commendation for Brave Conduct

Volunteer T. E. O'LEARY
(L.G. 21.x.1941)

For bravery and devotion to duty in helping to rescue a survivor after S. S. *Lunan* hit a mine and sank on 4th July 1941.

[At about 1.20 a.m. on 4th July 1941 a loud explosion was heard by personnel on duty at Victoria Wharf, Cardiff. A cloud of black smoke began to form some two hundred yards from the dockside and it was clear that a mine or delayed-action bomb had exploded. A small coaling vessel, S. S. *Lunan* (379 tons), had in fact been sunk with the loss of six of her seven crew. The single survivor could be heard shouting for help.

Volunteer O'Leary and Police Constable 9B Everett of Cardiff City Police at once went in search of a boat. They found a delapidated rowing boat and set out with Volunteer O'Leary rowing and Police Constable Everett baling out water. The rowing boat was directed to the wreck by means of flash lights and the survivor, who was in poor condition, covered with coal dust and oil and suffering from shock, was brought to the shore and taken to hospital. Shortly after landing the survivor Volunteer O'Leary collapsed, suffering from shock and lacerated hands, and was taken to hospital.

Volunteer O'Leary and Police Constable Everett were instrumental in saving the life of the only survivor in difficult and dangerous conditions.]

> *Note:* Police Constable W. J. Everett received a civilian King's Commendation for Brave Conduct *(L.G. 26.ix.1941)*.

1st CITY OF GLASGOW BATTALION

King's Commendation for Brave Conduct

Staff-Sergeant D. B. MILNE
(L.G. 7.vii.1944)

"On 16th January 1944 Staff-Sergeant Milne was in the throwing bay at a bombing range when a No.36 grenade was thrown which did not clear the parapet but hit the corrugated iron revetting. The grenade rebounded and hit the back wall of the bay, from which it dropped to the ground. Without hesitation Staff-Sergeant Milne pushed the thrower towards the bombing officer who was standing between the throwing and priming bays and who pulled him into the priming bay. The grenade was lying in such a position that if it exploded it might still endanger those in the priming bay so Staff-Sergeant Milne kicked it into the front of the throwing bay and himself took cover with the others.

It was undoubtedly due to the coolness and presence of mind of this n.c.o. that a serious accident was averted." *(H.G.I.C. No.55—16.viii.1944/Air 2/9001)*

2nd CITY OF GLASGOW BATTALION

King's Commendation for Brave Conduct (Posthumous)

2nd Lieutenant W. COOK
(L.G. 9.vii.1943)

["On 3rd April 1943 2nd Lieutenant Cook was instructing in the throwing of live No. 36 grenades set with four second fuses. One grenade fell short, struck the parapet and dropped back into the bay at the feet of the thrower, who stooped to retrieve it.

2nd Lieutenant Cook, realising the danger of delay, dashed into the bay, pushed the man to safety, and himself seized the grenade but before he was able to throw it from the trench it exploded. He was mortally wounded and died three hours later.

By his unhesitating action this very gallant officer, at the cost of his own life, undoubtedly saved that of one of his men."]

Note: 2nd Lieutenant Cook, who died on 3rd April 1943, is buried in North Merchiston Cemetery, Edinburgh.

3rd CITY OF GLASGOW BATTALION

King's Commendation for Brave Conduct

Volunteer W. A. MOODIE
(L.G. 22.vii.1941)

"On the night of 13th/14th March 1941 while on duty in Glasgow as battalion headquarters runner during a severe air raid he displayed great courage and coolness in carrying out his duties throughout the night, although twice knocked out by exploding bombs." *(P.R.O.—Air 2/9504)*

4th CITY OF GLASGOW BATTALION

King's Commendation for Brave Conduct

Section Leader E. GIBLIN
(L.G. 22.vii.1941)

["On the nights of 13th/14th and 14th/15th March 1941 while on duty in the shipbuilding yard of Mechans Ltd., Glasgow during severe air raids Section Leader Giblin displayed great devotion to duty and disregard for danger.

A land mine exploded immediately outside the yard forming a crater thirty feet across within which a gas main caught fire. Section Leader Giblin led a party which tackled this fire, shovelling sand and earth on the pipe outlet and covering it with bags, running a considerable risk in so doing, not only from the blaze but from continual bombing and falling shrapnel. If this action had not been taken the fire would have attracted further aircraft, which were in the vicinity for some hours.

His courage and energy throughout a continuous spell of fifty-two hours duty were an inspiring example to all."]

1st HAMPSHIRE (ANDOVER) BATTALION

British Empire Medal

Sergeant W. R. GREEN
(L.G. 23.xii.1943)

"On 3rd October 1943 Sergeant Green and an officer were conveying a projectile, which was thought to be defective, for demolition. A short distance from their destination the projectile exploded. The truck in which they were travelling continued on its course until it hit a hedge. Sergeant Green, though badly wounded, bleeding heavily and in great pain and unable to walk, succeeded in getting the officer out of the truck as he was too seriously wounded to move himself. Sergeant Green then crawled about one and a quarter miles to a farm for assistance. It is considered that unless Sergeant Green, by his fortitude and presence of mind under circumstances in which he might have thought the condition of the officer to be hopeless, had striven to crawl that long distance to secure help the officer would not have survived to receive medical attention." *(H.G.I.C. No.43—1.iii.1944) (Inv. 16.ii.1945)*

14th HAMPSHIRE (FAREHAM) BATTALION

King's Commendation for Brave Conduct (Posthumous)

Lieutenant L. B. BRUDENELL
(L.G. 28.ix.1943)

For bravery and devotion to duty in saving life at the cost of his own during live grenade practice. *(P.R.O.—Air 2/9289)*

Note: Lieutenant Brudenell died on 28th February 1943 and is buried in Porchester (St. Mary) Churchyard, Fareham, Hampshire.

16th HAMPSHIRE (HAVANT) BATTALION

King's Commendation for Brave Conduct

Sergeant C. E. H. HUTCHINGS
(L.G. 16.x.1942)

["Sergeant Hutchings, who lost both legs in the Great War, was involved in a road accident while riding his motor cycle combination on duty on the night of 17th April 1941 during an air raid. He received serious head injuries and one of his artificial legs was smashed. While he was recovering serum fever intervened and at one stage it was doubtful if he would survive. On 6th May he was allowed out of doors for the first time.

The same night incendiary bombs fell in his garden, a few feet away from the back of the house, and set fire to a wooden fence and a cycle shed. Although deprived of the use of his artificial legs, Sergeant Hutchings, with the aid of his wife, fought the fire with sandbags and a stirrup pump. When it was under control he was told that a neighbour's shop was on fire. He immediately climbed into his invalid chair, put the stirrup pump on board and trundled round to the shop where he gave assistance. Subsequently he patrolled The Broadway, Havant Road in his chair and helped other fire watchers."]

18th HAMPSHIRE (DOCKYARD/PORT) BATTALION

King's Commendation for Brave Conduct

Colour-Sergeant V. G. WHITE
(L.G. 7.vii.1944)

"During live grenade practice on 13th February 1944 Colour-Sergeant White, the instructor, prevented a very serious accident and probably loss of life through his very prompt action in disposing of a burning grenade which had fallen into the throwing bay. After landing in the bay the grenade became lodged amongst the loose chalk.

Colour-Sergeant White immediately ordered the detail to take cover, extricated the grenade after some difficulty and threw it over the top. It exploded in mid air."
(P.R.O.—Air 2/9001)

VOSPER FACTORY UNIT
[later part of 31st HAMPSHIRE (COSHAM) BATTALION]

British Empire Medal

Section Leader J. CHANTLER
(L.G. 18.xi.1941)

["During an air raid on the night of 10th/11th January 1941, Section Leader Chantler was on Home Guard duty at Vospers.

Although not trained as a fireman, his organising ability and splendid example could not have been bettered. His very prompt action prevented a serious outbreak in the machine shop and thousands of pounds worth of irreplaceable machinery engaged on urgent Admiralty work was thereby saved from destruction. Without his fearless energy and prompt action against continuous attacks with incendiaries, it would have been impossible to leave the machine shop mentioned under his care whilst the fire brigade concentrated on the blazing timber store and boat building shed at the other end of the works. He led his section with the greatest energy wherever it could be used most effectively, and a nearby delayed action bomb was completely disregarded during the whole of these operations. The bomb subsequently exploded very shortly after the raid without harm to anyone, as the area around it had by then been cleared.

The particular efficiency of this Home Guard unit, when it was needed to the very utmost, was undoubtedly greatly due to Section Leader Chantler's nerve and qualities of leadership."] *(Inv. 29.ix.1942)*

8th KENT (CINQUE PORTS) BATTALION

Member of the Order of the British Empire

Lieutenant A. J. WHITTINGSTALL
(L.G. 17.ii.1942)

"On 12th October 1941 Lieutenant Whittingstall was in command of a platoon of the Kent Home Guard when the platoon was being exercised in throwing live Mills grenades. A volunteer slipped and dropped a four second grenade. Lieutenant Whittingstall immediately ordered the men of his platoon to lie down and, with great presence of mind, placed himself with his feet against the grenade helping thereby to localise the effects of the explosion and the area of danger. When the grenade burst Lieutenant Whittingstall was wounded in the left foot, but by his courageous action he saved the rest of the platoon from casualties." *(P.R.O.—Air 2/8908/Graves) (Inv. 12.v.1942)*

1st BATTALION 'P' ZONE, LONDON
[later 51st KENT BATTALION]

British Empire Medal

Volunteer S. W. Anthony
(L.G. 22.i.1941)
"In October 1940 at Bromley a house received a direct hit from a bomb. When Anthony was told that people had been trapped he went through a ground floor window, although the house was collapsing, and found an injured man trying to rescue his child. He helped the man out and then, with the aid of another helper, began the work of rescuing the child." *(Bromley and West Kent Mercury 31.i.1941/Graves) (Inv. 3.iii.1942)*

Volunteer W. E. Whybrow
(L.G. 22.i.1941)
"In September 1940 at Shortlands he clambered into the ruins of a bombed house without the slightest regard for his personal safety and the fact that portions of the building and the outside walls were collapsing and the gas main blazing, and extricated an injured man." *(Bromley and West Kent Mercury 31.i.1941/Graves) (Inv. 3.iii.1942)*

3rd KESTEVEN (GRANTHAM AND SPITTLEGATE) BATTALION

King's Commendation for Brave Conduct

Platoon Commander A. L. Dawrant
Volunteer R. W. Ellacott
Volunteer G. A. M. McNicoll
Platoon Commander R. H. T. Ridler
(L.G. 17.vi.1941)
"On 3rd December 1940 an enemy aircraft was engaged by the British Manufacture and Research Company's factory defence guns during a daylight low-level bombing attack. The plane was hit, damaged and driven off.

On 27th January 1941 another enemy aircraft was engaged by the factory defence guns in a daylight low-level bombing attack and was shot down.

All these men were in action in the open on the factory roof without any protection whatsoever. Bombs and machine gun bullets fell all around. They displayed great gallantry and coolness in moments of great stress when their own lives and those of hundreds of their colleagues depended on their actions.

It should be observed that these men perform their daily duties at the factory and give up considerable time at night to factory defence. Mr Dawrant is the secretary of the company, Mr Ridler is chief accountant, Mr McNicoll an accountant and Mr Ellacott a clerk." *(P.R.O.—Air 2/9504)*

1st COUNTY OF LANCASTER (BARROW) BATTALION

King's Commendation for Brave Conduct

Volunteer V. BLACKBURN
(L.G. 16.xii.1941)

["When the 'alert' sounded on 16th April 1941 Volunteer Blackburn volunteered for duty. He helped restore some order in the hall and before the arrival of the A.R.P. services rescued some people trapped in a room which was on fire. Later he was instrumental in rescuing others from houses demolished by a land mine.

Only twenty four hours previously he had been doing similar work continuously for eighteen hours in a wrecked area, refusing to stop until he was satisfied everyone was accounted for."]

Sergeant E. WHALLEY
(L.G. 16.xii.1941)

["When the 'alert' sounded on 16th April 1941 Sergeant Whalley volunteered to augment the guard at C Company Headquarters and helped to maintain a watch on the roof of the hall.

While he was patrolling a land mine exploded in Union Street and blew him over. He then returned to the hall, only to be blown down the stairs by another land mine which exploded in Abbey Road. Finding out first if those in the building were injured, he put out the lights and helped secure some window frames which were in unsafe condition. He was then sent to ascertain where the mines had fallen and render such help as he could. Much damage had been caused in Carlisle Street and there he helped in bringing to safety elderly and bed-ridden people, put out two fires caused by blast and rescued a fire watcher trapped in business premises.

Despite continued enemy action he did not spare himself in his exertions and when more volunteers reported for duty he was an inspiration to all."]

77th COUNTY OF LANCASTER (BOOTLE) BATTALION

King's Commendation for Brave Conduct

Company Sergeant-Major S. N. LEE, M.M.
(L.G. 13.i.1942)

[For bravery and devotion to duty during an air raid on Bootle on the night of 20th/21st October 1941. C.S.M. (then Sergeant) Lee worked for over two hours rescuing injured people trapped in damaged Anderson shelters in Worcester Road, Bootle. Throughout the time that he was engaged in this work enemy aircraft were overhead and bombs were falling.]

86th COUNTY OF LANCASTER (LIVERPOOL) BATTALION

King's Commendation for Brave Conduct

Lieutenant A. F. L. HAGGART
(L.G. 26.viii.1941)

["At about 00.30 hours on 4th May 1941 a large number of incendiary bombs fell on the Breck Park railway sidings, Liverpool, causing several fires in the area. An ammunition train loaded with 250-lb bombs caught fire and at intervals until about 06.30 hours the bombs exploded, with devastating effect on the immediate neighbourhood. During the whole of this time Sergeant Ankers of the Liverpool Fire Brigade, Lieutenant A. F. L. Haggart, Home Guard and Miss M. R. Williams, a lady air raid warden, displayed great courage in the performance of their duties.

Sergeant Ankers was calm and resourceful and, acting as leader in the operations, he was an inspiration to all who assisted him. In attempting to control the fires and remove the burning ammunition train from the area he showed complete disregard for his own safety and acted with courage and resource.

Lieutenant Haggart and Miss Williams were conspicuous for the way in which they helped to evacuate people from the area. Although Lieutenant Haggart was injured and bombs fell very close to Miss Williams both held tenaciously to their tasks and only ceased when danger had abated."]

Note: Sergeant Ankers received the British Empire Medal (Civil Division) and Miss Williams was commended "for brave conduct in Civil Defence" *(L.G. 1.viii.1941)*.

UNIDENTIFIED COUNTY OF LANCASTER (LIVERPOOL) BATTALION [MINISTRY OF SUPPLY HOME GUARD COMPANY]

British Empire Medal

Lance-Corporal J. A. W. PIPER
(L.G. 17.vi.1941)

"On the night of 12th/13th March 1941 Lance-Corporal Piper was Corporal of the Guard at Oceanic House, Liverpool, when an enemy air raid took place.

A number of incendiary bombs were dropped on the building and one of these set the roof alight. Without hesitation, Lance-Corporal Piper proceeded to the top of the building and at great personal risk slid down the steeply sloping roof and recovered six of the incendiaries. Owing to the steepness of the roof he had to be hauled back on the end of a stirrup pump hose. Although the guard was compelled to evacuate the building, Lance-Corporal Piper remained at his post to the last bringing out of the building, undamaged, all the Home Guard equipment.

His conduct throughout was an example to his squad and his leadership materially assisted in reducing the damage." *(The Times 18.vi.1941) (Inv. 24.ii.1942)*

3rd CITY OF LONDON (FARRINGDON) BATTALION

Member of the Order of the British Empire

Lieutenant W. J. R. Bolt
(L.G. 21.x.1941)

"Lieutenant Bolt displayed conspicuous courage and devotion to duty in the early morning of 11th May 1941, when, during a heavy enemy attack from the air, a large bomb fell in the W.C. district of London and demolished several houses.

Lieutenant Bolt burrowed a tunnel under the debris and managed to reach a woman and two men. With the aid of a volunteer he managed to extricate one of the men and got him to safety. He then turned his attention to the woman, who had been pinned to a table by a heavy beam lying across her shoulders. The only way to free her was by sawing through the beam, but this involved the danger of the whole ceiling and superstructure collapsing upon the rescuers. Nevertheless the risk was taken and under great difficulty the beam was sawn through and prised up to relieve the woman. She was successfully got out and passed up into the street. Attention was then given to the third victim, who was pinned under rafters and masonry, but he could be only partially freed. The task of completing his extrication was left to the A.R.P. rescue party.

Throughout these operations Lieutenant Bolt was subject to three perils—the collapse of the ceiling and masonry while the beam was being sawn through, asphyxiation by gas which was escaping freely, and fire which broke out while rescue work was in progress." *(The Times 22.x.1941) (Inv. 14.vii.1942)*

British Empire Medal

Volunteer F. Nicholls
(L.G. 21.x.1941)

"Volunteer Nicholls displayed great personal courage and devotion to duty in the face of grave perils in the early morning of 11th May 1941, when, during a heavy enemy attack from the air, a large bomb demolished several houses in the W.C. district of London.

The aid of the Home Guard being requested, a volunteer of slender build was called for to crawl through a tunnel in a mass of debris, to the interior of a collapsed basement where several people were trapped. Volunteer Nicholls at once volunteered to go, taking with him a saw which had already been asked for by a Home Guard officer, who had already secured an entry to the basement. Acting under the instructions of the Home Guard officer, Volunteer Nicholls sawed through a heavy beam which had pinned down a woman. He did so despite the fact that his action threatened to bring down the ceiling and whole superstructure on top of him. Having sawn through the beam he helped to release the woman and to pass her out to the street. He then helped in rescue operations of another person who had been trapped under rafters and masonry.

Throughout these operations Volunteer Nicholls ran the risk of being crushed by falling masonry, asphyxiation by gas which was escaping freely, and fire which broke out before the rescue operations were completed." *(The Times 22.x.1941) (Inv. 24.iii.1942)*

1st BATTALION 'K' ZONE, LONDON
[later 12th CITY OF LONDON (BARKING AND ILFORD) BATTALION]

George Medal

Volunteer S. J. FERGUSON

(L.G. 11.ii.1941)

"On the night of 17th/18th October 1940 during a heavy enemy attack from the air, in the Barking area, Volunteer Ferguson, who was on duty at his company headquarters, proceeded to a group of houses which had received direct hits.

It was reported to him that a woman—a resident of one of the houses—was imprisoned under the wreckage. Despite the fact that the walls of the dwelling were collapsing, he made his way without hesitation into the ruins and found a woman bleeding from a severed artery. Ferguson at once applied first aid amid the flames of incendiary bombs and gave every help to her, at risk of his own life. He remained beside her until it was possible to remove her for conveyance to hospital." *(The Times 12.ii.1941) (Inv. 25.vii.1941)*

2nd BATTALION 'K' ZONE, LONDON
[later 13th CITY OF LONDON (WEST HAM) BATTALION]

Officer of the Order of the British Empire

Company Commander A. W. RICHARDS, M.M.

(L.G. 22.vii.1941)

"During a phase of intensive air attack, Company Commander Richards, commanding a Home Guard company in Barking, displayed consistent devotion to duty and complete disregard of his own safety, by rendering assistance on several occasions to victims of enemy bombs.

On one occasion he organised a party of volunteers from his company to render succour to patients of a hospital that had suffered direct hits. By skilful direction of the operations and his own participation in the work of clearing debris, though the whole district was under intense bombardment from the air, he was instrumental in saving a number of lives. He worked continuously throughout the night and only gave up when he was on the point of collapse from physical exhaustion.

On another occasion when large numbers of high explosive bombs and incendiaries were dropped in the area covered by his company, he formed a patrol to help extinguish fires. At great personal risk he climbed to the top of one house—as there were no ladders available he had to scale up the pipes of the house with high explosive bombs and shrapnel falling all round him—and gaining the roof, managed to extinguish the incendiaries. Afterwards he helped to extinguish several more fires, going from one to another, helping in rescue work, and organising the best possible assistance.

His ability, leadership, and total disregard of peril, cannot be too highly commended." *(The Times 24.vii.1941) (Inv. 10.ii.1942)*

King's Commendation for Brave Conduct

Sub-section Leader P. F. NEWMAN
(L.G. 11.ii.1941)

["Following the explosion of a land mine and the showering of incendiary bombs all over the district, Sub-section Leader Newman organised a party and entered a school building which was already ablaze. The caretaker and a number of other people were in the basement and did not know of the fire overhead. Sub-section Leader Newman told them of the danger and despite heavy bombardment from the air proceeded to climb to the roof, where he succeeded in dealing with a number of incendiary bombs.

His prompt and energetic action not only saved the building but a number of lives, for the occupants of the basement were asleep."]

Lance-Corporal W. DUNLOP
(L.G. 30.ix.1941)

["On the night of 8th March 1941 Lance-Corporal Dunlop was on fire watching duty during a heavy raid. The 'British Empire' public house in Barking Road received a direct hit and, realising that some people had been trapped, he immediately began to search the premises, despite falling masonry. Eventually the light of a warden's torch revealed one victim buried up to the head in the fallen debris. With total disregard for his own safety Lance-Corporal Dunlop dug his way under the debris and effected a rescue. He later succeeded in rescuing other people who had been completely buried. They were undoubtedly saved through his efforts."]

L.M.S. RAILWAY UNIT, ST. PANCRAS
[later part of 16th CITY OF LONDON (L.M.S. BROAD STREET) BATTALION]

British Empire Medal

Volunteer C. E. CORNWELL
(L.G. 11.iii.1941)

"A bomb explosion extinguished the lights of the guard room and Volunteer Cornwell and three others came out to see what was happening. They were directed to the scene of the explosion by Machine Attendant Tubbs and discovered that an engine had been struck and the boiler pierced, causing steam to enter the cab and imprisoning both driver and fireman.

Volunteer Cornwell, who is a goods checker, climbed into one side of the cab while Machine Attendant Tubbs endeavoured to get in the other side. Eventually both the crew were successfully extricated, although the fireman was found to be dead. The driver, who suffered severe injuries, also died while having his wounds dressed." *("Carry On"—L.M.S. War-time Newsletter Vol. 2, No.18—April 1941) (Inv. 24.iii.1942)*

28th CITY OF LONDON (7th G.P.O.) BATTALION

King's Commendation for Brave Conduct

Lieutenant P. A. SMITH
(L.G. 19.xi.1943)

["Lieutenant Smith was the Home Guard duty officer at Mount Pleasant on the night of 17th/18th June 1943 when the Parcel Office was set on fire by enemy action and eventually destroyed.

He showed complete disregard of personal danger in the flames, smoke and dust caused by the bomb explosion in the Parcel Station Basement and was tireless in his search for, and rescue of, casualties. He prevented further disaster by safeguarding the ammunition store and saved official property from the flames, besides organising effective patrols in and around the burning building.

His courage, resourceful leadership and presence of mind were an inspiration to all engaged in minimising the effects of the bombing."]

29th CITY OF LONDON (8th G.P.O.) BATTALION

British Empire Medal

Corporal A. V. JONES
(L.G. 26.viii.1941)

"Corporal Jones was in charge of a Home Guard detachment on duty during an air raid. Two buildings were damaged by incendiary bombs and by direct hits or blast from high explosive bombs. He displayed great personal courage and devotion to duty in a critical situation of some hours duration and inspired his men by personally engaging in various measures to meet the emergency which arose. In addition to fighting a fire for three hours with an improvised water supply and finally subduing it, despite suggestions that the buildings should be evacuated, Corporal Jones also dealt with an outbreak of fire on the roofs of other buildings nearby. But for his untiring efforts these buildings would undoubtedly have suffered much more serious damage, if not complete destruction, as the fire-fighting services were all heavily engaged in dealing with serious fires which were raging in the neighbourhood and were unable to render assistance." *(The Times 27.viii.1941) (Inv. 19.v.1942)*

2nd BATTALION 'H' ZONE, LONDON

George Medal

Volunteer D. LAZARUS

(L.G. 11.ii.1941)

"During an enemy air raid in the Aldgate district Volunteer Lazarus, a Home Guard aged 17, was on his way to report for duty when a bomb fell on a block of tenement flats. The explosion caused great havoc and the building was reduced to ruins. Masonry and other debris was falling continuously but Volunteer Lazarus, with complete disregard for his own safety, entered the ruins and began to remove quantities of wreckage with his hands in order to get to four people who were imprisoned. He managed to bring them all out, despite the fact that he had already sustained injuries. Instead of seeking first aid for himself, however, he made an attempt to rescue a fifth occupant of the flats, but a wall collapsed and buried him. He was taken to hospital suffering from multiple injuries to the head, arms and body." *(The Times 12.ii.1941) (Inv. 18.vii.1941)*

Volunteer D. LAZARUS, 2nd Battalion 'H' Zone, London. At the age of only seventeen rescued several people from a block of flats in Aldgate that had received a direct hit. He was buried when a wall collapsed and suffered multiple injuries. Awarded the George Medal.

1st BATTALION 'A' ZONE, LONDON
[later 1st COUNTY OF LONDON (WESTMINSTER) BATTALION]

King's Commendation for Brave Conduct

Company Commander J. I. COWAN

(L.G. 26.viii.1941)

["During an enemy bombing attack on Westminster on the afternoon of 11th November 1940 Company Commander Cowan was told that several people were buried in a printing works which had received direct hits. He at once went to the scene and took charge of operations, helping to extricate five people, of whom one was dead and the others badly injured. On learning from one of those rescued that other victims were buried elsewhere in the wreckage, he at once sent for help to his headquarters and then, with complete disregard for his own safety—for there were heavy falls of debris throughout the operations—he crawled to the assistance of a woman whom he discovered pinned under the wreckage which threatened every moment to crush her. He saw that by holding up a heavy beam to relieve the pressure on her it might be possible to save her life. By this time there was the added peril of fire but without hesitation he made for the beam, placed himself under it at the risk of being crushed himself, and managed by the exercise of his full strength to support it. By doing so he placed himself in a position of the greatest peril. Throughout the operations he displayed gallantry, resource, leadership and initiative."]

Platoon Commander T. D. WILLIAMS, M.V.O., D.C.M.

(L.G. 26.viii.1941)

["Following three separate air attacks on Buckingham Palace Platoon Commander Williams displayed conspicuous courage and devotion to duty.

After the first attack on 13th September 1940, when the Royal Chapel was severely damaged, he at once took charge of rescue operations and ensured not only the removal of the injured but the safety of others from falling wreckage.

On the second occasion on 15th September 1940 a bomb fell close to Their Majesty's appartments. It did not explode and without hesitation Platoon Commander Williams arranged to remove it to a spot where it was likely to do little damage. It was later destroyed by a bomb disposal squad.

Platoon Commander Williams again took charge of rescue operations after the third attack and worked amid the falling debris of the part of the Palace which had been wrecked. His conduct on this and other occasions cannot be too highly commended, for he not only helped to rescue life himself under conditions of the greatest danger, but inspired others to do so by his selflessness."]

'D' ZONE, LONDON
[later 5th COUNTY OF LONDON BATTALION]

British Empire Medal

Volunteer W. C. G. PETTIT
(L.G. 22.i.1941)

["Volunteer Pettit was on duty during a heavy air raid on the night of 16th September 1940. High explosive and incendiary bombs were dropped in Acacia Road and set fire to stables in which about fifty horses were kept. The roof began to blaze fiercely and the flames spread rapidly, threatening to gut the stables and destroy the horses, which were in a state of panic and were kicking and plunging wildly. Debris was falling and the stables soon became dangerous to approach but Volunteer Pettit, with complete disregard for his own safety went into the burning building and began coolly and methodically to supervise the rescue of the horses. In the process of so doing he was kicked by one of the horses and cut on the head by falling debris. Although in considerable pain he kept to his task and did not leave the stables until the last horse had been led out. He then reported to his headquarters and continued his spell of night duty."] *(Inv. 24.iii.1942)*

5th BATTALION 'R' ZONE, LONDON
[later 23rd COUNTY OF LONDON BATTALION]

British Empire Medal

Volunteer E. T. WISTOW
(L.G. 27.v.1941)

["On 29th December 1940 Volunteer Wistow was detailed for duty at a building which became the target of an intense enemy attack from the air, high explosive and incendiary bombs being concentrated upon it. He was on the roof when two high explosive bombs went through the building, carrying him with the debris. He disregarded his injuries and set to work to clear the exit of a shelter in which a number of people were trapped. These were taken to another shelter by himself and another man. At this point Volunteer Wistow had to be taken to hospital to have his injuries attended to, but he reported back for duty again at 3 a.m. the next morning.

He had helped to fight a serious fire a few days previously when incendiary bombs had set a building alight. Not only that, but he worked through a whole week-end to repair the damage.

He is deserving of high commendation for his devotion to duty and entire disregard of his own safety. By clearing the exits to the shelter during the enemy bombardment, though wounded and suffering from severe shock, he ensured the safety of his fellow citizens."] *(Inv. 24.iii.1942)*

Volunteer E. T. SMITH

(L.G. 27.v.1941)

["On 29th December 1940 Volunteer Smith was detailed for duty at a building which became the target of an intense enemy attack from the air, high explosive and incendiary bombs being concentrated upon it. Volunteer Smith was on the roof when two high explosive bombs went through the building, carrying him with the debris. He disregarded his injuries and set to work to clear the exit of a shelter in which a number of people were trapped. These were taken to another shelter by himself and another man. Volunteer Smith refused medical aid and carried on.

He had helped to fight a serious fire a few days previously when incendiary bombs had set a building alight. Not only that, but he had worked through a whole week-end to repair the damage.

He is deserving of high commendation for his devotion to duty and entire disregard of his own safety. By clearing the exits to the shelter during the enemy bombardment, though wounded and suffering from severe shock he ensured the safety of his fellow citizens."]
(Inv. 3.iii.1942)

> *Note:* Some details of Volunteers Smith's and Wistow's gallantry are given in *Graves*.

King's Commendation for Brave Conduct

Volunteer R. H. TIERNEY

(L.G. 8.vii.1941)

For bravery and devotion to duty during an air raid on the Royal Victoria Yard, Deptford [on the night of 19th-20th March 1941]. The building in which he was on duty was hit and set on fire. Although ordered to take cover he remained at his post, receiving injuries which resulted in the loss of a leg. He showed great courage and cheerfulness throughout. *(Graves).*

> *Note:* The incident at the Royal Victoria Yard attracted a number of civilian awards for gallantry. Messrs. J. A. Jones, C. F. Williams, and E. J. Wood were awarded the British Empire Medal; Messrs. E. J. Greave, and R. H. Shipway received King's Commendations; and Messrs. D. C. Bain and O. Hitchen Posthumous King's Commendations. *(L.G. 30.v.1941).*

6th BATTALION 'P' ZONE, LONDON
[later 31st COUNTY OF LONDON (STREATHAM) BATTALION]

Mentioned in Despatches

Volunteer P. D. WILLERINGHAUS

(L.G. 21.i.1941; amended 18.ii.1944)

"In October 1940 Volunteer Willeringhaus, who was on duty as a despatch rider at Headquarters 6th Battalion, 'P' Zone, was sent to deliver a message to a company headquarters. While he was on his way enemy aircraft appeared overhead and a high exposive bomb dropped near him, demolishing business premises and causing heavy casualties. Volunteer Willeringhaus was blown off his motor cycle by the explosion and sustained injuries to his head, face, both hands and legs. Despite the fact that he was suffering severely from shock and loss of blood he abandoned his machine, which had been rendered useless, secured the despatch with which he had been entrusted and dragged himself on foot to the company headquarters, a distance of three quarters of a mile. On arrival there he saw his despatch safely delivered and then collapsed." *(P.R.O.—Air 2/9537/Graves/The War Illustrated—14.ii.1941)*

Note: Volunteer Willeringhaus was only sixteen years old.

Volunteer W. T. WHITLOCK, L.M.S. Railway Home Guard. Although severely injured when bombs fell on Hampstead Heath station he pulled his section leader from the wreckage at great personal risk—19th October 1940. Awarded the George Medal.

L.M.S. RAILWAY UNIT, EUSTON
[later 37th COUNTY OF LONDON (L.M.S. EUSTON) BATTALION]

George Medal

Volunteer W. T. WHITLOCK
(L.G. 29.iv.1941)

"On 19th October 1940 a building [Hampstead Heath Station] received two direct hits from high explosive bombs. Volunteer Whitlock, who was on Home Guard duty, received severe injuries to an arm, leg and side; his eyes were also injured by the blast. He was thrown more than twenty feet and over a wall but, ignoring his injuries, he made his way back to the offices which had been wrecked. At great personal risk he pulled his section leader from the wreckage, thus saving his life." *(The Times 30.iv.1941/Graves) (Inv. 15.vii.1941)*

40th COUNTY OF LONDON (GAS, LIGHT AND COKE) BATTALION

British Empire Medal

Volunteer W. L. BADCOCK
(L.G. 27.v.1941)

["Volunteer Badcock was on Home Guard duty during an enemy air raid when a large number of incendiary bombs were dropped. The majority of the bombs were easily put out, but two lodged on top of a gas holder, which was at that time about 90 feet in the air. These incendiaries were lighting up the works and offering a target to the enemy airmen, who were circling round and subsequently dropped more bombs. In order to quench the blaze he and another man climbed to the top of the holder and scooped up the fire bombs in their helmets."] *(Inv. 24.iii.1942)*

42nd COUNTY OF LONDON (L.P.T.B.) BATTALION

Member of the Order of the British Empire

2nd Lieutenant W. B. G. EDWARDS
(L.G. 14.iv.1942)

["Second-Lieutenant Edwards displayed great gallantry during a bombing practice at East Grinstead on 4th October 1941. He was supervising the practice when a volunteer misthrew a bomb which lodged between the parapet and an officer's back. The officer moved and the bomb fell into the trench. Second-Lieutenant Edwards seized the bomb and threw it out of the trench. At the same time he saw that the volunteer had jumped out of his trench and was proceeding in the direction of the bomb. Second-Lieutenant Edwards ran after the volunteer, seized him and dragged him into the trench. The bomb exploded a fraction of a second later."] *(Inv. 7.vii.1942)*

> *Note:* At the time of the action for which he was decorated Second-Lieutenant Edwards was attached to the 17th Sussex (East Grinstead) Battalion.

3rd BATTALION L.P.T.B. HOME GUARD
[later 43rd COUNTY OF LONDON (L.P.T.B.) BATTALION]

King's Commendation for Brave Conduct

Corporal F. M. McCarty
(L.G. 17.vi.1941)

["When a delayed action bomb fell near his garage in Victoria on 15th November 1940 electric cables were set on fire immediately over the bomb. With complete disregard for his own safety Corporal McCarty stood on the edge of the crater and extinguished the fire. He has always shown coolness and disregard for his own safety under air raid conditions."]

48th COUNTY OF LONDON (L.C.C.) BATTALION

Member of the Order of the British Empire

Lieutenant G. D. Eccles, M.C.
(L.G. 18.xi.1941)

["During the time that St. Olave's Hospital has been subjected to hostile air attacks, Lieutenant Eccles has consistently shown the utmost courage, inspired leadership and devotion to duty, in dealing with all incidents.

On 7th November 1940 the Maternity Block was severely damaged by a high explosive bomb, and Lieutenant Eccles was prominent in the rescue of patients and the organisation of their evacuation to a safe place.

On 19th April 1941 high explosive and incendiary bombs caused many fires. One of these occurred in the main linen and blanket store, and was of a very serious nature owing to the inflammability of the stores, and to the fact that the room is situated in the centre of the hospital and the Administration Block. With great gallantry Lieutenant Eccles tackled the fire single-handed and, though blinded and choked with smoke and fumes, he succeeded in limiting the conflagration till further help was available. On the same night he subsequently discovered a further fire in the roof space of the Medical Officers' quarters, and again, with complete disregard for his personal safety, he succeeded in extinguishing it.

On the night of 10th May 1941 a shower of incendiary bombs fell in the hospital grounds. Lieutenant Eccles was blown over by the blast from a high explosive bomb which fell in the adjoining park. He picked himself up and tackled a fire in the mortuary, single-handed. Despite intensive overhead activity he succeeded in extinguishing the blaze and then carried on in putting out smaller outbreaks throughout the hospital."] *(Inv. 7.vii.1942)*

Note: Correspondence relating to Lieutenant Eccles's eventual appointment as M.B.E. is included in L.C.C. Records, H.G.-57.

46th COUNTY OF LANCASTER (SOUTH MANCHESTER) BATTALION

British Empire Medal

Section Commander F. McEwen
Section Commander J. McKeown
(L.G. 17.vi.1941)

"On the night of 22nd/23rd December 1940 the Home Guard company headquarters in Hulme Town Hall was partially destroyed by a landmine, and three civilians were buried under many tons of debris.

Section Commanders McEwen and McKeown had been on duty for fourteen hours at various wrecked houses and fires when they heard cries from the wreckage at Hulme Town Hall. Despite the fact that they were told that an A.R.P. Rescue Party had given up an attempt at rescue, the two section commanders organised a party and after working seven hours under a dangerously over-hanging wall they managed to contact, and finally extricate alive and not badly injured, two women and a man.

They showed exceptional gallantry and indefatigable devotion to voluntary duty during and after an enemy air raid. There is no doubt that the gallantry and determination displayed by these two men in the face of great personal danger had a tremendous moral and steadying effect on a badly shaken community." *(The Times 18.vi.1941) (Invs. McEwen—2.xii.1941; McKeown—13.x.1942)*

49th COUNTY OF LANCASTER (MANCHESTER) BATTALION

King's Commendation for Brave Conduct

Company Sergeant-Major P. A. Bennett
Company Commander A. G. P. Collings
Corporal B. Grayson
Platoon Commander L. J. Shepley
Corporal J. Westray
(L.G. 8.vii.1941)

For bravery and devotion to duty in dealing with unexploded bombs in a Ministry of Aircraft Production Factory. *(Graves)*

[Official records show that the factory was that of A. V. Roe and Co. Ltd., Greengate, Middleton, Manchester and that the date of the incident was 14th April 1941. Also involved in the improvised bomb disposal was the works A.R.P. officer, Mr. H. A. Marsden, who received a civilian King's Commendation *(L.G. 27.vi.1941)*

After the attack had ceased Company Commander Collings and Mr. Marsden searched the wreckage for bombs that were known to have fallen but not detonated. They found one bomb and as they were unable to determine the type of fuse decided to carry out a jerking test. Mr. Marsden attached a rope to the bomb and Company Commander Collings applied the test by pulling on the rope with a lorry which he drove himself. The bomb did not explode so he backed the lorry up to it and after shortening the rope to only twelve yards for ease of manoeuvre he pulled the bomb several hundred yards into a safe position in an adjoining field. At one point the bomb fouled the edge of a footpath and the rope broke. Mr. Marsden and Platoon Commander Shepley freed the bomb and reattached the rope and the operation was completed without further difficulty.

Company Commander Collings and Mr. Marsden then searched for and found a second bomb and in view of the doubtful state of the fuse decided to apply the jerking test again. Mr. Marsden, Platoon Commander Shepley and Mr. Leach attached a pulley and rope to the bomb and Company Commander Collings again drove the lorry while the rest of the squad took cover. Then Platoon Commander Shepley, C.S.M. Bennett and Corporals Westray and Grayson, under the direction of Mr. Marsden, manhandled the bomb on to a trolley. Company Commander Collings reversed the lorry to within five yards of the bomb and attached the rope. With Mr. Marsden in the cab and Platoon Commander Shepley sitting on the trolley to ensure that the bomb did not shift from its lashings, he drove the lorry for several hundred yards into the adjoining open ground.

Company Commander Collings showed complete disregard for his personal safety and owing to his courage and his efficient handling of a heavy lorry, and the example he set to the personnel under his command, a dangerous situation was quickly and adroitly dealt with.

Platoon Commander Shepley, C.S.M. Bennett and Corporals Grayson and Westray also showed complete disregard for their own safety, in as much as portions of the roof were still falling around them as they cleared a path through the debris in the vicinity of the first bomb and they were in immediate danger of injury from glass, broken asbestos and steel work dropping from a height of fifty to sixty feet. Throughout the operations they carried out their duties with coolness and quiet efficiency.]

63rd COUNTY OF LANCASTER (MANCHESTER) BATTALION

British Empire Medal

Sergeant W. H. PRITCHARD
(L.G. 30.v.1944)

"During live grenade practice a grenade struck the parapet and fell back into the bay. Sergeant Pritchard, who was in charge of the throwing bay, appreciated the danger. Without hesitation he flung the thrower out of the bay, picked up the grenade and threw it over the parapet where it immediately exploded without doing any damage.

Sergeant Pritchard departed from the prescribed procedure owing to the muddy and slippery condition of the throwing bay and because he realised that it was unlikely that two people would be able to get clear quickly enough." *(H.G.I.C. No.53—9.viii.1944/Air 2/9001)*

4th BATTALION 'T' ZONE, LONDON
[later 4th MIDDLESEX BATTALION]

British Empire Medal

Assistant Section Leader H. T. MORRIS
(L.G. 27.v.1941)

["During a bombing attack by enemy aircraft in Middlesex on a night in September 1940 Assistant Section Leader Morris was proceeding to the Headquarters Post when high explosive bombs began to fall at 80 to 100 feet distance. Almost simultaneously there fell at about 30 feet distant and just outside a large nearby building a large incendiary bomb of the oil type. The explosion threw Assistant Section Leader Morris violently into the air and he sustained injuries which rendered one of his arms useless. The building was in great danger of being destroyed by fire owing to the proximity of much inflammable material to the woodwork of the building, but Assistant Section Leader Morris at once rallied reserve men and returned to the spreading fire, displaying great courage in helping to keep it under control, thus saving the building and much material. By his disregard of all danger he set a fine example of devotion to duty and to his men."] *(Inv. 24.ii.1942)*

Section Leader G. TURNER
(L.G. 27.v.1941)

["During a bombing attack by enemy aircraft on a night in September 1940 Section Leader Turner was proceeding to Headquarters Post near a large building when high explosive bombs began to fall at 80 to 100 feet distance; almost simultaneously there fell at about 30 feet distance and just outside the building, a large incendiary bomb of the oil type. The explosion threw Section Leader Turner violently into the air and on the fringe of the pool of oil, some of which had scattered over one part of the building which was partly constructed of wood. He had his hip badly injured through falling on the concrete. Realising, however, the great danger of fire, he dragged himself to the building, put on the fire alarm and gave instructions to rally reserve men to assist the fire brigade. He himself went back to the centre of the fire which was rapidly gaining a hold, kicked away several blazing sacks of paper, dismantled the sandbags framing the Headquarters Post, and threw the sand on to the spreading fire, using the sandbags themselves to put out the flames. The situation had been rendered the more perilous by the bursting and ignition of a gas main, and realising that this main continued to act as a beacon to the enemy aircraft, he procured asbestos sheeting and placed it over the blaze and took steps to have the gas turned off at its source.

By his prompt assessment of the whole situation and courage and initiative in dealing with it while suffering great pain and shock Section Leader Turner undoubtedly saved the whole building."] *(Inv. 24.ii.1942)*

2nd BATTALION 'S' ZONE, LONDON
[later 20th MIDDLESEX BATTALION]

British Empire Medal

Volunteer M. STOCKLAND
(L.G. 17.vi.1941)

"On 29th January 1941 Volunteer Stockland performed a very gallant action as the result of which he himself suffered severe injuries. During a heavy enemy air attack an explosive incendiary bomb fell in a position which seemed to make a serious outbreak of fire inevitable. It was seen that the bomb was of the explosive type, but it was essential that it should be dealt with at once, because of highly inflammable material which surrounded it. Although he was perfectly aware of the risk he ran, Volunteer Stockland approached the bomb at close quarters and with entire disregard for his own safety, moved it away from the danger zone. He had no sooner accomplished this task when the bomb exploded inflicting upon him serious injuries. His courage cannot be too highly commended." *(The Times 18.vi.1941) (Inv. 24.ii.1942)*

21st MIDDLESEX BATTALION

British Empire Medal

Sergeant H. H. T. RYAN
(L.G. 28.vii.1944)

"On no fewer than three occasions Sergeant Ryan, who is a battalion bombing instructor, has been the cause of the probable saving of life or injury by the cool and expeditious manner in which he has handled situations arising whilst practice with live grenades has been carried out, regardless of his own safety. On 10th August 1943 a man under instruction threw a grenade which rebounded into the throwing bay. Sergeant Ryan removed the man into the shelter bay before the grenade exploded. On another occasion later a similar incident took place but this time the thrower of the grenade stood still, rigid with fear. Although physically a powerful man, Sergeant Ryan had to use every ounce of force to get the man clear of the bay, showing great presence of mind by throwing the man outside the perimeter wall. A precisely similar accident occurred on another occasion, when Sergeant Ryan managed to get the thrower out of the throwing bay before the grenade exploded." *(H.G.I.C. No.55—16.viii.1944)*

3rd MONMOUTHSHIRE (NEWPORT) BATTALION

Military Medal

Volunteer G. JONES

(L.G. 19.ix.1940)

"On 12th/13th July 1940 Volunteer Jones was a member of a guard posted in defence of a vital point. The post was bombed, one man being killed and another seriously wounded.

Volunteer Jones, who was himself in a place of safety, heard the groans of the wounded man and at once left shelter and carried him on his back under cover. During this time bombs, debris, large pieces of steelwork and heavy glass were still falling and Volunteer Jones carried out his task with complete disregard for his own safety. His courageous behaviour set a fine example to all those present." *(The Times 18.ix.1940/Graves)*

> *Note:* Volunteer Jones was only eighteen years old at the time of the action for which he received his Military Medal.

Volunteer G. JONES, 3rd Monmouthshire Battalion, who rescued a seriously wounded comrade during a heavy air raid on Newport—12th/13th July 1940.
The first member of the Home Guard to be decorated for gallantry and the only one to receive the Military Medal.

9th MONMOUTHSHIRE (PONTYPOOL) BATTALION

King's Commendation for Brave Conduct

Sergeant D. W. SEABOURNE
(L.G. 5.v.1944)

"During a live grenade throwing exercise on 6th February 1944 Private B. J. Curtis of B Company accidentally dropped the grenade which he was about to hurl from the throwing bay. Although Sergeant Seabourne ordered 'take cover', Private Curtis attempted to pick up the bomb. Sergeant Seabourne, with total disregard of personal danger, pulled him away and got him under cover just as the grenade exploded.

This n.c.o. displayed great courage and coolness in danger and undoubtedly saved the life of Private Curtis." *(H.G.I.C. No.51—28.vi.1944/Air 2/9001)*

6th NORFOLK BATTALION

King's Commendation for Brave Conduct

Volunteer R. C. V. GEORGE
Volunteer C. S. GUNTON
(L.G. 25.iii.1941)

[For bravery and devotion to duty when a Blenheim bomber of the Royal Air Force crashed near Horsham St Faith on the night of the 23rd December 1940. As a result of their actions the only member of the crew who survived the crash was extricated from the burning wreckage. Machine gun ammunition was exploding at the time and it was afterwards discovered that live bombs were still in the aircraft.]

> *Note:* C. C. Benns, Senior Warden H. W. Brundish, Police Constable B. S. Hardesty and Special Constable G. C. Wiley, all of whom were involved in the same incident, received civilian King's Commendations "for attempting to rescue the crew of a crashed and burning aircraft" *(L.G. 21.iii.1941)*.

5th SOMERSET (BATH CITY) BATTALION

British Empire Medal

Sergeant B. BROWN, M.M.
(L.G. 18.ix.1942)

"During an air raid the Home Guard were called to help with rescue work. The district was very heavily bombed and machine-gunned from a low level. A bomb struck a building and Sergeant Brown, without a moment's hesitation, went into the demolished building. He released a man who was trapped and got him outside, and he also rescued three women from the same building. The building subsequently collapsed, but Sergeant Brown's instant action proved an example to the whole contingent, and a considerable number of people were eventually rescued, some with great difficulty.

Sergeant Brown's gallantry and extremely quick and efficient action resulted in the saving of many lives." *(Bath and Wilts Chronicle and Herald 19.ix.1942) (Inv. 16.iii.1943)*

King's Commendation for Brave Conduct

Corporal E. E. WEBB
(L.G. 18.ix.1942)

For bravery and devotion to duty during and after an air raid on Bath, 25th/26th April 1942.

[Corporal Webb left his home at about 11.30 p.m. to report for 'stand-by' duty at Messrs. Stothart and Pitt Ltd. Near the top of Shaftesbury Road he saw that assistance was required at a demolished house and helped police officers to rescue a man.

The Oldfield Park district had suffered very heavy damage and he then went into Lower Oldfield Park where he rescued two elderly women from a house which had been partially demolished. Shortly afterwards he went with police officers to No. 20 Lower Oldfield Park, where a light had been seen flashing from the debris at the rear of the house. It was discovered that eight people were trapped in the basement. The adjoining house was on fire and was being dealt with by the Fire Brigade. An opening was made at the rear of No. 20 and Webb was able to get into the part of the building where the inhabitants were trapped. Having crawled through another aperture he was able with the aid of a saw which was passed through to him to release the eight people one by one and hand them over to the police for attention. A good deal of smoke was entering No. 20, which made the rescue work even more difficult.

The rescue work at No. 20 took over an hour, beginning just after the first raid had subsided. Had it not been for Corporal Webb's courage and determination it is doubtful, in view of the fire in the adjoining house, whether the rescue could have been completed in time to save the lives of those who were trapped.]

6th SOMERSET (BATH—ADMIRALTY) BATTALION

George Medal

Company Sergeant-Major J. A. LESLIE
(L.G. 3.xii.1942)

"Company Sergeant-Major Leslie showed outstanding courage and personal bravery in rescue work during the night of 26th/27th April 1942, and on the following days at Bath. The Regina Hotel had been hit and although the raid was still in progress he made his way into the basement through a small hole which allowed only one man to enter at a time, and himself rescued a number of people. A woman was trapped by falling masonry and hanging by her knees. Company Sergeant-Major Leslie supported her for a considerable time while other men worked at the masonry to release her. During this time there was such danger that both might be killed by falling masonry that they were covered with a sheet so that they could not see the blocks if they fell. There was imminent danger of fire and at one period Company Sergeant-Major Leslie had to be doused with water to prevent his clothes catching fire, but throughout it all he never wavered. During the same night Company Sergeant-Major Leslie swarmed up the side of a shop and tore down the blazing shop blind and fixture in an attempt to prevent the spread of fire after the firemen had given up the task as hopeless." *(Bath and Wilts Chronicle and Herald 4.xii.1942) (Inv. 16.iii.1943)*

British Empire Medal

Private N. W. S. BAKER
(L.G. 3.xii.1942)

"At the Regina Hotel, Bath, on the night of the 26th/27th April 1942, in company with Company Sergeant-Major Leslie and Private Martell, Private Baker made a number of rescues after having worked on the fire at the Assembly Rooms. He spent 4½ hours in a small hole releasing trapped persons. Later, hearing sounds from the upper rooms, he searched them although they were in danger of collapse, and found and rescued two persons." *(Bath and Wilts Chronicle and Herald 4.xii.1942) (Inv.16.iii.1943)*

Private J. M. MARTELL
(L.G. 3.xii.1942)

"Private Martell was a co-worker with Company Sergeant-Major Leslie at the Regina Hotel, Bath, on the night of the 26th/27th April 1942. He showed great bravery in forcing another entrance into the hotel and ascertaining that there was a large number of people buried in the basement. At great personal risk he freed a number of people, being himself in danger from falling masonry. He often had to work alone with no more than a hand torch for light. The building was smouldering throughout the rescue work." *(Bath and Wilts Chronicle and Herald 4.xii.1942) (Inv. 16.iii.1943)*

Private H. D. REES
(L.G. 3.xii.1942)

"Private Rees was involved in the incident at the Regina Hotel, Bath, on the night of 27th/28th April 1942, with Company Sergeant-Major Leslie. He helped to rescue the woman supported by Company Sergeant-Major Leslie. He worked in great danger without a break, from the time the hotel was hit (early in the morning of 27th April) until 7.30 p.m. on the 28th April, and helped to bring out altogether 25 persons, five of whom were found to be alive." *(Bath and Wilts Chronicle and Herald 4.xii.1942) (Inv. 16.iii.1943)*

Company Sergeant-Major J. A. LESLIE, 6th Somerset Battalion was among several members of his battalion who worked in very dangerous circumstances to rescue survivors trapped in the wreckage of the Regina Hotel, Bath, following an air raid—26th/27th April 1942.
Awarded the George Medal.

70

27th STAFFORDSHIRE (WALSALL) BATTALION

King's Commendation for Brave Conduct

Corporal H. KITSON
(L.G. 3.xii.1942)

["At about 01.45 hours on 31st July 1942, during an air raid on Walsall, a shower of some three hundred incendiary bombs fell on and around the Walsall Corporation Transport Depot at Birchills and a number of buses were set on fire. Corporal Kitson, commanding the Home Guard picquet on duty at the depot, showing great courage and disregarding the danger of bursting petrol tanks and falling glass, drove several burning double-decker buses out of the garage and so prevented the fire spreading. The last bus that he brought out was ablaze from end to end with only the glass at the back of the driver's cabin separating him from a blazing inferno. Throughout the raid and its aftermath Corporal Kitson showed the greatest courage and devotion to duty and was an inspiration to the other fire fighters."]

3rd SURREY (3rd SOUTHERN RAILWAY) BATTALION

King's Commendation for Brave Conduct

Volunteer C. E. LAZELL
(L.G. 8.vii.1941)

["On 29th November 1940 at about 12.20 hours Volunteer Lazell was on Home Guard duty at Sunbury Station when bombs fell on either side of the booking office, burying three members of the railway staff—the booking clerk, a porter and a signalman. With the assistance of Volunteer Lazell the porter and the signalman were able to crawl out of a small opening. Volunteer Lazell then burrowed through fallen timbers and broken glass with his hands to enlarge the opening and after about twenty minutes was successful in rescuing the booking clerk. Throughout Volunteer Lazell acted without regard for his own safety, as bombs were still dropping close by setting up vibrations which were liable to cause loose or broken timbers and debris to collapse."]

7th SURREY (DORKING) BATTALION

Member of the Order of the British Empire

2nd Lieutenant G. V. WALKER
(L.G. 15.ix.1944)

British Empire Medal

Lance-Corporal E. T. MONK
Corporal E. C. SARGENT
(L.G. 15.ix.1944)

["In April 1944 an aircraft flew over Home Guard personnel training near Lowfield Heath, Surrey and was seen to crash; a terrific explosion followed. The aircraft had come to rest on its back and caught fire. Second Lieutenant Walker and Corporals Monk and Sargent rushed to the scene and, regardless of the burning wreckage and the possibility of exploding bombs and petrol tanks, Second Lieutenant Walker crawled under the wing and, assisted by the two n.c.o.s, succeeded in releasing the pilot from his harness and dragging him clear of the flames. Had it not been for the prompt and courageous action of these three men the pilot would undoubtedly have been burned to death."]

Section Leader A. H. TILYARD-BURROWS, Vickers-Armstrong Factory Unit, Weybridge. Assisted in the removal of a delayed action bomb to a place where it would not damage the factory if it exploded—21st September 1940.
The first Home Guard to receive the George Medal.

VICKERS ARMSTRONG AIRCRAFT FACTORY UNIT, WEYBRIDGE
[later part of 10th SURREY (VICKERS ARMSTRONG) BATTALION; then part of 3rd SURREY (WEYBRIDGE) BATTALION]

George Medal

Section Leader A. H. TILYARD-BURROWS
(L.G. 22.i.1941)

British Empire Medal

Volunteer W. J. AVERY
Volunteer C. E. CHAPLIN
Volunteer E. A. MASLYN
(L.G. 22.i.1941)

"On the morning of 21st September 1940 at about 08.30 hours the Vickers Aircraft Factory at Weybridge was attacked by an enemy aircraft. Three bombs were dropped, two of which exploded, doing slight damage. The other, a 500-lb. bomb, penetrated the factory roof, passed through a wall at the end and came to rest on the concrete driveway outside the erecting shed, having failed to explode. As the explosion of the bomb at the position where it rested would have caused considerable damage, its immediate removal was a matter of national importance.

Lieutenant J. M. S. Patton, Royal Canadian Engineers, undertook to remove the bomb to a place of comparative safety and Section Leader Tilyard-Burrows together with Volunteers W. J. Avery, E. A. Maslyn and C. E. Chaplin, with complete disregard of personal safety and having no previous experience of handling unexploded bombs, immediately volunteered to assist.

The bomb was lashed to a sheet of corrugated iron, attached to a truck by wire cable and towed to a crater about 200 yards away where it could do no harm. The task was accomplished in little more than half-an-hour from the time the bomb had fallen. The bomb exploded the following morning.

Throughout the operation these men displayed cool courage of the highest order and contributed largely to the removal of a serious threat to the production of this factory."

(P.R.O.—Air 2/9537) (Invs. Tilyard-Burrows—18.vii.1941; Avery, Chaplin, Maslyn—24.ii.1942)

> *Notes:* Lieutenant J. M. S. Patton was awarded the George Cross and Captain D. W. C. Cunnington, also of the Royal Canadian Engineers, the George Medal for their gallantry on this occasion *(L.G. 13.xii.1940).*
>
> Section Leader Tilyard-Burrows subsequently enlisted in the Royal Engineers and served as 14404353, Lance-Corporal with 858 Quarrying Company. He lost his life on 27th July 1944 in Normandy and, having no known grave, is commemorated on the Bayeux Memorial.

55th SURREY (SUTTON AND CHEAM) BATTALION

King's Commendation for Brave Conduct

Sergeant C. WINCHESTER
(L.G. 7.vii.1944)

"On the afternoon of 30th January 1944 live grenade throwing was being carried out. During the practice a man slipped when throwing a grenade, with the result that the grenade hit the front wall of the throwing bay and bounced back. The officer in charge immediately ordered the detail out of the bay, whereupon Sergeant Winchester, who was the instructor in the throwing bay, picked up the smoking grenade with his left hand and threw it clear. There is little doubt that his ready action, calm demeanour and disregard for his own safety saved what might have been a nasty accident." *(H.G.I.C. No.55—16.viii. 1944/P.R.O.—Air 2/9001)*

4th BATTALION 'Z' ZONE, LONDON
[later 61st SURREY (NORWOOD) BATTALION]

British Empire Medal

Volunteer A. E. PRITCHARD
(L.G. 8.vii.1941)

"On the night of 11th January 1941 a heavy enemy air attack developed in South London. A high explosive bomb of the heaviest kind fell on a group of houses and demolished them; all that remained being masses of debris and a very large crater.

Volunteer Pritchard, who was on Home Guard duty, began at once to rescue the survivors. He managed, at great personal risk, to rescue several people from one house and then turned his attention to a man and his wife who were trapped in a collapsed building. His task was particularly perilous as the shop in which they had sheltered was on the very edge of the bomb crater, the sides of which were of slipping clay, and very deep, with a gas main alight at the bottom. Debris was falling all the time as the bombardment continued. After working a full hour under conditions of the greatest danger Volunteer Pritchard succeeded in extricating the two people. His action cannot be too highly commended." *(The Times 9.vii.1941) (Inv. 24.ii.1942)*

King's Commendation for Brave Conduct

Lance-Corporal G. HOWARD
(L.G. 17.vi.1941)

["On the night of 11th January 1941 during a heavy enemy air attack on the Norwood district a high explosive bomb of the heaviest weight fell at the junction of two roads, demolishing a large number of houses and forming a gigantic crater.

Lance-Corporal Howard was on duty at the time and at once proceeded with the work of rescuing people who were trapped in the debris. In one instance he displayed the greatest courage. Hearing that there was a woman buried in a partly demolished house he ignored falling masonry, and the fact that the floors above, one of which carried a large piano perched on the edge, were likely to fall on top of him and worked to rescue her for nearly half an hour. He managed to get her out, but only just in time.

His devotion to duty and total disregard for his own safety were an inspiration to all other rescue workers."]

14th SUSSEX (HOVE) BATTALION

Member of the Order of the British Empire

Captain G. HOWARD
(L.G. 7.vii.1944)

"On the morning of 26th March 1944 Captain Howard was instructing a company in live grenade practice. A private under instruction entered the throwing bay with two No. 36 grenades primed with four-second fuses. Seeing that the safety pin of one of them was in the wrong way Captain Howard took the grenade and withdrew the pin to reinsert it properly. The man under instruction put the other grenade in the front pocket of his battledress trousers. As he did so Captain Howard heard the striker go down and saw smoke coming from his pocket. Without hesitation Captain Howard struck the man on the jaw and, pulling the grenade out of his pocket threw it out of the throwing bay. The grenade exploded on the parapet before Captain Howard could get down himself and he sustained minor injuries to his face. By his cool and prompt action Captain Howard undoubtedly saved the life of the man under instruction as well as his own." *(H.G.I.C. No.55—16.viii.1941/P.R.O.—Air 2/9001)*

17th SUSSEX (EAST GRINSTEAD) BATTALION

For an award to an officer attached to this battalion see 42nd County of London Battalion, page 61.

UPPER THAMES PATROL

King's Commendation for Brave Conduct

Volunteer J. GREENMAN
(L.G. 21.i.1941)

["Commended for his brave action when a bomb fell on a private house near the lock where he was on patrol. The debris was still falling when Volunteer Greenman went to the rescue of its occupants. He dug with his bare hands to a depth of four feet to find and release a woman buried under fallen beams and bricks. Six people in all were rescued by Messrs. Watercraft's Home Guard, although the gas and water mains had burst and debris was falling."]

1st WARWICKSHIRE (WARWICK) BATTALION

King's Commendation for Brave Conduct

Corporal J. GRIFFIN
(L.G. 18.ii.1944)

"On 13th June 1942 Corporal Griffin was on duty as leading gunner/observer at the Lockheed Works, Leamington. He displayed marked bravery and devotion to duty in maintaining fire on a Dornier 217 which attacked his post with cannon and machine gun fire.

Again on 16th July when another attack developed his quick action in recognising the hostile aircraft and warning the workers when he recognised the attacking machine undoubtedly saved many lives." *(P.R.O.—Air 2/9001)*

4th WILTSHIRE (TROWBRIDGE) BATTALION

British Empire Medal

Sergeant F. C. LEE
(L.G. 20.iv.1943)

["On 30th December 1942 Sergeant Lee was supervising a practice with live grenades. In the bombing trench at the time was a recruit who, through nervousness, retained the grenade too long in his hand, with the result that it fell into the trench. Sergeant Lee at once tried to pick it up in order to throw it away, but found that it was wedged between two stones. Thereupon he stamped the grenade into the ground to lessen the explosion, and dragged the recruit to safety into the priming bay, thereby undoubtedly saving his life. An instant later the grenade exploded."] *(Inv. 6.vii.1943)*

6th WILTSHIRE (MARLBOROUGH) BATTALION

British Empire Medal

5567971 Sergeant G. E. SMITH, Wiltshire Regiment
(L.G. 21.iv.1942)

["On 7th December 1941 Sergeant Smith was instructing members of the Home Guard in the throwing of live No. 36 grenades. About twenty-five men were under instruction. One of the men, while throwing a grenade struck the sand bags which were on top of the throwing bay and the grenade lodged on the sand bags. Sergeant Smith ordered all the men to lie down, but the grenade, which was fizzing, meanwhile rolled down among other live grenades and detonators. Sergeant Smith then ran forward, picked up the grenade and just managed to throw it clear before it exploded. His prompt action in a dangerous situation prevented what might have been a very serious accident."] *(Mackay)*

Sergeant F. J. L. ROSIER

(L.G. 4.viii.1942)

"During hand grenade practice by members of the Wilton Platoon, on the 24th May 1942, one of the men under instruction dropped a grenade after he had withdrawn the safety pin. The grenade rolled under a board by which stood a box of live grenades. Sergeant Rosier, who was instructing the platoon, immediately ordered all those nearby to take cover. He then recovered and threw the grenade, which exploded immediately it reached the ground. The prompt and courageous action of this n.c.o. prevented what might have been a serious accident.

What made Sergeant Rosier's action particularly meritorious in this instance was that the grenade fell under some boards into the trench, and therefore, there was a certain amount of delay, which would not have occurred if it had fallen clear." *(Graves/Mackay)* *(Inv. 16.iii.1943)*

Lieutenant W. FOSTER, M.C., D.C.M., 7th Wiltshire Battalion, who sacrificed his life to save the lives of others when a live grenade fell back into the throwing bay during practice—13th September 1942.
Posthumously awarded the George Cross.

7th WILTSHIRE (SALISBURY) BATTALION

George Cross (Posthumous)

Lieutenant W. FOSTER, M.C., D.C.M.

(L.G. 27.xi.1942)

"When Lieutenant Foster was instructing a class in throwing live grenades a Mills bomb rebounded to the firing position. Without hesitation Lieutenant Foster threw himself on the bomb one second before it exploded, thus saving the lives of his comrades nearby. This officer's gallant action was not carried out in the heat of battle, but deliberately in cold blood, and with full knowledge of the consequences. As a result of this action Lieutenant Foster lost his life." *(The Times 28.xi.1942/Mackay)*

Note: The incident in which Lieutenant Foster was killed took place on 13th September 1942. He is buried in St. Mary's Churchyard, Alderbury, Wiltshire. His widow received his George Cross at an investiture on 2nd March 1943.

3rd BATTALION DONCASTER GROUP
[later 43rd WEST RIDING OF YORKSHIRE (HATFIELD) BATTALION]

British Empire Medal

Volunteer R. H. JUBY
(L.G. 22.i.1941)

"On 27th September 1940 an aircraft from the Royal Air Force Station at Finningley struck the ground near Misson and immediately burst into flames. The pilot, after being thrown from his seat, was caught by his parachute harness and remained hanging from the aircraft. Volunteer Juby, who immediately ran to the aircraft when it crashed and burst into flames, cut away the parachute harness and freed the pilot. He then carried him to the windward side of the aircraft. The pilot was later taken by ambulance to hospital but he died from the injuries he had sustained in the accident.

Volunteer Juby disregarded personal safety and danger when he approached the burning wreckage and entered the flames to cut away the pilot's harness. Had it not been for the injuries which he had received in the accident, there is little doubt that Volunteer Juby's prompt action would have saved the pilot's life." *(P.R.O.—Air 2/9537) (Inv. 23.ii.1943)*

ULSTER HOME GUARD

British Empire Medal (Civil Division)

Platoon Sergeant W. B. ANDERSON
(L.G. 4.ii.1944)

"On 16th May 1943 when Sergeant Anderson was acting as an instructor at a live grenade practice a grenade thrown accidentally in the wrong direction by a pupil in an adjacent bay unexpectedly fell into the bay occupied by Sergeant Anderson and an officer under training. Despite clear instructions from Sergeant Anderson, the officer, instead of leaving the bay, sought to protect himself by crouching where he was. Realising the perilous situation in which the officer had placed himself, Sergeant Anderson lifted the officer bodily from the bay to cover in the rear traverse, although he was well aware that the grenade (a 4-second No. 36) was due to explode.

As time only permitted the barest margin of safety when they had reached the entrance to the bay Sergeant Anderson thrust the officer behind the retaining wall and threw himself down on him, covering him with his own body regardless of the fact that he himself was exposed from the waist downwards to fragmentation from the explosion, from which both fortunately escaped injury.

Sergeant Anderson afterwards continued to carry out his instructional duties unperturbed." *(L.G. 4.ii.1944/P.R.O.—Air 2/9001) (Inv. 18.vii.1945)*

INDEX OF RECIPIENTS

Pettit, W. C. G.	B.E.M.	58	Thomas, T. H.	M.B.E.	43
Piper, J. A. W.	B.E.M.	51	Tidball, L. I.	B.E.M.	30
Pritchard, A. E.	B.E.M.	74	Tierney, R. H.	K.Comm.	59
Pritchard, W. H.	B.E.M.	64	Tilyard-Burrows,		
			A. H.	G.M.	73
Rees, G. E.	B.E.M.	43	Topham, J.	B.E.M.	26
Rees, H. D.	B.E.M.	70	Tozer, C. W. L.	G.M.	23
Rhodes, C. J.	K.Comm.	34	Treen, G. J.	K.Comm.	27
Richards, A. W.	O.B.E.	53	Turner, G.	B.E.M.	65
Richards, J. R.	M.B.E.	33	Tyler, S. A.	K.Comm.	28
Ridler, R. H. T.	K.Comm.	49			
Rosier, R. J. L.	B.E.M.	77	Wainwright, W. L.	M.B.E.	42
Rowe, G. H.	K.Comm.	30	Walker, G. V.	M.B.E.	72
Roxburgh, H. W.	G.M.	36	Webb, E. E.	K.Comm.	69
Ryan, H. H. T.	B.E.M.	66	Westray, J.	K.Comm.	63
			Whalley, E.	K.Comm.	50
Saragine, W.	B.E.M.	26	White, S. J.	M.B.E.	41
Sargent, E. C.	B.E.M.	72	White, V. G.	K.Comm.	47
Seabourne, D. W.	K.Comm.	68	Whitlock, W. T.	G.M.	60
Searle, H. A.	B.E.M.	37	Whittingstall, A. J.	M.B.E.	48
Shelton, J. M.	B.E.M.	22	Whybrow, W. E.	B.E.M.	49
Shepley, L. J.	K.Comm.	63	Willeringhaus, P. D.	M.i.D.	59
Simpson, T.	G.M.	25	Williams, T. D.	K.Comm.	57
Smith, E.	B.E.M.	40	Wilson, G.	K.Comm.	27
Smith, E. T.	B.E.M	59	Wilson, T. F.	M.B.E.	42
Smith, G. E.	B.E.M.	76	Winchester, C.	K.Comm.	74
Smith, P. A.	K.Comm.	55	Wistow, E. T.	B.E.M.	58
Stewart, J.	B.E.M.	39	Wright, F.	B.E.M.	32
Stockland, M.	B.E.M.	66			
Taylor, R. L.	K.Comm.	40	Yeomans, J. A.	K.Comm.	36

INDEX TO UNITS

"A comprehensive and authoritative overview of authentic, reflective coaching, this is an essential volume for anyone who is serious about the quality and continuous development of their coaching."

—Professor David Clutterbuck, David Clutterbuck Partnership

"Benjamin Disraeli once said, 'The greatest good you can do for another is not just to share your riches but to reveal to him his own.' Erik de Haan and Yvonne Burger have done the coaching community a great service by offering a much-needed panoramic view of the field. Reading this book is a must."

—Manfred F. R. Kets de Vries, Distinguished Clinical Professor of Leadership Development and Organisational Change, INSEAD

"*Coaching with Colleagues* is ambitious in its depth and range, written with passion and enthusiasm, and rich in metaphor... All in all, it is a rigorous and valuable guide for managers and professional coaches alike."

—Ann Lewis, Director, Ann Lewis Coaching

"This book will provide a useful perspective for anyone involved in coaching who has learned a collection of techniques and interventions from a variety of methodologies without fully understanding where they come from and how they fit together."

—Nigel Harris, Partner, Burton Sweet Chartered Accountants and Business Advisers

"This is a really comprehensive and detailed analysis of the different approaches to coaching. It really 'brings it all together'. But more than this, the book sets out an agenda for a more integrative approach to coaching."

—Andrew Atter, Business Coach

"Professionals today, in whatever field, have an increasing need for lifelong learning... What de Haan and his collaborators give us is a clear framework to better organise, supervise and facilitate our own professional development, and to advise our own colleagues and their organisations."

—Geof Cox, Author and Consultant, New Directions Ltd

Coaching with Colleagues

An Action Guide for One-to-One Learning

Second revised edition

Erik de Haan
*Director of Centre for Coaching, Ashridge Business School,
and Professor of Organisation Development and Coaching,
VU University, Amsterdam*

and

Yvonne Burger
Professor of Executive Coaching, VU University, Amsterdam

First published 2014 by
PALGRAVE MACMILLAN

Palgrave Macmillan in the UK is an imprint of Macmillan Publishers Limited, registered in England, company number 785998, of Houndmills, Basingstoke, Hampshire RG21 6XS.

Palgrave Macmillan in the US is a division of St Martin's Press LLC, 175 Fifth Avenue, New York, NY10010.

Palgrave Macmillan is the global academic imprint of the above companies and has companies and representatives throughout the world.

Palgrave® and Macmillan® are registered trademarks in the United States, the United Kingdom, Europe and other countries

ISBN: 978–1–137–35919–3 paperback

This book is printed on paper suitable for recycling and made from fully managed and sustained forest sources. Logging, pulping and manufacturing processes are expected to conform to the environmental regulations of the country of origin.

A catalogue record for this book is available from the British Library.

A catalog record for this book is available from the Library of Congress.

Contents

Appendices

Figures

Tables

Preface

Coaching with colleagues

The era of coaching with colleagues

A book about learning with colleagues is entirely in keeping with the
spirit of our times. Both the nature and role of 'work' have changed
radically in the West in recent decades. Where we work can no
longer be predicted on the basis of family background and education. How we work changes almost from month to month, if only
due to new developments in the field of information and communications technology. What we expect from work is no longer clear
either: for most of us, it is not just about earning a living. Work now
serves other purposes, for example satisfying our
more personal needs (Maslow, 1962) such as recognition, influence,
self-expression and self-fulfilment. As a result, we now expect more
and more from work and, by the same token, work has come to
'expect' more of us. Our working lives are gradually becoming more
exciting and interesting. It is becoming increasingly difficult to take
refuge behind unique expertise or customised approaches – instead,
we now have to find a tailored solution for every job or client, to
show more of our personal side in our work and to make that
personal side 'effective'. 'Work' is becoming more like 'school', in
two respects:

- In the contemporary sense of school: a place of training and education, a learning environment or study centre. A place we go to
  seeking self-development and self-fulfilment.
- In the original sense of the Greek *scholè*: leisure, rest, pleasure
  and, paradoxically enough, free time and ease. A place we go to
  find ourselves, to reflect and to spend time doing things that
  really matter to us.

The illustration in the frontispiece was chosen as a reminder of ancient Athenian civilisation, where 'school' was still an intellectual pastime and where one-on-one supervision, not to mention 'coaching' of leaders and high potential individuals, emerged and flourished. The photograph shows the entrance to the Temple of Athena Aphaia (the 'invisible'), erected in the late sixth century BC on the Greek island of Aegina. For us, the two pillars represent the two foundations of a coaching session: the coach and the coachee. The photograph also expresses, for us, the way in which each of these coaching pillars is accompanied by an 'alter ego' or 'guardian angel' ('daimonion' in Ancient Greek), a sort of 'internal coach' who whispers reflections and inspiration in your ear.

Not surprisingly, more and more people are feeling the need for a sanctuary where they can reflect on their work, and professionals have higher and higher expectations of such a sanctuary. What they want is a good conversation – a conversation that helps them to think things through systematically and understand them better, to reinforce the connection between themselves and their context, and to help them tackle things differently and more effectively the next time. In the same way as Plato elevated dialogue to an art form for the Ancient Greeks, the aim of many modern professionals is to elevate these 'good conversations' to an art form.

Which brings us to *Coaching with Colleagues*, as a sequel to *Learning with Colleagues* (de Haan, 2004). This book is not concerned with performance appraisal, planning or clearing-the-air conversations. Coaching with colleagues goes much further and involves:

- building up a coaching relationship and making it so strong that both parties can say what is really at issue
- paying attention to the link between work issues and the personality of the colleague
- considering fundamentally different working methods and tailoring their contribution to the colleague, issue and context
- being aware of your own strengths, pitfalls and preferred approaches – and knowing what assumptions underpin your coaching style
- exploring and discussing the limits of your effectiveness as a coach, and making this process of exploration and investigation itself part of the helping conversation.

How are you going to stay 'professional', if not by means of 'helping conversations' with fellow professionals? What are you going to learn from as a professional? Training programmes and courses, which you have already completed? Textbooks, which are outdated almost as soon as they reach the shelves? Clients and customers, who often aren't quite sure themselves what questions they want to ask you?

In our view, coaching is both the easiest and the most complex form of learning with colleagues. Easy: after leafing through these pages for even just ten minutes anyone can apply the most basic yet effective of methods (see the techniques in Chapter 6). And difficult: in the narrow confines of the one-on-one conversation, every contribution – indeed every facial expression or minor shift in attention – can send the conversation off in a completely different direction. This, for us, is what makes coaching such a subtle and wide-ranging craft.

In our view, coaching is an activity that fits in with both meanings of 'school': the learning environment and the place of leisure. The pleasure lies in taking a playful approach to serious and dramatic issues and, conversely, in a serious approach to fantasy and play. The learning aspect lies in the fact that coaching has an advantage over many other methods of professional development in that it can be organised with and through colleagues (from inside or outside the organisation), it can take place close to the place of work, and it affords an opportunity for much-needed peace and concentration.

The structure of this book

This book, *Coaching with Colleagues*, consists of three parts:

1. Part I, *Context for coaching*, contains a brief introduction to coaching and explains a number of central concepts ('What are we actually talking about?').
2. Part II, *Approaches to coaching*, examines a number of approaches to coaching in greater depth and provides a link to the main currents of psychotherapeutic thinking ('How do you go about it?').
3. Part III, *Reflection on coaching*, illustrates some of the skills of the coach and considers the context within which coaching often takes place ('And who is coaching where?').

Writing this book was a valuable learning process for us, and one which involved a great deal of mutual coaching. Now that the writing is behind us, we notice that many of our pet subjects have found a home in the book. The final result:

- is integrative, and therefore places a minimum of restrictions on the reader's freedom of choice
- starts from the reader's own coaching practice and the invitation to develop, from a variety of perspectives, a personal approach to coaching
- contains specific checklists and aids as well as references to underlying theory and research
- describes applicable methods and specific, ready-to-use coaching styles
- includes many examples from our own experience of coaching a wide variety of clients.

Besides the full, cover-to-cover reading that we, of course, heartily recommend, the reader can take other routes through this book:

- Readers who are looking for a brief introduction to the subject of coaching and are keen to hone their own abilities and skills as coaches in an organisational setting can opt for the route via Chapters 1 (definitions of coaching, mentoring, supervision, etc.), 3 (conditions for coaching), 4 (structure of coaching relationships), 12 (capabilities of the coach) and 14 (organisation coaching).
- Readers who wish to deepen and broaden their own practice as a more experienced coach can opt for the route via different approaches, applications and frameworks, i.e. Chapters 2 (layered communication during coaching), 5, 6, 7, 8, 9, 10 and 11 (different coaching approaches and what works for whom) and 15 (limitations of coaching, both internal and external).
- Readers who wish to develop the role of coach in their own organisation, looking at different approaches and the choice between internal or external coaching, can opt for the route via Chapters 1 (differences between coaching, counselling, mentoring and supervision), 5 (different approaches), 11 (choices between different approaches), 13 (impact of coaching on different learning styles and professional careers) and 15 (limitations of coaching, both internal and external).

The authors as mouthpieces

Who are the authors of an action guide to coaching with colleagues? Developers of coaching methods? Innovators in their field? Coaches with a distinguished record of service? That would be nice. The authors of this book see themselves primarily as editors of work done by others, 'mouthpieces' for methods and specialist knowledge which are often as old as the discipline of coaching itself.[1] All of the coaching approaches in this book – other than, perhaps, the IRONIC METHOD which we developed ourselves (see Chapter 9) – have a long history. Our own contribution is to have translated these approaches into simple methods. As often as possible, we include source references to the authors who actually developed the concepts and methods discussed.

While writing this book we were very involved in learning about coaching – through doing it a lot, reading about it and, together with many colleagues, organising seminars on the subject. We would like to thank some of the colleagues who made this possible:

- The business schools Sioo and De Baak for the many opportunities given to us to develop, for the benefit of participants in coaching courses, some of the material for this book. Since 2001 Erik has been involved as a developer and co-trainer of the second module of De Baak's programme *The Professional as Coach*, and Yvonne and Erik together have been developing and facilitating Sioo's professionalisation module *Coaching!* since 2002. Both programmes have been running twice a year for several years now, and are attracting considerable interest. On a more personal note, we would like to thank Debbie Molhuizen and Tamara van Duin (De Baak) and Marguerithe de Man (Sioo) for taking on the management of these programmes.
- Ina Smith and Bill Critchley of Ashridge Consulting and Charlotte Sills of the Metanoia Institute for their 'mentoring' in applying many of the ideas from this book in Ashridge Consulting's programme *Coaching for Organisation Consultants* and for the opportunity to work with verbatim reports (see Appendix B) in the Ashridge accreditation process for professional coaches.

1. Or 'young' in fact, compared with any other fields. Coaching – individual consultation, mentoring and supervision – really became a discipline only in the latter half of the twentieth century.

- Sarah Beart of Ashridge Consulting for her idea of applying the ladder of inference method within analytic coaching. We have now gained experience with it ourselves, and the LADDER METHOD has found a home in Chapter 8.
- Lorraine Oliver for her patience in looking for quantitative, 'outcome research' articles about coaching, the needle in the proverbial haystack, at which she has been wonderfully successful.
- Our Canadian-Dutch colleague Nico Swaan for countless detailed suggestions for the English translation, many of which made us rewrite the original Dutch text.
- Trevor Ashwin of Curran Publishing Services for exceptionally careful and patient editing, and for coming up with detailed suggestions regarding every single page of the manuscript.
- Our colleagues Charlotte Sills of the Metanoia Institute and Eunice Aquilina of the BBC's Internal Coaching Services for many helpful and supportive comments and suggestions on the first English draft.
- Selma van Vemde for her ability to bring coaching in all its varied forms – and more! – to life in her attracti\ve illustrations.

In the revised second edition

Our comment at the start of this Preface about the spirit of our times appears to be borne out by sales of this book. The second edition has come along quickly and coaching appears more than a trend. Coaching seems nothing less than a cultural revolution at the intersection between personal development and organisational development. And this book is not only an expression of that revolution, but is increasingly inspiring it as well.

For the revised second edition we have thoroughly revised and adapted this book in line with current requirements. Quantitative research within coaching, which this year marks its twentieth anniversary (after Peterson, 1993), has undergone a great expansion in recent years. In Chapter 11, therefore, we are able to give a more detailed account of this research and what we as coaches can learn from it already. We also emphasise the consensus in the field that it is crucially important for any coach (whether internal and external) to practise with mature and reliable ethics. As a result, we have added to Chapter 15 (the chapter about ethics and boundaries of the profession) ten examples of ethical dilemmas as regularly observed or faced by us in practice, accompanied by our best insights and suggestions.

We have resisted the temptation to write new chapters. In our view, it is precisely the compact structure of this book that makes it so usable as a guide and manual for the practitioner. Moreover, in *Relational Coaching* (2008), Erik has already written a comprehensive follow-up to this book.

We have also added four appendices: Appendix F is the 'coachee' version of the coaching behaviours questionnaire from Appendix E, designed to make it easier to collect feedback from your own coachees. Appendix G is an example of a coaching contract. Appendix H is an account of a complete series of coaching sessions. Together with eight new practical examples, this was added in response to requests from many readers. Finally, Appendix I gives an introduction to the very contemporary practice of 'telephone coaching', which we see as a positive development.

We hope that, with these changes and adjustments, *Coaching with colleagues* will serve as a modern, up-to-date guide to this exciting field for some time to come.

This book is dedicated to our own coaches with whom we have learned so much: Erik with Ric Oostburg, Gerard Wijers and Anton Obholzer, and Yvonne with Hanneke Elink Schuurman and, last but not least, Peter Janssen.

Erik de Haan and Yvonne Burger

Erik.DeHaan@Ashridge.org.uk
www.ashridge.org.uk\erikdehaan
info@yvonneburger.nl
www.yvonneburger.nl

Part I

Context for coaching

Introduction:
'Helping' conversations

We all have experience of conversations that are helpful to us. Conversations in which we can open our hearts, in which we feel truly understood, in which things become clearer, or in which we can hear ourselves think. These are conversations in which we gather the courage to face difficult issues – and which fill us with gratitude towards the people we have been talking to, even though the latter have often done little more than listen and offer a candid opinion. These are conversations in which we ourselves can take centre stage and ponder out loud on our main preoccupations. Such 'helping' conversations have certain features in common, features which we will try to identify and formalise in this part of the book. As an illustration of the form taken by such 'helping' conversations and how they may arise, this first section contains a brief but fairly comprehensive summary of the coaching profession.

Part I consists of four chapters which go together in pairs:

1. Chapter 1 outlines the breadth of coaching, as regards the type of problem and the corresponding coach's role: as mentor, supervisor, consultant, internal and external colleague. We give an initial indication of the limitations of coaching and of the main skills of the coach, subjects to which we return in more detail in Chapters 12 and 15.

2. Chapter 2 outlines the richness of coaching: richness in the subtlety of the communication and richness in the network of interconnections and references within what is expressed. We provide a window onto the contribution made by the coachee, from verbal, explicit input to the conversation, via implicit and non-verbal input, to things of which the coachee is

less aware. We also provide a
window onto the contribution
made by the coach, which ranges
from exploring to suggesting and
from supporting to confronting.

3. Chapter 3 illustrates the external
    conditions which are important
    for coaching conversations, by
    outlining in chronological order
    the kind of process the coach
    and coachee go through together.
    We give a summary of the basic
    principles of coaching, from
    making preparations and struc-
    turing the conversation to the
    ingredients of coaching con-
    tracts.

4. Chapter 4 illustrates the internal
    involvement which is important
    for the development of a coaching
    relationship, by outlining in chron-
    ological order the way in which the
    relationship between coach and
    coachee can develop. This gives a
    checklist for the intake of a new
    coachee, a summary of different
    forms of relationship during coach-
    ing, and a list of points for atten-
    tion when evaluating coaching.

The aim of this first section is therefore to give a straightforward indication of the way in which a cycle of 'helping' conversations can be
structured, and what the most striking events and elements within it
are. This first section is aimed in principle at every coach and every
coachee. As a result, it is rather general and lacking in direction in
terms of interventions and approaches. We hope to add sufficient dif-
ferentiation and depth later, in Parts II and III, to enable the reader to
feel more at home as a unique coach or coachee.

1

A wide scope for conversation

What do we mean by coaching?

Coaching is a method of work-related learning which relies primarily on one-to-one conversations. The two colleagues in the coaching conversation have different roles. The coach is focused on facilitating the coachee's learning and development process. As such, the coach's primary concern is that the coachee takes care of him- or herself. The coach may be a more experienced colleague, an outside professional with the same expertise as the coachee, or an outside adviser who is experienced primarily in 'coaching professionals' and is not – and has never been – active in the coachee's field of expertise. Coaching by one's own manager ('coaching leadership') is usually not geared solely towards learning, as in the definition above, in view of the judgmental nature of the managing relationship. In general, 'managing by coaching' means applying coaching techniques in the practice of leadership.

The aim of coaching is to improve the coachee's professionalism by discussing his or her relationship with certain experiences and issues. The coach's intention is to encourage reflection by the coachee, to release hidden strengths and to overcome obstacles to further development. The focus is on topics such as:

- how the coachee works with others
- how the coachee acts in specific situations, such as those involving managing, negotiating, giving advice or exerting influence
- how the coachee handles difficult situations, with colleagues and clients for example
- how the coachee forms judgments and makes decisions.

Figure 1.1 The coach is at your disposal

These topics are linked not only to the content of the specialist area but also to the person and the knowledge and skills at the coachee's disposal, the way in which (s)he acts, forms judgments, and so on. This makes coaching suitable for many different professional roles.

The coaching process roughly consists of the following phases (see also Chapter 3):

1. Intake and establishment of a coaching contract.
2. Building and maintaining the relationship.
3. Raising awareness.
4. Refining the contract.
5. Facilitating change.
6. Integration, review and evaluation.
7. Closure.

The first and sixth of these, those of intake and integration, often take place together with colleagues of the coachee, or with the coachee's manager.

During the coaching conversation the coachee raises issues related to recent experiences, such as experiences and queries relating to:

- leading others, or managing professionals
- drafting and evaluating proposals
- maintaining relationships with clients, customers or colleagues
- rejected proposals
- internal evaluation of services rendered per customer
- external evaluation: gauging customer satisfaction
- advising customers and clients
- handling differences of opinion with direct reports, customers or clients.

The main feature of coaching is therefore that a professional is given an opportunity to reflect, with the coach's assistance, on his or her own actions and thoughts.

A characteristic feature of coaching is that issues arising from the coachee's professional practice always provide the starting point. The conversations are not therapy sessions during which individuals' personalities are delved into deeply. It is useful, however, to consider the way in which the person contributing an issue deals with that issue personally, and to investigate the extent to which aspects of his or her behaviour are causing or prolonging the issue. The conversation can therefore centre on personal performance, but always in the context of practice.

1. Questions where content and specialist knowledge are at the centre, in which this knowledge needs to be applied in specific, difficult situations.	2. Questions with a content-related component, but where the way in which the coachee relates to and handles the content is important.	3. Questions where personal characteristics of the coachee are at the centre.

$$\longleftarrow \text{———————————————————} \longrightarrow$$

Range of coaching questions

'Coaching conversations' therefore cover an area similar to peer consultation (see Chapter 2 of *Learning with Colleagues*):

1. Issues where content is at the centre will often relate to unexpected experiences, for example in drafting proposals and giving advice.

These are often put forward in terms of 'what' questions: 'What kind
of system should I use here?'

2. Issues where the actions of the issue holder and the way in which
    (s)he handles a problem are central, are often put forward in
    terms of 'how' questions: 'Will you, as my coach, help me to
    decide how to do this, or how to tackle this issue?'

3. Issues where the very person raising the issue is at the centre are
    often put forward in terms of 'what' questions too. 'What kind
    of assignments suit me?' 'What is it about me that makes me
    come up against this time and again?' As these are more per-
    sonal 'what' issues, they can also be put forward as 'who' ques-
    tions, along the lines of 'Who am I, and what type of work is
    suitable for me?'

Because there is a personal component, it is important for the coachee
to become aware of his or her actions and to consider alternatives
open to them. The coach will help in this respect, primarily by clarifying the problem. The coach therefore has a consultative role and aims
to support the coachee in developing a personal approach to a personal issue or problem.

Different forms of coaching

Coaching is an 'umbrella' or 'container' term.[1] A variety of forms of
facilitation, mentoring and supervision can be differentiated.[2] What
these forms of guidance have in common is the fact that they centre

1. To be precise, coaching is both a 'container' and a 'containment' term.
    Coaching affords scope and containment to a broad variety of issues and
    concerns. We see coach and coachee as the 'container' and 'contained'
    within a 'dyadic' relationship (see Chapter 8 and Bion, 1963).

2. When considering the distinction between mentor and coach, it is inter-
    esting to look at the original meanings of both words:

    • *Mentor* is introduced in Homer's *Odyssey* as an old friend of the family.
      The goddess Pallas Athena assumes his form as a disguise in order to
      help Odysseus' son, Telemachus, find his father. Both Mentor and
      Athena have wide experience and knowledge of the situation, and
      advise and assist Telemachus. A typical example of Mentor's coaching
      style can be found in Book 22: 'Come hither, friend, and stand by me,
      and I will show thee a thing'. It is astounding how much insight can be
      gained from the *Odyssey* – one of the oldest works in Western literature,

on a relationship between a coachee and a coach ('one-to-one') and that that relationship is focused on the coachee's learning in his or her work. Table 1.1 contains an overview of a number of forms of coaching; we should emphasise that the same terms are defined slightly differently in different places.

In Table 1.1, coaching methods are differentiated by objective, target group, subject matter, working method, qualifications of the coach and level of intervention. This final distinction, *level of intervention* (see Chapter 2 of *Learning with Colleagues*), is an important issue in personal guidance. It relates to the degree in which personal characteristics and behaviours of the coachee form a part of the learning process.

The 'depth' of coaching conversations

In general, there is a link between the person who has an issue and the nature of the problem. For example, a given question can be very difficult for one individual to address, while someone else barely registers it or is able to resolve it with no problem. The degree to which a problem affects us, makes us insecure, causes sleepless nights or intrigues us, says something about the problem, of course, but also something about the person who perceives and 'owns' the problem. The following possibilities can be distinguished:

> dating to the eighth century BC – about a concept as modern as 'mentoring'!

- *Coach*, on the other hand, is defined in the dictionary as: 'A large, closed, horse-drawn carriage with four wheels which conveys esteemed individuals from where they were to where they want to be.' The coach is therefore a vehicle, a way of getting from A to B, and not a person who contributes knowledge or experience and gives instructions. In our view, this is the main difference between a mentor and a coach: one is a more experienced professional who contributes her own expertise; the other is an instrument in the coachee's learning who is not necessarily familiar with or experienced in the coachee's field of work. It is interesting that the word 'coach' comes from the name of the Hungarian village Kocs, where in the 15th century AD a distinctive cart was produced. For us the history of the word symbolises the gradual change in our society from craftsmanship to industrial ('railway coach') to knowledge-intensive (educator-coach) to emotionally intelligent production methods.

In this book we assume that mentoring is a special form of coaching. As a result, we do not refer specifically to mentoring, except in Chapter 11 where we cite research by Ragins et al. (2000), which is particularly concerned with the mentoring relationship.

Table 1.1 Forms and levels of coaching

Different forms of coaching	Objective	Target group	Qualifications of coach	Subject matter	Working method	Level (1–10)
Supervision	Becoming more professional	Professionals	Coach is often simultaneously the manager	Specific work-related issues	Based on case material	1–4
Individual training/ On-the-job training	Reinforcing skills	Anyone	Subject-matter expertise Training expertise	Behaviour and understanding	Learning by doing, transfer of knowledge and feedback. Limited number of sessions	2–5
Mentoring	Guided learning by doing Action learning	Anyone	Subject-matter expertise	Behaviour and understanding	Observation, feedback. Practice in workplace	4–7
Individual advice	Support in problem-solving	Managers	Expertise as a consultant Management experience	Work in relation to the person	Broadening in context (reading, observing)	3–7
Individual consultation	Becoming more professional Reinforcing knowledge, attitude and skills	Professionals	Mature professional	Person in relation to the work	Individual conversations, upon request of the coachee	5–8
Counselling	Personal development Increasing understanding	Anyone	Psychological expertise	The person within the work environment	Prior agreement on number of sessions (minimum 5)	7–10

1. Some problems are 'objective' or technical in nature. For example, if someone is having trouble with certain software packages this might relate to resistance to information technology, or simply to a lack of knowledge or skill. Sometimes, therefore, there is simply a need to acquire knowledge or learn a particular skill. Expert advice can provide a solution here.
2. Sometimes, however, acquiring knowledge or learning new behaviour is not enough. There are underlying patterns which suggest that, though this specific problem may be solved, the same problem (possibly in a different form) will reappear the next day. Here it is important to consider not the incident, but the work context and the pattern generated by the incident. This is not always easy, because a feature of such patterns is that they often go unrecognised by the person concerned. Many people have a tendency to define problems as separate from themselves: 'It's not my fault; it's the work environment; it's my colleagues'. Coaching can provide a solution here.
3. Sometimes issues and problems are so personal that a thorough exploration within the context of work and professional experience is insufficient. An individual's abilities and limitations underlie the problems and issues at hand. A characteristic aspect of such problems is that they are experienced as much privately as they are at work. Therapy can provide a solution here.

In coaching, a number of different levels are present simultaneously (a matter also considered in Chapter 2). The focus is not only on the issue raised, and on ways of dealing with it, but also on the patterns underlying such issues. The coach can often choose which of these levels to pursue, or at which level to make a personal contribution. In making that choice, the coach determines to a large extent how the conversation will continue. The importance of choosing the 'right' level of intervention therefore often becomes clear only in retrospect.

A much-used summary of levels of intervention is shown in Figure 1.2.

Role and competencies of the coach

Clearly with such a variety of issues the demands placed on a coach depend on where the emphasis is placed. An 'all-round' coach understands the main principles of organisation, change and intervention management, and also of clinical psychology. As the depth of intervention increases, the coach must rely increasingly on his or her intuition,

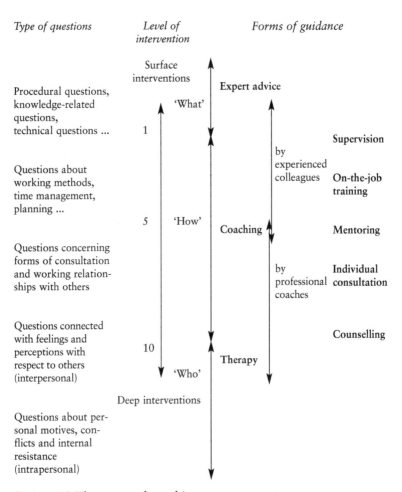

Figure 1.2 The scope of coaching

psychological understanding and experience, and on 'shadow coaching' by another coach or a peer consultation group. These enable the coach to recognise patterns and mental models, both in the processes described by the coachee and in the meetings between coachee and coach. Bringing these patterns up for discussion can yield significant insights.

Generally speaking, a coach is able to

• identify with the coachee's problem and support the coachee in the search for a solution or an approach,

- encourage the coachee to find new perspectives on his or her problem,
- explore relationships between the problem and the organisational context,
- view his or her own interaction with the coachee as if from the 'outside', and give a transparent account of it when asked,
- relate the issue raised by the coachee to what happens during the coaching conversation, and raise that relationship during the conversation with the coachee.

Part III of this book focuses on the skills a coach can be expected to have, and on the manner in which the coach can bring those different skills to bear.

Summary: a wide scope for conversation

Coaching is a method of work-related learning which relies primarily on one-to-one conversations.

The aim of coaching is to increase the coachee's professionalism by discussing his/her relationship to the experiences and problems raised.

The scope of coaching is fairly wide, embracing:

- Supervision: approach, procedures, results.
- On-the-job training: approach and behaviour.
- Mentoring: approach, forms of consultation and working relationships.
- Individual consultation: the person in relation to work.
- Counselling: the person within the work.

Coaching is therefore situated somewhere between expert advice and therapy, at different levels of intervention.

The main skills required of coaches are:

- Listening skills: identifying with the coachee's problem.
- Intervening choicefully: encouraging the coachee to find new perspectives and solutions.
- Organisation development: exposing links between problem and organisational context.
- Psychological understanding: exploring and raising the coachee's interaction during the conversation.

2
A rich field of exploration

This chapter sets out to provide a clear explanation of the complex and multi-layered nature of coaching conversations. It starts with a window onto the coachee used by both coach and coachee: this is an extended version of the Johari window (see Luft, 1969, or *Learning with Colleagues*, Chapter 10). It then introduces a window onto the coach, which gives an idea of the different emphases that coaches can apply in their approach.

In our experience, coaching conversations are very rich and full conversations. They often deal with issues of real importance to the coachee – issues with a broad background, and issues the coachee has worked on previously, either alone or with friends and colleagues. In addition, the coachee reveals not only something about the issues and situations, in words and in gestures, but also something about themself in the way in which they handle those issues. In the way in which he or she tells a story, the coachee invites the coach to contribute in a specific manner – for example by listening, asking questions, being stern, empathising or lending expertise. Clearly, the attitude of the coach makes a real difference. By the way in which he or she asks questions and listens – and, more generally, by every contribution to the conversation (not contributing is not an option![1]) – the coach influences the conversation both intentionally and unintentionally. An orderly, well-controlled conversation is out of the question – there are simply too many variables. It sometimes feels as if we are 'playing' in a very confined space where every tiny movement, every glance and gesture acquires meaning, a meaning that interacts with other meanings and causes ripples in pre-existing patterns of meaning. For us, coaching conversations are quite literally a

1. See Watzlawick et al. (1967) on the fact that we cannot *not* communicate.

'craft of skill and precision', offering access to an extremely rich field of exploration for those who open themselves up to it. A good coach does precisely that.

Window onto the coachee

In a coaching conversation, both coach and coachee are focused on what is going on in the coachee's mind. They are therefore working together on the same territory: the 'material' which is the coachee. It is useful to have a 'map' of that territory, or a 'window' onto everything the coachee is contributing to the conversation at each moment. Figure 2.1 is a map of the playing field between coach and coachee, derived from the 'Johari window' (see *Learning with Colleagues*, Chapter 10).[2]

At any one moment in a coaching conversation, coachee and coach are standing side by side on the map and looking out at what

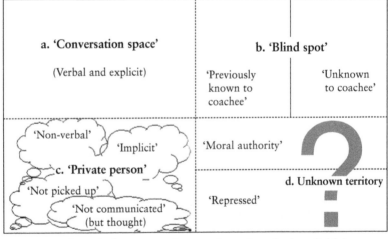

Figure 2.1 The window onto the coachee: the playing field between coach and coachee

2.   There are good alternatives to our map, such as the Comparative Script System in Lapworth, Sills and Fish (2000) or the more complex Grid used by Bion (Bion, 1962). The use of one of these maps can be 'liberating' for coaches as they will be able to 'place' new information quickly, thereby freeing themselves for what is to come. Maps also help to summarize what is *not* said, to trace what is perhaps being overlooked both by the coach and by the coachee.

Figure 2.2 Coach and coachee walk side by side on a map provided by the coachee. Together they discover the landscape *and* the map.

is going on within the coachee. This is not a conventional model of communication, with a sender, a receiver and numerous distortions in the communication process (as, for example, in Schulz von Thun, 1982). Such models fall short when it comes to coaching: all too easily we give in to the tendency to experience our communication with other people as our interaction with the things that surround us. Sure enough, 'things' send out 'signals' – and, sure enough, those signals come through clearly or less clearly – and, sure enough, we receive those 'signals', process different aspects of them, construct some sort of internal 'representation' of the things and react to that in turn. Yet this representation does not do full justice to the complexity of our interaction with things, and definitely falls short as a representation of our communication with people, where something fundamentally different is going on. People literally become absorbed in each other when they communicate, and create a communicative unit (Watzlawick et al., 1967) – even a hermit is not a hermit without the group of people with respect to which (s)he assumes the role of hermit. It is this communicative unit which we attempt to illustrate below. It consists of four 'fields', discussed in the following sections.

a. The conversation space or 'free space'

The *conversation space* is the field worked out in most detail on our map (see Figure 2.3). This represents the explicit and visible part of the coachee's contribution. The coachee's 'story' always has both 'expressive' and 'appellant' aspects simultaneously (Schulz von Thun, 1982):

- *Expressive* describes the part that reveals something about the coachee and their issues. The coachee expresses him- or herself and so provides personal insights. The stories told by the coachee – for example about the background to an issue, or things that have happened this week, are expressive. The opinions, feelings and facts (s)he contributes are also expressive.
- *Appellant* describes the part where the coachee makes an appeal to the coach. In other words, (s)he implicitly or explicitly conveys an expectation or hope of a particular response. At the simplest level the coachee tells his or her story, assuming the coach is listening. Or the coachee asks a question and then usually expects an answer from the coach – unless it is a rhetorical question, when the coachee rather expects agreement from the coach. Or else the coachee has an overt request for help ('I'd like your opinion on this!'). At a subtler level the appeal may be implicit, as in 'I'm absolutely hopeless at this', which often implies 'will you do it for me?' Appellant behaviour becomes even subtler, and often more interesting for the

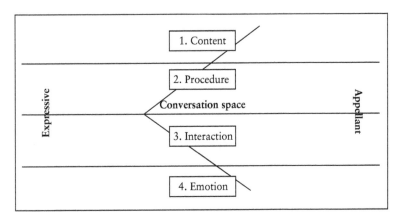

Figure 2.3 The conversation space in the Johari window in more detail

coaching process itself, when the coachee appeals to the coach for help in a specific way – for example, by pressing for solutions, or by adopting a superior stance.

Expressive and appellant elements of conversations are not easy to distinguish. Most typically expressive comments also have an appellant aspect (for example, 'I think it's a good idea to take another look at that' implies 'and I hope you will go along with me'). Conversely, the most strongly appellant comments also have an expressive significance (for example, 'I would like to hear your opinion about a conversation that I had this week' also communicates 'because I am preoccupied with it at the moment').

Another useful distinction in the conversation space is that between the different *levels* in the conversation, from factual to personal. We normally assume four levels of conversation, or four different levels of explicit communication that qualify each other:

1. Contributions concerning the *content* of the conversation, that is, the story being told by the coachee, and facts and statements (s)he provides. This concerns all sorts of information being conveyed at any particular moment in the conversation. Contributions on this level are often expressive.
2. Contributions concerning the *procedure* of the conversation, in other words, its different stages, structure and working method. This concerns attempts by the coachee to organise the conversation. Contributions at this level are often appellant ('How would you like me to tell my story?'), but are not necessarily so ('First I will talk about the meeting and then I will say something more about my colleague herself').
3. Contributions concerning the *interaction* in the conversation: how the parties to the conversation respond to each other, what roles they adopt and their attitude towards each other.[3] Contributions at this level are often appellant ('Yes, but you are my coach ...'), and can also be partly expressive ('I think we're stuck here ...').
4. Contributions concerning the *emotion* in the conversation, i.e. about feelings currently being experienced by the coachee or

3. This aspect of communication is often also classified under the *relationship aspect*, which concerns not only this conversation but also the relationship between coach and coachee more generally (Schulz von Thun, 1982).

coach. Contributions at this level are often largely expressive ('I still feel angry about it now'; 'Your response moves me').

In general, these four levels are easier to distinguish than the expressive and appellant aspects of communication, even if it is not always easy to separate the third and fourth levels (see, for example, the last example under 'emotion', which could also have appeared under 'interaction'!). An important boundary between these levels is that between the first and the other three, between:

- statements concerning the coachee's 'case' (content), and
- statements concerning this conversation, at this moment (procedure, interaction, emotion).

The first level (content) always concerns 'there and then' and the other levels always concern 'here and now' – the procedure now, the interaction now and the feelings now. Other procedures, interactions and feelings remain more remote and cannot be distinguished from the content of the conversation. If a contribution relates to the structure of the conversation, it is purely procedural. If it relates to the way in which the two parties to the conversation respond to each other, it is purely interactive. If it relates to the feelings of individual parties in the conversation, it is purely emotional.

As with the distinction between 'expressive' and 'appellant', it is clear that all four levels are always present implicitly in every conversation. The coachee and coach can answer the four accompanying questions at any moment:

- What is the content of the conversation now?
- What is the structure of the conversation now?
- What is the interaction within the conversation now?
- What are my feelings in this conversation now?

All parts of the conversation space which are not explicitly on the table at this moment and which concern the coachee remain safely hidden in the 'private person' quadrant in the Johari window, where they await (possible) communication in the future.

b. The private person
In Figure 2.1 (page 15) we drew thought bubbles in this quadrant. Ultimately this quadrant concerns what happens within the coachee

during the conversation but is not directly communicated or picked up by the coach. This is therefore the part of the map where the coachee is more at home than the coach. The following levels can be identified in this quadrant, in order of decreasing accessibility to the coach:

1. *Non-verbal information* from the coachee (Mehrabian, 1972), such as:
   • proximity, attitude, movement, gestures and facial expressions
   • intonation, volume, strength and tone of voice
   • interjections such as 'mmm', 'er' and 'um'.
   It is well known that our non-verbal communication conveys an enormous amount of information. In the event of contradictory verbal and non-verbal signals, the non-verbal impression generally appears to be the stronger.[4] Non-verbal information is generally implicit and therefore leaves a lot to intuition and guesswork. As a result, non-verbal communication occurs primarily in the space of the private person.

2. *Implicit information* from the coachee, that is, information which can be read 'between the lines'. This information is again both expressive and appellant. Here too, a wealth of information is expressed through word choice, word repetition, word stress and internal contradictions.[5] In fact, implicit communication forms a grey area between all four quadrants. Think of vague, barely audible words: do they belong to the 'conversation space', or the 'private person' space? Do they reveal something about the coachee in the 'blind spot', or do they make coach and coachee guess about their origin, which means that they remain 'unknown territory'? To a large extent, coaching results in implicit communication of this kind becoming more explicit, and the coachee literally being able to find a place for it.

3. *Information from the coachee that remains unheard*: information which is explicitly communicated by the coachee, but is not picked up or consciously registered by the coach.

4. Mehrabian (1972) – with regard to the communication of 'liking' in words, voice and facial expression – describes how subjects' reactions can be described as 0.07 × (influence of words) + 0.38 × (influence of voice expression) + 0.55 × (influence of facial expression). The non-verbal signals appear to dominate strongly!

5. The coachee is unaware of much of his/her own implicit information, which therefore then belongs in the 'blind spot'.

4. *Uncommunicated thought* – this is all of the information that the coachee has decided to keep to him- or herself.
5. *Everything that is not currently on the table*: the entire remaining private person of the coachee, including everything (s)he has experienced and is able to retrieve. This field is connected with the unknown territory, which contains all sorts of experiences which the coachee can no longer recall.

Clearly, the 'size' of the private person decreases the more the coachee is prepared to reveal personal details, but also the better the coach is able to register less obvious signals.

c. The blind spot

The blind spot is that part of the coachee (or of his/her contribution) that the coach can observe but that the coachee is unaware of personally. It is therefore the part of the map where the coach is more at home than the coachee. For example, certain emotions may become visible on the face of the coachee; or the coachee may omit certain aspects of a story, or have forgotten them entirely.

This area can be divided into two general areas (Freud, 1923):

1. The part previously known to the coachee, sometimes called the 'preconscious'. The coach has only to mention or recall a fact and the coachee remembers it. An example is the 'homework' for a particular session, with which the session was intended to begin. Imagine that the coachee starts off on a completely different tack. When the coach mentions the homework, a surprised and slightly guilty expression may appear on the coachee's face: an indication in the blind spot that the homework was in his or her preconscious mind.
2. The part unknown to the coachee. The coachee has a lot to learn here, by definition, so the coach can make a valuable contribution by raising aspects from this field in the conversation.

d. Unknown territory

The coachee's 'unknown territory' also contains a 'preconscious' area. This area concerns information which may come to the coachee's attention accidentally and is then recognised as the coachee's reaction shows. This preconscious is connected with the preconscious in the 'blind spot', which is known to the coach, but not to the coachee at this moment.

Leaving aside this 'preconscious' area, the unknown territory is in fact one great unknown: we don't actually know for sure whether there is anything in it. This is where coach and coachee embark on a voyage of discovery together. The area as such remains fundamentally, and by definition, unknown: if coach or coachee are indeed able to say something about it, it appears immediately in one of the other quadrants of the Johari window. However, there are many signs that there is 'something else' in addition to these quadrants, if only because memory ebbs and flows, or because new feelings and ideas sometimes present themselves initially in an incomplete state. The generation of new ideas and the unearthing of memories seem to be based on an activity which itself lies outside our own awareness. Chapter 8 shows that there are many pointers to the existence of a personal 'unknown territory' and that we can find pointers to the existence of this unconscious in our Freudian slips, humour, emotions and dreams. Freud wrote about this at length, and was also bold enough to classify the content of this unknown – and in principle unknowable – zone using the following main distinction (Freud, 1923):

1. The *moral authority* that influences what ends up in the unknown territory, and what can emerge from it. This area consists of the 'unconscious conscience' (an internal representation of 'evil') and the 'ego ideal' ('an internal representation of good') and exercises a sort of controlling influence on memories, utterances and emotions, in terms of what is 'permitted' or 'not permitted'. Freud referred to this as the 'super-ego' (Über-Ich). We believe it is helpful if the coach is aware of the possible existence of a super-ego, which opens the possibility that a coachee is unknowingly not permitting thought about certain things, or does not allow him/herself to find and implement certain solutions.
2. The *hidden or repressed material* itself: the facts, desires, feelings and fantasies being created or dismantled. This material is indeed present but the conscious mind has no access to it, nor is it visible in the coachee's blind spot. Sometimes we are capable of perceiving the existence of something like this within ourselves: for example, while scanning a newspaper or magazine our thoughts may suddenly be drawn to something or someone, but only later do we notice that the relevant name was printed on the very page we were reading. Evidently, we did perceive the key word but did not initially admit it into our conscious mind.

This simple classification of the unknown area can sometimes come in handy. The simultaneous presence of so many fields – in the 'conversation space', the 'private person' and the 'blind spot' as well as in the 'unknown territory', all at the same time – gives an indication of the richness of a coaching conversation at any moment in time. Bear in mind too that the fields also qualify and comment on each other, and it becomes clear that the sheer number of possibilities is incalculable.

An example
A coachee who says 'I have a pain in my big toe' is reporting all of the following simultaneously:

- a fact
- a topic for a conversation
- an implicit qualification which may say something about the seriousness of the conversation
- an implicit relationship definition ('I talk about my pain and you listen')
- an appeal to the coach ('Help me endure my pain!')
- a feeling
- a non-verbal qualification which may say something about the severity of the pain
- the need not to continue with previous topics of conversation
- an expression of him- or herself as coachee.

All of these things come together at the moment of the conversation. The coach has the choice of doing nothing, following up any of these messages, or indeed continuing with or proposing a completely different type of conversation or conversational content. An overwhelming variety of choices.

We hope, of course, that our 'map' has brought some clarity and order to coaching conversations. At the same time, however, such a simple map skims over much of the subtlety, misunderstanding, incomprehension and fantasy that also enter coaching conversations. The different fields in the map often refer to each other, and the coachee's communication may bring together meanings on many levels at the same time (a phenomenon known as 'condensation' – see Malan, 1995). Moreover, the coachee tells personal stories which (s)he has already self-censored to a large extent; these stories lead the coach to think about the coachee in a certain way, again coloured with a mixture of interpretations, self-censorship and misconceptions. One might say that the distortions and misconceptions of the coachee are still somewhere in the 'private person' and that the distortion and (mis-)understanding on the part of the coach lie somewhere in the 'blind spot' – but that too would be to skim over all of the destructiveness and creativity inherent in one-on-one conversations. Our aim has been to show how rich the playing field of coaching is – all the simultaneously present ambiguity and uncertainty simply provide more evidence of that richness!

Window onto the coach

In the coaching conversation the coachee continually produces new information which can find a place somewhere in the Johari window. At the same time, the coach has great freedom in the way (s)he responds to that information. To bring some structure to that freedom, we also offer a window onto the contribution made by the coach. Later, in Part II of this book, we will introduce at least one specific coaching method for each quadrant in this window. We will also examine in greater depth the effects of the different methods, the similarities between the methods, and their correspondence to combinations of coachees and coachee issues.

It is assumed that the coach makes two fundamental contributions:

1. *Direction* of contribution: exploring or suggesting? The coach can choose at each moment to follow and liberate the coachee's thoughts and contributions, or to constrain them and introduce his or her own thoughts and contributions. This enables the coach to influence the direction of the conversation, by deciding whether to 'lead' or to 'follow' the coachee. In the first instance the coach will suggest or propose something; in the second the coach will put him- or herself at the service of a joint exploration or discovery process.
2. *Nature* of contribution: supporting or confronting? The coach can decide at each moment to build on and reinforce the coachee's strengths, or else to bring up the coachee's weaknesses and help him or her overcome them. This enables the coach to influence the construction or deconstruction of the conversation, by deciding to support or challenge the coachee more. In our experience, most coachees expect both support and confrontation from their coaches. The coach can decide when to contribute one or the other.

Figure 2.4 The coach attempts to portray the coachee as faithfully as
possible. Coaching means observing with great clarity and
then painting in minute detail.

Combining each of these possibilities gives a minimal playing field for
the coach encompassing four options:

1. Exploring and supporting, or facilitating the coachee with encour-
    agement and understanding. The coach attempts to explore the
    issue together with the coachee and contributes warmth and under-
    standing to the conversation. This approach is referred to hence-
    forth as *person-focused*.
2. Exploring and confronting, or facilitating the coachee at a greater
    distance. The coach attempts to look at what the coachee is leav-
    ing out and cannot appreciate personally, thus contributing
    understanding and objectivity to the conversation. This approach
    is referred to henceforth as *insight-focused*.
3. Suggesting and confronting, or helping the coachee with sugges-
    tions and instructions. The coach attempts to offer the coachee a
    new framework or approach to the problems being considered,
    and contributes ideas and recommendations to the conversation.
    This approach is referred to henceforth as *problem-focused*.

4. Suggesting and supporting, or helping the coachee with options and positive feedback. The coach attempts to send the coachee off on a more positive, constructive train of thought and to help with suggestions for the future. This approach is referred to henceforth as *solution-focused*.

As Figure 2.5 shows, each of the four orientations on the playing field results in a different orientation on the part of the coach.

Interestingly, the orientations in the quadrants, to which we return later (in Chapters 5 and 12), show other familiar polarities which are relevant to coaching:

1. The *level* of addressing coaching issues (from top left to bottom right) – ranging from the coachee's problem to the coachee as a person, from 'what' to 'who' questions, and from superficial to more personal levels of intervention (see Chapter 1). This is a dimension that runs from content to person. The coach makes a choice, with regard to intervention level, by adopting a *problem-focused* or *person-focused* stance.
2. A *time orientation* from past to future (from bottom left to top right) – from the current situation, how it came about and what can be learned from it, to solutions and suggestions for the future. This is a dimension that runs from causes to options. The

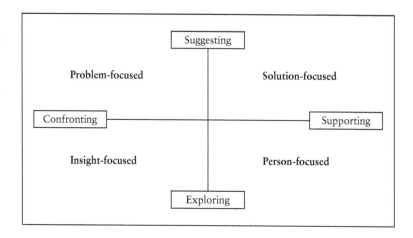

Figure 2.5 The window onto the coach: different contributions from the coach. A similar model has been proposed for mentoring by David Clutterbuck (1985).

coach makes a choice, on this time dimension, by adopting an *insight-focused* or *solution-focused* stance.

In Figure 2.6, these intervention levels and time axes have been added.

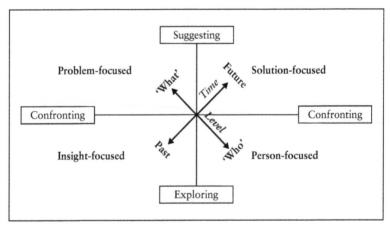

Figure 2.6 The window onto the coach, showing intervention level and time axes.

Summary: a rich field of exploration

During coaching conversations, *both* coach and coachee are focused on the coachee's issues.

These conversations are extremely rich and complex in nature, because the coachee offers a great variety of 'material' simultaneously and because all sorts of information and behaviours are interwoven and qualify each other.

The 'material' that is the coachee can be presented with somewhat deceptive clarity using the *Johari window*:

1. The conversation space, containing:
    - expressive and appellant aspects
    - four levels of communication: content, procedure, interaction and emotion.
2. The private person, containing:
    - non-verbal information
    - implicit information
    - information which remains hidden
    - thoughts which are not expressed
    - everything else the coachee might contribute but does not.
3. The blind spot, containing:
    - that of which the coachee is unaware at this moment but of which the coach is aware (the 'preconscious')
    - that of which the coachee is entirely unaware but of which the coach is aware (the actual blind spot).
4. The unknown territory, containing:
    - a moral authority
    - that which is repressed on behalf of the moral authority.

The coach's contribution can be presented clearly using the *window onto the coach*.

1. Person-focused: observing and supporting the coachee from the coachee's perspective.
2. Insight-focused: considering the coachee from an independent perspective.
3. Problem-focused: helping the coachee with an approach to the problem.
4. Solution-focused: supporting the coachee in his/her search for solutions.

3
Structuring the coaching journey

This chapter outlines a number of aspects that we generally attend to at the start of coaching and when structuring our coaching conversations. We give generally applicable suggestions for structuring and conducting the whole process and individual conversations and point out that different approaches to coaching are dictated by different initial conditions. Some coaching approaches can be applied during a stroll with the coachee; for others, taking notes during the conversation is vital. The differences between approaches are dealt with in Part II.

At Ashridge, we usually assume an underlying coaching process which is basically circular, spiralling upwards, and has seven intuitive and sometimes overlapping phases:

1. *Intake and establishment of a coaching contract*
   In every intake there should be some check for boundary issues and conflicts of interest. Coach and coachee clarify their mutual expectations as much as possible. A coaching contract has three areas of significance: administrative, professional and psychological. At the very least, the contract contains a mention of the objectives, the number of sessions (often between five and twenty), the frequency, duration and location of sessions, and the range of learning methods to be utilised.
2. *Building and maintaining the relationship*
   This 'working alliance' means agreement in practice – and not only in the letter of the contract! – about such things as tasks and goals of the coaching relationship, and the establishment of empathy, genuineness and efficacy in the relationship.

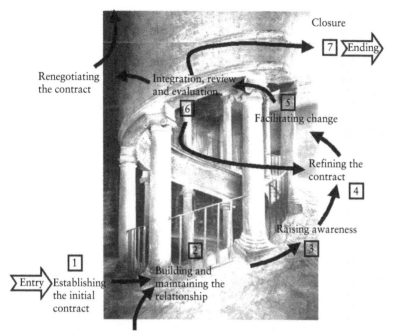

Figure 3.1 The coaching process, as seen through the eyes of the coach:
with the help of the famous spiral staircase of Bramante we
have tried to express the circular, and at the same time pro-
gressive, nature of a coaching journey

3. *Raising awareness*
   Where coach and coachee explore key issues, needs, gaps, patterns and problem triggers. The coaching serves largely to
   strengthen insight and self-acceptance.
4. *Refining the contract*
   Where coach and coachee review the coaching process up to a given
   point, take stock of the outcome in the light of the original goals,
   and explore options for the future. This may take place halfway in
   the coaching journey and may be a moment to liaise with other
   involved parties.
5. *Facilitating change*
   The coach helps the coachee to build commitment and enthusiasm for practice and experiment.
6. *Integration, review and evaluation*
   Coach and coachee explore together the results of the journey and
   implications of the outcome. The coachee evaluates the coaching

and a decision is taken towards either renegotiating the coaching contract or ending the journey.

7. *Closure*
    Where coach and coachee appreciate their common achievements, perhaps look once more at forestalling relapse and – more or less ceremoniously – make their farewells.

Basic principles

General principles

- The coach and the client are equals (i.e. they are not in a reporting relationship).
- Clients ultimately know best what is good for them and can decide themselves what they do or do not want, both in their private and in their professional life – clients are therefore responsible for the choices that they make and accountable for their actions.
- The responsibility of the coach is to give the client an opportunity to explore, discover and clarify ways of living and working more satisfyingly and resourcefully.
- During coaching the goals, resources and choices of the client have priority over those of the coach.

For the coach

- Individual coaching conversations aim to support the coachee in his or her continued professional development.
- The conversation is shaped by the coachee's learning objectives; however, the coachee remains personally responsible for achieving those objectives.
- The coachee's contribution is the starting point for the conversation, not what the coach thinks the coachee should learn or do.
- Everything the coachee contributes is completely confidential. The person being coached must be able to and dare to be vulnerable.
- Adequate time, peace and quiet are a *sine qua non* for coaching.

For the coachee

- Everything can be raised and subsequently may serve as 'material' in order to explore the coachee's own role and approach.

- Before the start, the coachee concludes a 'contract' with the coach specifying learning objectives, and how they will work together to achieve those objectives. The coachee also agrees the frequency (for example, once a month or every six weeks), the length (for example, an hour and a half) and the number of sessions. After that, coach and coachee decide jointly whether to continue or terminate the sessions, and conclude a new contract if necessary.

Making an appointment and preparations

Conversations are the methodological basis of coaching. The first conversation starts even before it has actually begun. Coach and coachee have expectations, questions, and conscious or unconscious impressions of each other. The first step on the coaching journey has been taken when the coachee decides to enter into a conversation with you here and now.

The first action is usually taken by the coachee, namely making an appointment for a time and a place. A lot can happen during a short telephone conversation. From their interaction with you, you learn something about the coachee's emotional involvement in the issue they wish to address , and how they deal with time and space Sometimes you immediately notice something that will prove later on to be a very significant detail.

Points for attention during such first contact situations include the following:

- Set a time limit for the process, to monitor its effectiveness and to protect the space and focus needed for the conversation.
- On a practical note: take the coachee's telephone number, so you can get back to him or her.

After the first conversation, the coachee will know if there is a 'click' – if there is sufficient contact for you to work together. In addition, coach and coachee will have gained an initial impression of the basic themes. If you think that you are not the most suitable coach for these themes, or for particular coachees, you can still help them by referring them to someone else.

Preparation for a conversation
Novice coaches sometimes have a tendency to want to prepare for a conversation. The risk here is that you will be concerned primarily

with your own agenda during the conversation. It is more important to 'empty your mind', so that you can concentrate fully on your coachee, as well as:

- being aware of your own involvement (how do you feel and what does that mean?)
- putting yourself in the role of coach (not colleague, manager, consultant or trainer, for example).

Venue and set-up
The coach is generally the host or hostess. Consider the venue for the coaching. Do you go to the coachee or does (s)he come to you? What are the possible implications of this? In general, the following are recommended:

- some distance from the coachee's workplace: in your office or on neutral territory
- a quiet room with pleasant lighting and atmosphere, where you yourself feel comfortable
- a seating arrangement where you are at an angle to each other, so that the coachee can choose to look away and does not feel put on the spot
- chairs in which you can easily keep your balance.

Ask yourself who is sitting nearest the door and what the implications of this might be.
  The following set-up is recommended:

- seating position: 120 degree angle
- table not too large (moveable)
- chairs in which you can relax, but not slouch
- room tidy, well-lit, not too cold.

Starting the conversation

The first five minutes are often critical. There is no such thing as a neutral introduction. The coachee's theme often comes up right at the start of the conversation. The first question should therefore be as open as possible. In his or her first sentences, a coachee often outlines a relevant problem and offers a personal view on it. But this can also happen in *the last five minutes*, when the 'door-knob phenomenon'

Figure 3.2 The coach organises the most appropriate set-up for the
conversation

may operate: some people may be unable to say what is really bothering them until the last five minutes, so that they don't have to talk
about it any further during this session.

Try to establish why the coachee is coming to you at this point in
time with this issue. Be clear and check that the other person understands you. It is not the intention that this conversation should result
in further confusion on the part of the coachee.

Taking notes during the conversation has advantages and
disadvantages:

Advantages of note-taking	Disadvantages of note-taking
• Helps to focus attention	• Diverts attention from non-verbal information
• Helps to structure the coachee's contribution	• Distances the coach from the coachee
• Helps to prepare for the next conversation	• Provides a form of foothold for the coach that can be deceptive

Often, it comes down to the coach's personal choice: whatever (s)he is more comfortable with. It can also depend on the approach and working method that you choose as coach (see Part II of this book).

Some coaches ask their coachee to make notes during or after the conversation. Similar advantages and possible disadvantages apply here too, this time for the coachee.

Continuing the conversation: the art of listening

Coaching is mainly a matter of listening and asking questions, although a whole range of different interventions also enter into it (summarised in Chapter 12).

The following points are important *when asking questions* (see also Chapter 3 of *Learning with Colleagues*):

- *Open questions* are the most effective way to increase awareness and accountability. Open questions start with 'what', 'when', 'who', 'how many'. 'Why' is not recommended because it often puts others on the defensive. A better approach is to ask questions such as: 'What are your reasons?'; 'In what stages?'; 'What does that achieve?'. Leading questions are not recommended – if you have a suggestion, better to just come out with it.
- In principle, start with *general questions* and concentrate increasingly on *specific details*. This allows you to uncover important (hidden) factors.

The following points are important *when listening*:

- Be aware of the different aspects attached to a message (see previous chapter):
  - the content-related aspect (things, facts, other people)
  - the expressive aspect (own feelings or judgments)
  - the appellant aspect (appeal to the coach to behave in a certain way)
  - the relationship aspect (how the coachee defines the relationship with the coach, for example as a relationship based on trust).

You can raise these aspects with the help of 'meta-communication'; then the listening moves from the content to the way in which the coachee communicates.

- Listen for intonation and word choice.
- Pay attention to body language.
- Show that you are listening to your coachee by offering small encouragements (gestures, posture, facial expressions) and by following the coachee verbally (in your responses, using the other person's language as much as possible).
- Give back what you hear by mirroring or summarising and checking ('So, if I understand you correctly ... is that right?').
- Bring things back to specifics if the coachee has a tendency to generalise problems (in terms of 'everyone', 'always', 'everywhere', 'never'). Ask for examples, precise details, and so on.
- Reflect the feelings of the coachee by naming them, so that listening becomes more explicit and the coachee also has an opportunity to 'listen to' his or her own emotions.
- Be aware of how you are feeling yourself! Your own feelings may yield additional information about the coachee, but may also affect your impartiality or objectivity.
- Be aware of possible projection(s) or (counter-)transference (see Chapter 8) which may get in the way of pure listening.

The coaching contract

After the first conversation, coach and coachee usually conclude a contract. In the case of internal coaching, it is usually sufficient to make (verbal) agreements concerning:

- the objectives of the coaching
- the topics to be addressed by the coaching, including the way in which you are to work on specific topics, in relation to working on underlying patterns and career or management development issues
- the approach and methods to be used
- the intended effects of the coaching in the workplace
- the method of checking or evaluating whether the objectives and intended results have been achieved
- the length, frequency and duration of the coaching sessions
- the venue for the sessions
- unconditional confidentiality

- reference to an applicable Code of Conduct and conditions (see also Chapter 15).

In the case of external coaching, the usually formal, written contract covers all of the above plus an agreement of the fee, specifying:

- the level of the fee
- any reimbursement of other costs
- the method of payment
- financial arrangements for cancelled sessions.

Summary: structuring the coaching journey

The coaching process involves the following steps:

1. Intake and establishment of a coaching contract.
2. Building and maintaining the relationship.
3. Raising awareness.
4. Refining the contract.
5. Facilitating change.
6. Integration, review and evaluation.
7. Closure.

Preparation by the coach:

- 'empty your mind'
- be aware of how you are feeling at this moment
- decide whether or not you intend to take notes.

Setting for the conversations:

- comfortable chairs set at a wide angle to each other
- moveable table
- tidy, well-lit, pleasant room.

During conversations:

- asking questions
- listening, to the coachee's body language as well as their statements
- mirroring, including the coachee's feelings
- maintaining awareness of yourself as coach.

Ingredients of the coaching contract:

- the objectives and topics of the coaching
- the intended outcomes of the coaching in the workplace
- the method of checking or evaluating intended objectives and outcomes
- the length of each session; the number of sessions and the interval between them
- the venue for the sessions
- unconditional confidentiality
- the level of any fee and reimbursement of other costs.

4

Entering into and ending the coaching relationship

Coach and issue often enter into an interesting interaction with each other. This often begins right at the start of coaching: for example, if the coachee presents an issue *and* an opinion on it, or an interpretation of it. Issue and issue holder become entangled and one wonders where to begin in a coaching conversation – with the issue, with the relationship between coachee and issue, or with the coachee? Just as issue and issue holder in coaching often enter into these patterns and play out recurring 'scripts', the coachee often plays fascinating games with his or her coach – games which are normally related to the initial issue(s) and to the subject matter of the coaching. For the coach, the dynamic of the coaching relationship may give clues to the relationship between the coachee and others and to the relationship between the coachee and his/her issues. For the coachee, the coaching relationship may develop into something meaningful – into a significant relationship which frequently springs to mind even outside the coaching conversations. More than enough reason to enter into, develop and wind down the coaching relationship as carefully as possible, and to take regular time out to consider the nature of the evolving relationship. In addition, minor frustrations in this relationship can have significant consequences for the results of the coaching. For a consideration of really difficult relationships between coach and coachee, and how to interpret and handle them, see Chapter 9.

Entering into a coaching relationship as a theme of coaching

The first impressions that people gain of each other have a significant impact on the course of their subsequent communication. First impressions can, after all, be strong and persistent. They can tell you a lot about the underlying themes, but can also be deceptive. A particularly positive or negative first impression often indicates that something is going on that might obstruct an open, exploratory approach. It is worthwhile registering a number of things consciously right at the outset, such as:

- Are both parties on time, or does one arrive early or late?
- Do they shake hands? What does it feel like? Do they look at each other?
- What associations does this person have for you? Who does (s)he remind you of?
- How do the two parties get on? What body language do you notice?
- Do you use first names? Do you break the ice, or give a formal introduction?

There is no one correct answer to these questions, but it is important to consider them because experience shows that 'minor' impressions at the start can have major consequences later on.

The start of a coaching relationship is often dominated by the needs of both coachee and coach, and on their degree of openness about those needs. The coachee often needs help, and it is quite possible that (s)he may also have a clear need for a specific type of help and a specific approach from the coach. In a sense, such a coachee supplies the problem and the solution right at the outset! The coach needs a coachee in order to be a coach – he or she often has a need to be helpful to someone and to consolidate that helpfulness.

It helps to be aware of the existence of such needs, their translation into specific wishes or their concealment using diversionary tactics, right from the start. Managing them explicitly and in a productive way can then commence, if necessary, right at the start of the coaching relationship.

An example

One of us receives a call from the executive secretary of a large company. She says that one of the directors wants to make an appointment for a coaching conversation. Strikingly, he doesn't call himself but has his secretary make contact. It is also striking that the coachee won't come to the coach: the coaching has to take place in his office.

When it comes to it, the coach is welcomed by the secretary and has to wait a while until the coachee is available – a revealing start, with hindsight! The coachee finds it difficult to make contact. He comes across as somewhat single-minded and pays little heed to the interaction between the people in his department. He finds people difficult, in fact, and looks for ways to avoid people if he doesn't get on with them, instead of discussing the issues openly with them. He feels threatened easily and comes across as anxious. In the first conversation he says that he wants to learn from coaching how to exercise influence better in different contexts. He adds that he wants to come across more forcefully. The coach tells him how he has come across to her, and what influence he has had on her so far, and asks whether there are similarities with the behavioural patterns between him and his colleagues. This generates understanding. Later, the coachee experiments cautiously with different behaviour, paying more attention to interpersonal processes and making them the subject of conversation.

After a hesitant beginning, things gradually get better. He feels more influential and more valued by his colleagues, but still finds it difficult to make contact. Suddenly, the coach is informed that the coaching is over! Saying goodbye, as a form of contact, is also difficult for this coachee. He could have been better prepared for that by the coach.

It is advisable for you, as the coach, to enter into and build up the relationship as consciously as possible. To that end, it may be useful to investigate for yourself – patiently and almost a little suspiciously – how the coachee arrived at his or her issue, and what role you are seen to play in handling the issue and therefore in the life of the coachee. The following thought experiment may be useful in this connection:

- 'What does this coachee actually want? Does (s)he want to get away from something, or to achieve something? To explore something, or to arm themselves against something ...?'
- 'How has the coachee arrived at the situation in which (s)he is recounting their issue? What else might this issue relate to? What does it point to? What might be hidden behind the issue? What is the history of the issue and what attempts have already been made to address it ...?'

- 'Why coaching? What has led to this request? What does (s)he expect from it? What recommendations does (s)he generally accept, and from whom ...?'
- 'And why me? What expectations does this coachee have of me – what prejudices, perhaps – what assumptions about my method? What is the coachee hoping for ...?'
- 'What feelings does this coachee prompt in me? Do I think we get on? What do I think of the quality of our contact? What is (s)he appealing to in me? Can I and do I want to offer it? What is my own interest? And what am I hoping for myself ...?'
- 'What approach is the coachee requesting? What approach do I think myself is best? Coaching or no coaching? Person-focused or problem-focused? Solution-focused or insight-focused? Does the coachee have sufficient strength to handle my preferred approach ...?'
- 'What does this mean for our relationship? How is it going to develop? How am I to enter into that relationship itself? How can I show in my behaviour what kind of relationship I envisage? How can I adopt this coaching approach from my very first meeting ...?'

Once the coaching has started, many types of coach/coachee relationship can develop, often geared very specifically to the specific interaction between this particular coach and this particular coachee. Technically, we refer to *positive transference* or *working alliance*[1] – in other words, to replicating previous helpful relationships in someone's life, making use of the coachee's previous experience of other helpful conversations. The following typical forms of positive transference can be differentiated:

- The *guild master/freeman relationship*, in which the coachee presents practical issues and the coach immerses him- or herself in those issues and says something meaningful about them. This relationship is often seen between mentor and mentee, or in supervision.
- The *doctor/patient relationship*, in which the coachee turns him- or herself inside out, revealing uncertainties and emotions as completely as possible; the coach interprets the problems and outlines possible

---

1. These terms come from Freud (*inter alia* 1912b), who also provides other useful phrases such as *zärtliche Übertragung* (tender transference) and *erwartungsvoll bereitgehaltene Libidobesetzung* (expectantly maintained libidinal cathexis).

solutions. This relationship often arises with more emotional themes and issues.

- The *midwife/mother relationship*,[2] in which the coach anticipates the coachee's problems and seeks to help provide strength to tackle them. This relationship is characteristic of a very concerned and caring coach.

- The *peer review relationship*, in which coach and coachee look together at the coachee's day-to-day practice and subject it to as independent an examination as possible. They 'dot the i's' together and take a critical look at the coachee's approach and proposals. This relationship often arises in a more insight-focused setting.

- The *old boys relationship*, in which the coachee seeks out the coach as a sparring partner in order to exchange experiences and try out ideas. The coachee often rehearses certain approaches and conversations with the coach. This relationship often arises in the coaching of senior managers.

Of course, in our day-to-day practice we see various mixtures of these typical relationships and we often see a coaching relationship evolve from one to another, depending on changes in the nature of the themes.

Take care that coaching relationships do not deteriorate unnoticed into 'ordinary' significant relationships, like that of a courting couple, rival scientists, a rich uncle and favourite nephew, or a parent and dependent child. The coaching relationship comes into everyone's life after many other important relationships have already been entered into. Almost inevitably, the coaching relationship comes to resemble one or more of its predecessors. This is not a problem in itself, as long as

- it does not happen completely unnoticed, and
- it does not undermine the essence of the coaching relationship (as helping, delineated and for the benefit of the coachee).

This is also considered in our discussion of transference and counter-transference in Chapter 8. As long as the coach continues to reflect –

2. This is the relationship that Socrates entered into with ambitious young men in ancient Athens – see, for example, Plato's *Theaetetus*. However, Socrates combined this welcoming and caring role with that of the 'gadfly' that saw through any gratuitous stories and excuses.

Figure 4.1 Coaching relationships already exist within most house-
holds; the coachee is therefore prepared very early for
working alliances of the kind necessary for coaching

patiently and almost suspiciously! – on the nature of the relationship
and is not led astray into non-coaching interventions, any resemblance
to other, earlier relationships can only be enriching and instructive.
Forces that exert an influence in all other relationships, such as the
quest for inclusion, control, or affection (see Schutz, 1958 and
Learning with Colleagues, Chapter 12), will unavoidably also come
into play in this coaching relationship. What those forces are, and
how and when they surface, often depends on the coachee's issue and
how the coachee deals with it personally. Following on from this, it is
worth viewing the nature of the evolving relationship (implicitly and
explicitly) as a theme of the coaching itself.

Saying goodbye as a theme of coaching

Most coaching literature does not devote much attention to the end of a
coaching journey, yet the end of coaching is certainly an important
moment and an important theme it its own right. In the following

paragraphs we examine this theme, the actual 'goodbye' and the evaluation of a coaching journey.

The psychoanalytic literature, compared with that on coaching, devotes more attention to termination, parting and loss. Growing up always entails saying goodbye: to breastfeeding, nappies, primary school, the parental home, and parents themselves. The process can be a difficult one and ambivalent feelings come into play each time we say goodbye. Saying goodbye is something we have to do throughout our lives and it can sometimes be very traumatic. Saying goodbye within significant relationships is a particularly painful process.

Malan (1995) mentions a number of quite different responses by clients to endings – which can always be related to the main issues in the coaching process:

- Simple gratitude, or a last session very similar to the others – which is the more likely to occur the shorter the coaching.
- A sense of having received 'enough', even though the coach may have misgivings and feel there is more to work on.
- The so-called 'flight into health', where the coachee suddenly has no more issues and says (s)he has resolved them all. This can only be 'apparent health', and may be a way to end the coaching before the coach can announce the ending him/herself.
- Premature withdrawal, where the coachee comes to the penultimate session fully intending to come again and then suddenly decides not to attend the last session. This often represents a way of avoiding feelings about the ending itself (see the example on pages 37–8).
- Intense grief and anger, which seems much more serious that the limited scope of the coaching relationship would indicate. This is a 'transference phenomenon' (see Chapter 8); like the previous response it usually stems from earlier difficult endings in the coachee's life experience when 'normal mourning' was not possible.

Every coaching process has boundaries. As a coach, you want to handle this boundedness professionally. Be aware that saying goodbye can be difficult for your coachee, and try not to add a new negative experience to other painful experiences of saying goodbye. It should not be a simple repetition of old pain – saying goodbye must be made manageable by the departing coachee personally. Ideally, therefore, the coachee herself should say goodbye to the coach and not feel abandoned or rejected. If you are aware that

saying goodbye is a relevant theme for the coachee, it is important
to facilitate it carefully.

A number of points may help make it easier to say goodbye:

- Make clear arrangements in advance about saying goodbye, so
  the coachee knows what will happen.
- Bring up the subject of what saying goodbye means to the coachee,
  if you notice that (s)he finds it difficult to stay or to go away.
- Ask specifically what it means to the coachee to say goodbye to
  this particular coach, to yourself.
- Be aware that saying goodbye involves a sort of 'mourning process' which can be broken down into phases: denial, anger, depression, acceptance and renewed forward impetus ...
- Think about what saying goodbye means to you: what are you
  losing, and what holds you back from letting a coachee go?

The actual goodbye

And then it is over: the end of the journey. To be able to round off a
coaching relationship well, it is advisable to arrange a final meeting in
which you and the coachee can discuss the working relationship, and
its meaning to the coachee and his or her future development.

Some coaches ask their coachee to describe their process of development in pictures, in a drawing. Others ask for a reflective report
or a learning log. Still others request a verbal conversation. Whatever the case, it is useful to take a look back together to the start
of the coaching journey, its stages of development, its outcome and
the coachee's future perspectives.

The evaluation of the coaching journey

Saying goodbye is not the same as evaluating a coaching process. By
evaluating the coaching after a period of time, the coach confronts the
coachee with where (s)he is at that time and the coach learns more
about his or her own coaching style. It also allows the coach to demonstrate reflection on his or her own practice and explore opportunities for development. Questions which might be asked in this context
include the following:

About the coachee:

- How does the coachee look back on the process and the outcome
  of the coaching?

- What became of the original objectives?
- What plans did the coachee make at the end of the journey?
- What became of those plans in the intervening period? What new plans, if any, has (s)he made?
- How does the coachee intend to continue the personal process of professional development?

About the coach:

- What has the coach contributed to the coachee's learning process?
- What is the evidence for that contribution?
- How did the coachee experience the interaction during the conversations?
- What were difficult moments in the coaching, and how did the coach handle them?
- What tips does the coachee have for the coach in his or her continued development?

We ourselves experience more and more clearly feelings of loss, or even pain, at saying goodbye at the end of every coaching conversation. This too feels like a break in the relationship and the start of a period in which the coachee is alone again. As a result, we are increasingly moving towards a brief review and evaluation at the end of each conversation, reviewing what went well in this conversation and what less so. A few minutes' evaluation at the end of each coaching conversation helps to facilitate the coachee's transition to the 'world outside'.

It has also proved to be a good idea for the coaching contract to incorporate a formal evaluation and possible refining of the contract halfway through the coaching, especially when other parties such as the coachee's manager were closely involved in setting the objectives for the coaching. The coachee can then go back to these other parties and check if they think the coaching is on track and whether they already experience something changing.

Summary: entering into and ending the coaching relationship

The coaching relationship itself is always a theme of coaching, because:

- the coachee's issues overlap with the way in which the coachee handles them
- the way in which the coachee handles the issues overlaps with how the coachee handles him/herself and others
- the way in which the coachee handles others overlaps with how the coachee handles the coach.

When entering into a coaching relationship, the following factors are crucial:

- the first impression that coach and coachee make on each other
- the different needs that coach and coachee have on entering into the relationship
- the expectations and assumptions that coach and coachee have about each other
- the initial skirmishes which mark the entrance into a coaching relationship of a specific type.

Later on, the coaching relationship often evolves into a significant relationship for the coachee which is reminiscent of, for example:

- a guild master/freeman relationship
- a doctor/patient relationship
- a midwife/mother relationship
- a peer review relationship
- an 'old boys' relationship.

Allowing a helping coaching relationship to deteriorate unnoticed into an ordinary, more two-sided relationship is extremely risky.

Saying goodbye itself is another theme of coaching, and is a painful process that needs to be facilitated and made explicit. It is helpful to spend some time evaluating the coaching, considering factors such as:

- the process and outcome of the coaching
- the coachee's learning process
- the interaction during conversations and the 'difficult moments'
- how the coachee can develop further in relation to his or her issues
- how the coach can develop further as a coach.

Part II

Approaches to coaching

Introduction: 'Authenticity'

Having built a picture of the characteristics and set-up of 'helping conversations' in the first part of this book we intend, in Part II, to outline different approaches taken by the coach in such conversations. This can only be done in a rather abstract and general way that fails to take account of some of the subtlety of coaching conversations. Haven't we seen earlier that coach and coachee exchange information at different levels simultaneously, and that such interwoven and interconnected patterns of information exchange can qualify and even contradict each other? How can we then make unambiguous statements about the approach taken by the coach? Only if the coach is consistent over time and also consistent in all of the various layers of communication? If so, then that is by no means always the case – which is why ironic and paradoxical descriptions, introduced later in Part II (in Chapter 9), are perhaps the most realistic ones.

In order to be able to comment on different coaching approaches, this part of the book assumes for the sake of convenience that the coach is sufficiently consistent:

- across different communication channels, i.e. in his or her own expressive and appellant communication, and in verbal and non-verbal communication, and
- over time; in other words, during all events taking place in longer sections of coaching conversations.

Certainly an inconsistent coach can make things unnecessarily difficult for the coachee, so these assumptions will carry a positive connotation for most readers in most situations.

In the next seven chapters we give a wide-ranging overview of coaching approaches. The different approaches are justified on the basis of our 'window onto the coach' (Chapter 2), and of the historical development of psychotherapy. Coaching may have grown out of management training and sports coaching, but we believe it has a sound foundation in principles and methods of psychotherapy.[1] We have therefore decided to place it within the context of the main currents of psychotherapy. We realise that, in so doing:

- Implicitly we are making great demands on coaches, demands to which we return in the chapter on the capabilities of the coach (Chapter 12).
- We cannot be exhaustive and will stick to the major trends. Some important contributions to the coaching profession, such as those that have come out of therapeutic schools like RET, NLP, TA and Gestalt, will not be covered in this book. This is partly because these approaches overlap significantly with approaches that we do introduce. It is also because some of these approaches do not fit into our definition of coaching (see Chapter 1), in which the coach facilitates the coachee's development and so leaves the giving of expert advice to the coachee him- or herself. On the basis of that definition, advice from the coach should serve primarily to stimulate the learning process, with less emphasis on telling the coachee what to do.

In Chapter 12, the approaches introduced in Part II are made more explicit by linking specific interventions – in other words, specific behaviour – to different coaching styles and approaches.

Our own position with respect to the different approaches is largely neutral and eclectic: it is as independent as possible and chooses what is most helpful or effective in a given situation. All of the methods given here, as in *Learning with Colleagues*, can be applied to every coaching issue in principle, although each method does of course have its own specific merits, drawbacks and preferred applications (see Chapter 11). We both have our own personal preferences as well, but we are aware that they are not set in stone, and vary with the coachees that we meet and the developmental process that we ourselves undergo. In addition, we believe emphatically that coaches and coachees must discover for

---

1. We recommend the book by Bruce Peltier (2001), which provides a more detailed theoretical foundation for coaching in both psychotherapeutical and sports coaching literature.

themselves which approaches suit them best. Such discoveries are among the most important outcomes of coaching, and we would not wish to deprive anyone of them by stating our own preferences.

In our view, the most important contribution that the coach can make to 'helping conversations' is genuineness – in other words, an honest and authentic interest in the coachee and his or her issues. We believe that spontaneous and genuine interest cannot be replaced by any form of training, study or supervision. In that respect, there is nothing to beat a unique, personal style of coaching.[2] We appreciate that trying out and practising new approaches can adversely affect that 'genuineness' in the short term. In the long term, however, we are confident that the genuine interest that a coach can demonstrate is only reinforced and broadened through increasing familiarity with, and study of, different approaches. We believe that another characteristic of genuineness, and hence of good coaches, is that they maintain close links between theory and application – in other words, they are who they claim to be and are happy to be held accountable for the way in which they work. We hope that this part of the book can help coaches to increase the genuineness of their approach.

Part II of the book is structured as follows. After a short historical summary, Chapters 6, 7, 8 and 9 describe four different coaching approaches. In Chapter 10 all four are translated into specific methods, as far as this is possible, in the form of consecutive steps in coaching conversations. In Chapter 11 we examine the applicability of the different approaches and methods and give suggestions arising from both research results and experience.

This structure is intended to give coaches the opportunity:

- to reflect on their own approach to coaching conversations and to pick up new ideas
- to increase their flexibility by considering a range of approaches and by investigating when to apply which approach
- to bring their genuineness more to the fore by harmonising reflection and action or theory and practice as far as possible
- to gain inspiration for (even) more authentic coaching, rather than to learn recipes for 'good' coaching.

2. Research has shown that even leading therapists such as Freud, Rogers and Erickson, in the approaches they described, introduced many methods and techniques which fitted in with their own personalities (Corsini and Wedding, 1989).

5
Historic roots and summary of approaches

I think any theoretically based psychotherapy is mistaken because each person is different.

A teaching seminar with Milton Erickson, J.K. Zeig (1972)

Personal development through coaching may have grown out of management training and sports coaching but it has much in common, in our view, with the older field of psychotherapy (see also Peltier, 2001). As a consequence, we look primarily to psychotherapy to find historic roots for various coaching approaches. In the history of psychotherapy different authors have made different choices and different recommendations, often related to their own approach or personality, or to the type of clients for whom their approach was developed. Strangely, research has shown that there is much more agreement between psychotherapists in practice than there is in theory (Corsini and Wedding, 1989). Therapists using completely different theoretical approaches therefore do largely the same things in the consulting room.

It is interesting to review the main currents of psychotherapy one by one, because the evaluations made by psychotherapists are also relevant to the choices you can make as a coach. We therefore propose a 'selectively eclectic' approach to coaching, where the coach considers various options and chooses the one that fits best in the given situation and with their own personality and expertise as a coach.

Historic roots

Table 5.1 offers a brief summary. In order to organise the different psychotherapeutic approaches, we consider how a number of important currents in psychotherapy handle the therapist's involvement in the client's learning objectives. In all psychotherapy, and also in coaching, the therapist/coach becomes part of the client's past and risks doing things that consolidate, instead of changing, problematic aspects from that past. This can happen, for example, if the coach only goes through the motions, or attempts to change from the outside things that can only be changed from the inside by the coachee.

An extremely clear-cut formulation of this basic dilemma within psychotherapy or coaching can be found in the book *Strategies of Psychotherapy* (Haley, 1963), where Haley asserts that clients generally seek out psychotherapy as a last resort in order *not* to change, in order to stay the same despite external pressure. What they then ask of the therapist is paradoxical: 'Change me without changing me!' This poses a dilemma for the therapist, who is being asked to intervene, on the one hand, but on the other hand to leave the client the same! Different currents handle this basic dilemma differently, as we see in the Table 5.1.

Table 5.1 The main currents of psychotherapy and their approach to the dilemma

	Some leading figures	Emphasis is on	How to handle the 'basic dilemma'
Analytic/ Psychodynamic	Sigmund Freud Carl Jung Melanie Klein	Primary process thinking Conflicts Transference Understanding and interpretation	Deferment, until: Emergence of the dilemma in this interaction
Cognitive/ Behavioural	Ivan Pavlov Albert Ellis Burrhus Skinner Aaron Beck	Rational analysis Step-by-step plan	Counter-question Finding solutions
Person-centred/ Humanistic	Carl Rogers Abraham Maslow	Internal (self-) evaluation Self-actualisation	Complete acceptance Relaxed
Paradoxical/ Provocative	Milton Erickson Gregory Bateson Jay Haley Frank Farrelly	Paradoxes Drawing on and mobilising defences	Posing a 'counter-paradox' Positive reinforcement

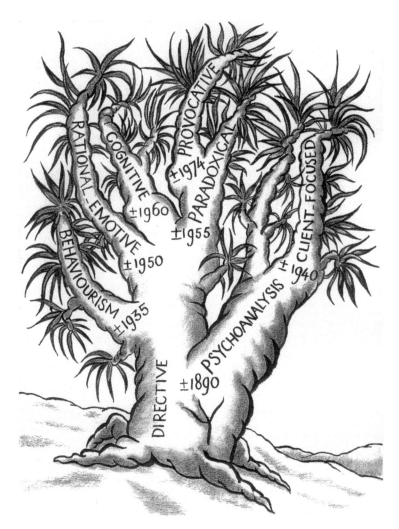

Figure 5.1 A 'family tree' illustrating the growth of different therapeutic trends

1890: The directive trunk splits into two, with the advent of psychoanalysis.
1935: The directive trunk sprouts a new branch – behaviourism.
1940: A branch splits off from the psychoanalytic trunk – client-focused or Rogerian counselling.
1950: The directive trunk sprouts a new branch – the rational-emotive approach.
1955: The directive trunk sprouts a new branch – the paradoxical approach, and (in 1974) the provocative approach.
1960: The directive trunk sprouts a new branch – the cognitive approach.

Each of these four main currents in psychotherapy has influenced the way in which professionals in organisations are coached. Each current has a different emphasis, which can be useful at different times and with different coachees. In the following chapters we show how these different approaches found their way into our own coaching practice. We introduce four approaches that follow on from these four main currents:

- *Directive coaching:* attempting to improve from the outside.
- *Person-centred coaching:* attempting to move the focus inside.
- *Analytic coaching:* attempting to understand from the inside.
- *Paradoxical coaching:* attempting to upset, surprise or manipulate from the outside.

Roots in the personality of the coach

Depending on his or her own personality, every coach has personal preferences which make certain approaches more attractive than others. It is a good idea to fill in your own coaching profile at this point (Appendix A) so that you can compare your own approach with the four approaches discussed here. But please note – if you do not ask your coachees or colleagues to fill in Appendix A as well, this will only be a self-report. Self-reports are of limited value because you are reporting only what you think about yourself, not what you actually do as a coach.

Table 5.2 illustrates the preferences that characterise four different approaches to coaching, within five different polarities. 'L' stands for the 'left-hand pole' and 'R' for the 'right-hand pole'.

Table 5.2 Preferred approaches in different coaching methods

	Directive coaching	Person-centred coaching	Analytic coaching	Paradoxical coaching
Directive ⟷ Non-directive	L	R	R	L
Analytic ⟷ Intuitive	–	R	L	L
Oriented towards the future ⟷ Oriented towards the present	L	R	R	L
Solution-focused ⟷ Development-focused	L	R	–	L
Focused on change ⟷ Accepting	L	R	R	L

The different approaches can also be placed in the 'window on the coach' matrix in Chapter 2. Under the horizontal axis, 'analytic' and 'person-centred' appear next to each other while above the horizontal axis are the 'directive' and 'paradoxical' approaches, except that they come out at roughly the same place. One special directive approach (see Chapter 6) is the only one to appear in the first quadrant – this is 'solution-focused' coaching, which is strongly influenced by solution-focused therapy.

Otherwise, the directive coaching approaches introduced in this book are less directive than most therapies in the behavioural and cognitive domain (see Hawton et al., 1989). The coachee generally submits less to the coach's authority, although this may take place to a greater extent in mentoring and 'coaching leadership'.

Figure 5.2 shows the 'window onto the coach' from Chapter 2 once again, with a number of different approaches described in the following chapters.

For more specific suggestions about coaching styles, interventions and conversational techniques appropriate to each of these approaches, see Chapter 12.

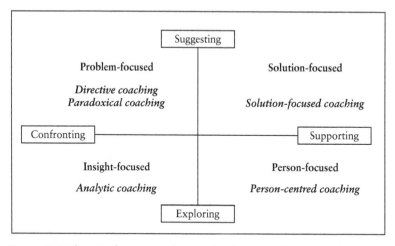

Figure 5.2 The window onto the coach with specific approaches

Summary: historic roots and summary of approaches

Our summary is based on the following four main currents in psychotherapy:

- analytic or psychodynamic therapies
- cognitive or behavioural therapies
- person-centred or Rogerian therapies
- paradoxical, ironic or provocative therapies.

Based on this distinction, and on different approaches developed in part by psychotherapists, we arrive at the following specific approaches:

- Directive coaching: attempting to improve from the outside, such as:
  - the GROW method
  - the solution-focused method.
- Person-centred coaching: attempting to move the focus inside.
- Analytic coaching: attempting to understand from the inside, such as:
  - the analytic and organisation coach method
  - the ladder method.
- Paradoxical coaching: attempting to upset, surprise or manipulate from the outside, such as
  - the ironic method
  - the paradoxical method
  - the provocative method.

6
Directive coaching: Structuring with an objective

> Your every separate action should contribute towards an integrated life; and if each of them, so far as it can, does its part to this end, be satisfied; for that is something which nobody can prevent. 'There will be interferences from without,' you say? Even so, they will not affect the justice, prudence, and reasonableness of your intentions. 'No, but some kind of practical action may be prevented.' Perhaps; yet if you submit to the frustration with a good grace, and are sensible enough to accept what offers itself instead, you can substitute some alternative course which will be equally consistent with the integration we are speaking of.
>
> Marcus Aurelius, *Meditations*

Introduction: the coach at the helm

The most basic and straightforward coaching approach is undoubtedly the *directive* approach, in which the coach keeps a grip on the conversations and puts the coachee on a leash, so to speak, providing encouragement and helping him or her resolve their issues.[1] This book

1. In fact, the directive approach has the longest history of all, because an age-old tradition of restraint, disciplining conversations and hypnosis of psychiatric patients is entirely in keeping with this approach. For an introduction to the field of modern directive therapeutic techniques, see Hawton et al. (1989). Otherwise, the description 'cognitive and behavioural' is a more common description, at least in psychotherapy, than 'directive'. This also highlights the distinction with the systemic and paradoxical approaches (see Chapter 9), which are also directive. We retain the word 'directive', nevertheless, because it appears more frequently in the coaching literature.

does not describe the most directive methods, which simply involve the coach answering the coachee's questions and explaining how to tackle the issues arising. These sorts of directive technique are not examined more closely because we believe that coaching always focuses on helping the coachee to find his or her own answers (see also the definitions in Chapter 1). We do discuss a number of extreme directive methods in Chapter 9, in which the coachee does receive answers to his or her questions, albeit highly absurd ones. These are given with a completely different aim in mind than that of providing a solution – namely, that of mobilising the coachee's own problem-solving abilities.

This chapter outlines two methods in which the coach is purely *directive* in the structuring of the conversation, but purely *facilitating* with respect to the content of the issue: the GROW method and the 'solution-focused' method. Both methods are directive with regard to the conversation itself but open or 'empty' with regard to the content of the conversation. These coaching methods can be used for any subject matter.

An example

The coachee has become bogged down in his job. He experiences himself as being controlled by the issues of the day while he feels a need to exert more control himself. He has become stressed and his employer has terminated his temporary contract. He has time to think about what he expects from a new job. He wants to learn how to avoid the same pitfalls and how to exercise more control in the future. His therapist refers him to a coach. They agree on a course of action: the coach will facilitate his search for a new job, where he hopes to adopt a different attitude.

In the subsequent conversations, and in the coachee's homework between sessions, they explore the sources of his energy (using an energy diary), how he has made decisions in his life so far (using a biography assignment), what he is looking for in a job (using a 'career drivers' questionnaire) and what his main qualities are. He starts his job hunt (via the Internet, newspapers, his own network and the coach's contacts) and is invited to attend a number of interviews. He rehearses the final interview with his coach and is offered the job.

Goal-oriented coaching: the GROW method

A coaching method which has been very successful in organisational settings is John Whitmore's GROW method (1992). The origins of the method betray the roots of 'coaching' in sports coaching: Whitmore based his book on *The Inner Game of Tennis* by the tennis coach Gallwey (1974). Thanks to its rigid structure and ease of use, with its pre-prepared questions, this form of coaching can be quickly learned and applied in a wide variety of situations. Even ten-minute informal coaching conversations can be fitted into the GROW format.

The structure of a GROW coaching conversation is an easily remembered acronym:

1. *G for Goal:* ask about the coachee's goal or objective, as far as the issue is concerned and as far as this conversation is concerned.
2. *R for Reality:* ask for a description of the reality relevant to this issue.
3. *O for Options:* ask about the different options open to the coachee.
4. *W for Will:* ask about the coachee's decision and the strength of his or her accompanying willpower.

In the following paragraphs we go through the different stages of the coaching conversation according to Whitmore (1992), step by step.

Step 1: the personal goal

The coach starts by asking the coachee about the goal of this conversation, even before coach and coachee explore the background and context. This helps the coachee to focus on the future and, right at the start of the coaching conversation, to state the direction (s)he wants the coaching session to take, as well as his or her ultimate personal goal. This goal may be adjusted after Step 2, the reality test.

The coach can ask about both potential goals: the goal for this session and the goal as far as the problem or issue is concerned. If the latter, the 'ultimate goal', also depends on external circumstances outside the coachee's control, the coach also asks about a 'personal target': what does the coachee hope to achieve personally en route to the envisaged ultimate goal.

The coach is looking for a positive formulation of the goal and checks that it is specific, measurable, attainable, relevant and time-bound (these are known as the 'SMART' characteristics).

Figure 6.1 Directive, goal-oriented coaching sometimes has a lot of
impact

Sample questions relating to G: the goal:

- What is the goal of this conversation?
- What exactly do you want to achieve - in the short term and in the long term?
- Is this an ultimate goal or a target?
- If it is an ultimate goal, what is the associated target?
- When do you want to have achieved it?
- To what extent is it positive – in other words, a challenge, attainable, measurable?
- What intermediate steps are involved, and which milestones?
- In how much detail do you expect to be able to work on this in this session?

Step 2: the underlying reality
The coach attempts to elicit an objective description of the coachee's
reality. The coachee is asked to describe, as objectively as possible, how

things stand at the moment with regard both to achieving the goal and other relevant factors. The intention is to gather as much factual and measurable information as possible about the context and background. In the face of value judgments, personal biases and indirectly expressed emotions, the coach perseveres with targeted open questions. Questions focusing on matters of fact, such as 'what', 'who', 'when' and 'how much', are more useful in this respect than questions that elicit opinions and rationalisations, such as 'why' and, to a lesser extent, 'how'.

The coach is looking for facts and circumstances, specific actions taken, obstacles standing in the way of fulfilment and specific sources which can be drawn on, in terms of time, money and manpower for example.

Sample questions relating to R: the reality:

- What is happening now? (What? Where? When? How much?)
- What is the situation exactly?
- Who are the parties involved?
- What exactly is the crux or essence of the problem?
- What exactly are you concerned about in relation to the current situation?
- What have you done about it so far, and with what results?
- What prevented you from doing more?
- How much control do you yourself have over the situation?
- Who else has control, and to what extent?
- What are the main obstacles in your path?
- What internal obstacles still exist?
- What sources can you tap into in order to overcome those obstacles?
- What other resources do you need? How can you get them?
- How does it feel exactly? What emotion is that? What effect does that emotion have on you?
- How would you rate your own confidence on a scale from 1 to 10?
- What exactly are you afraid of?
- What circumstances are reinforcing your self-confidence at this moment?

Step 3: the possible alternatives
The coach helps the coachee maximise his or her own freedom of choice, by asking for possible alternatives. The intention is to gather together as many options as possible, so once the coachee has made an exhaustive list, the coach generally asks for 'just one more'. All conceivable (and also inconceivable) options are welcome – the more the better.

The coach is looking for positive options, possibilities and alternatives. As soon as the coachee comes up with restrictions or reservations about certain options the coach asks: 'What would the option be like if those restrictions or reservations weren't there?' ('What if ...?'). The coach is hesitant to contribute personal suggestions because that would make him or her an expert advisor. Options provided by the coach may prompt resistance, or receive a disproportionately high rating in the coachee's estimation. The coach does not make any suggestions without checking that they are really welcome, and ensuring the coachee has already made a complete personal list.

Sample questions relating to O: the options:

- What are all the different ways in which you could approach this issue?
- What options do you have?
- Make a list of different alternatives, important and less important, complete and partial solutions.
- What else could you do?
- What would you do if you had more time, or a bigger budget, or if you were the boss?
- What would you do if you could start all over again?
- What would you do if all circumstances were under your control?
- Would you perhaps like to hear a suggestion from me?
- What are the pros and cons of all of these different possibilities?
- Which option would produce the best result?
- Which option appeals to you most or feels best?
- Which would give you the most satisfaction?
- Would it be convenient to combine options?

Step 4: determining commitment
The coach attempts to round off the conversation with a sound decision by the coachee – or, if necessary, with the conclusion that the original

goal was too ambitious and no decision can be taken. The coach helps the coachee to decide what to do and when – and how likely it is that (s)he will actually act on that decision. It is important for the coach to remain outside the decision-making process. There is a real risk that the coachee will take a 'decision' now only for form's sake or for the sake of the coach, which would of course be a decision of no actual value.

The coach aims to ask, in turn:

• which alternative or combination of options the coachee chooses;
• when the option is to be put into effect, and with what kind of assistance; and
• how great the coachee's commitment is.

Despite this orientation towards closure, the coachee should not feel rushed. If this is the case, it usually comes from a desire on the part of the coach, overtly or covertly, to push the coachee towards a specific decision or course of action. It is therefore a good test, at the end of the conversation, to ask to what extent the coachee has felt (s)he had worked on his or her own authority in this conversation.

Sample questions relating to W: the will:

• What are you going to do?
• Which option, or combination of options, are you going to choose?
• When are you going to do that?
• Will that meet your goal?
• Does this conclusion meet your goal for this conversation?
• What obstacles do you expect, and how are you going to overcome them?
• What internal obstacles do you perceive within yourself?
• How are you going to overcome that internal resistance?
• Who needs to know?
• What help do you need and how are you going to get it?
• What can I do for you in order to support you?
• Indicate on a scale from 1 to 10 how likely it is that you will carry out that action.
• If lower than 10: why not 10? What can you do to make it a 10?
• If lower than 8: is it not better to give up? (As it seems unlikely that you will actually do it.)
• Is there anything else we should talk about, or have we finished?

Positive coaching: the solution-focused method

Solution-focused coaching is an approach derived from solution-focused brief psychotherapy.[2] This current in psychotherapy developed as a reaction to many variants of behavioural and cognitive therapy which were invented as 'problem-focused therapies'. In those variants, therapists worked mainly on exploring problems, interrupting and replacing clients' ineffective solutions. The inventors of solution-focused therapy discovered that building on 'exceptional moments' (times when the problem did not exist or was less serious) had much more effect on their clients. Instead of advising clients to try out different solutions (therapist-centred), they encouraged clients to do more of what already seemed to be helping, or to do more of what they were already doing when the problem did not arise (client-centred). In so doing, they were working towards a form of therapy that had maximum effect in minimum time.

An important difference between solution-focused coaching and the conventional 'psychoanalytic' approach (Chapter 8) is that the latter establishes causal connections between past and present (phenomena emerge from an underlying structure). In the solution-focused approach, causal connections are not taken as the starting point; causes are regarded as 'narrative constructions' (stories) constructed by the coachee him- or herself. There is no absolute truth; on the contrary, we are constantly constructing our own world (Gergen, 1999). We do this by talking about it and by attaching our own meaning or interpretation to it. Language therefore shapes reality. The coach is not an expert, but explores the stories together with the coachee, challenges him or her to find new definitions and to construct a future in which the problem no longer

2. *Solution-focused* brief psychotherapy was developed at the Brief Family Therapy Center in Milwaukee and at the Institute for the Study of Therapeutic Change in Chicago, by Insoo Kim Berg, Steve de Shazer, Barry Duncan, Scott Miller and others. In management consultancy and coaching there is a very similar approach known as *Appreciative Inquiry* (see Cooperrider and Srivastva, 1987). This chapter borrows from *Keys To Solution In Brief Therapy* by De Shazer (1985) and *Interviewing for Solutions* by De Jong and Berg (2001).

arises. The coach can help by steering the conversation in that particular direction.

Basic principles of solution-focused coaching
The basic principles of this coaching style are:

- Coachees have access to all the resources they need in order to be able to change. Change is inevitable, because stability is an illusion. The coach encourages change by working together with the coachee.
- No problem is ever-present; there are always times when a problem does not present itself. The coach investigates what the coachee is doing differently or how (s)he is thinking differently, at those times.
- The coach can use coachees' fantasies about the future in order to construct achievable solutions.

In this approach, the coach's task is to accept the problem as presented by the coachee. There is therefore no need for an exhaustive diagnosis or problem analysis. It is not necessary to know precisely how problems came about. What is useful is to concentrate on solutions, asking appropriate questions. 'How would your work look then?' 'What would you be thinking?' 'What would you be doing?' 'How would you be feeling?' The art is to listen to the coachee's story without having any theories of your own in mind (because that would mean you pay less attention to the coachee's theories) and to construct new stories about the coachee's life together, starting from the premise that if you don't like your circumstances or your work, at least you can change your stories about it. By making new definitions, the coachee's experience changes and it becomes easier for him or her to start to act differently. Moreover, talking about solutions is a more motivating experience than talking about problems.

Approach
In order to construct a new story, it is best to start at the beginning. A coaching conversation in this style is characterised by questions focusing on what the coachee is good at, on the exceptions to the problem and on the hypothetical solutions (s)he is considering. You challenge the coachee to suggest specifically and in detail how

things could be improved. You draw on the coachee's own problem-solving skills. Understanding the problems and their origins is not necessary.

The coach is concerned with keeping a solution-focused conversation going, by:

- emphasising the coachee's abilities and praising his/her inherent strengths;
- asking for examples of situations in which the coachee did not experience the problem (exceptions); and
- asking about behaviours on the part of the coachee that made a positive difference (successes).

The coach disregards elaborate descriptions of the problem as far as possible. This also applies to blame attributed to third parties and solutions which are outside the coachee's control. The coach helps the coachee to set realistic personal objectives. Minor changes now are sufficient to bring about bigger changes later on.

The coachee embarks on a voyage of discovery around everything that (s)he is already doing right, so that the homework is often: 'Go away and do more of the same'. This leads to successful experiences which the coachee can talk about, and as a result, allow the coachee to take charge personally. The coachee is the expert and finds the solutions. The coach helps with support and praise for what has been achieved.

An important question in solution-focused coaching is the 'miracle question', which asks the coachee to imagine exactly how his or her situation will have changed once the problem is solved.

> *An example of the 'miracle question'*
> Imagine that a miracle occurs one night while you're asleep and the problem that you raised here is solved as a result. But you don't know that the miracle has occurred. What will be different at work the next morning? What will show you that the miracle has occurred and that your problems have disappeared?

The answer to this question gives a clear picture of what the coachee wants to change and what (s)he can do personally to achieve that goal. The coach can have the coachee rate the current situation on a scale from 0 (in which the problem is overwhelmingly dominant) to 10 (in which the problem has disappeared). This makes it possible to track small changes.

Each coaching session ends with the coach giving feedback, praising the coachee on progress and providing relevant homework assignments.

Types of questions
A coaching conversation in the solution-focused style follows the structure outlined below, which is derived from current protocols.

In the first conversation:

- *Problem:* 'What brings you here? How is this a problem for you? What have you already tried? What was useful? What helped?'
- *Objective:* 'What do you want to change as a result of the coaching?' ('Miracle question'; further questions about what would be different.)
- *Exceptions:* 'Are there times when the problem does not arise? When, and what happens then? Are there times when the problem is less serious? When, and what happens then?' (Ask for details; praise the coachee on what (s)he did at the time.)
- *Rating:* improvement since request for coaching; motivation; confidence (all on a scale of 1–10).
- *Feedback:* compliments, reason for the homework assignments (from reflection to doing, depending on whether the coachee is seen as *visitor, complainer* or *customer* – see below), setting homework.

In the follow-up conversation:

- Ask about improvements: 'What has improved since our last conversation?'
- Details: 'How is it going? How are you doing that? Is that new for you? What is the effect on X?'
- Compliments on behaviour.
- Continue to ask questions: 'And what else is better?'
- Positive suggestion: 'Do more of the same!'
- Rate the progress (scale 1–10).
- Feedback: compliments, reason for homework, homework itself.
- Signing up for another session: 'How much time do you need for that? When do you want to come back?'

Application
Clearly, the solution-focused method does not make any recommendations for an in-depth exploration and analysis of the problems. In some

cases it is necessary to find out more about the problem, but only if it cannot be done more simply and in a more solution-focused way. You can continue to persevere with the solution-focused style if:

- an improvement has already occurred between the request for coaching and the first conversation
- there are exceptions to the problem – in other words, occasions where the problem does not arise or is less serious
- a hypothetical solution can be formulated – a description in behavioural terms of what would be different if the problem were resolved completely.

In other words, according to solution-focused coaches, in the vast majority of cases you can work directly towards a solution without first analysing the problem itself in depth.

The solution-focused coaching style works best if the coachee is open to solution-focused suggestions relating to his or her own behaviour. In that respect, together with De Jong and Berg (2001), we distinguish between 'visitors', 'complainers' and 'customers'.

- *Visitors* are coachees who don't think they have a problem. They are often sent by their bosses and just want to be left in peace. Minimal coaching is possible in these cases. The coach can do no more than attempt to create a working relationship in which coaching becomes possible, by recognising the coachee's situation, supporting and praising him or her, and being as 'hospitable' as possible.
- *Complainers* do provide information about their problem, but see themselves neither as part of the problem nor of the solution. In such cases, the coach can encourage the coachee to reflect on the real possibility of personal change.
- *Customers* are the ideal coachees for the solution-focused coach. They say they want to do something about the problem themselves. The coach can give customers homework with some expectation that they will actually do it.

An example
The coachee works in a government department where she feels completely isolated. Like a dedicated professional, she churns out memoranda and reports, only for them to remain unread. What she does is clever, but she's doing it all on her own. She doesn't involve any colleagues because she's afraid they won't really be able to understand what she's doing. Gradually, she

Figure 6.2 Solution-focused coaching can put you back on the right track

starts to feel thoroughly miserable and under a lot of stress. She is not getting enough sleep, all sorts of ideas keep going round in her head, and she is touchy at home. She no longer finds any enjoyment in her hobbies.

This is no time for confrontational interventions, as this approach might only cause the coachee to become overly stressed. The coach therefore opts for reinforcing interventions: exploring when the coachee feels better and when things are going well. The coach tries to identify times when the coachee does experience collaboration and satisfaction and, together with the coachee, works out homework assignments which will enable closer collaboration.

These lead to positive experiences. The coachee notices that colleagues are open to her if she acts with greater initiative, and that it is inspiring to think about things together. She becomes more and more enthusiastic and finds that, as time passes, she is better able to make a real contribution. One small step at a time, she goes a long way.

Summary: directive coaching

A characteristic feature of directive coaching approaches is that the coach takes a strong lead, and either structures the conversations or comes up with solutions and hands out assignments.
Two directive methods are introduced:

1. The GROW method
Goal-oriented coaching, oriented towards the future: the coach facilitates the coachee and proposes ways of achieving a stated goal. Conversations are structured as follows:

- G for Goal: have the coachee formulate the outcome or objective personally.
- R for Reality: ask for a description of the reality relevant to this issue.
- O for Options: ask about the various options open to the coachee.
- W for Will: ask about the coachee's decision and commitment.

2. The solution-focused method
Solution-focused coaching, moving away from the problem: the coach tries to find situations when the problem does not arise, looks for reasons for those positive experiences, and attempts to build on them. Conversations are structured as follows:

- *Objective*: What do you want to achieve?
- *Solutions now*: What is going better already? How exactly? What positive exceptions do you experience?
- *Characteristics of solutions*: What tells you that things are going better ('miracle question')?
- *Feedback for solutions*: Positive evaluation and compliments.
- *Reinforcement of solutions*: Reinforcing what is already going well with the aid of homework.

The solution-focused method distinguishes three types of coachee, and can actually help only the third group:

- *Visitors*: don't think they have a problem.
- *Complainers*: don't see themselves as part of their problem.
- *Customers*: indicate that they want to do something about their problem.

7
Person-centred coaching: Facilitating the coachee

> The most personal is the most universal.
> Carl Rogers, *On Becoming a Person*

Introduction: counselling as a form of coaching

'Person-centred counselling' is a form of coaching in which the coachee is welcomed entirely on his or her own terms and is given a maximum of space to work in his or her own way on personal issues. The coach refrains as far as possible from any form of direction, contributes a minimum of new information or advice, and acts as a sort of partner and companion in the coachee's process of development. We might start by considering where counselling lies in terms of the various facilitating styles that we can identify (see *Learning with Colleagues*, Chapter 16), namely:

- *Expert:* focused on the coachee's issues and problems.
- *Process manager:* focused on the process between the coachee and his or her problems.
- *Trainer:* focused on the skills and abilities of the coachee.
- *Developer:* focused on the person and values of the coachee.

The counsellor is very much in the camp of the developer. Counselling is therefore a form of coaching in which the coachee is always at the centre; it focuses on increasing the self-confidence, strength and abilities of the coachee personally. In the counselling approach the coachee as a person is central from the outset, and coach and coachee tackle the problems and issues on that basis.

An example
The coachee is silent at the start of the conversation and looks at the coach in a wait-and-see mode. The coach looks back with a friendly smile and full of expectation. The situation starts to resemble a children's game in which players try to out-stare each other without blinking or looking away. Until the coachee shrugs her shoulders and bursts out slightly provocatively, 'Oh well, I suppose I'll have to do it myself then ... that's what you're trying to tell me, isn't it? I decide what to talk about.'

The coach ignores her own inclinations to, first, give a response, second, start to structure the conversation, and third, interpret the coachee's striking behaviour. Perhaps out of shyness, perhaps because no other specific option presents itself, she keeps smiling in a friendly and inviting way, until the following sentence issues forth: 'What do you want to talk about today? We agreed to look at specific practical issues, but also at your career development. Do you want to start somewhere?'

There is another short silence, until the coachee clears her throat and says: 'You know, I've prepared for this conversation and have already gone through a few things.' The unaccustomed openness, willingness and compliance of the coach at the start of this conversation makes such an impression that the coachee refers to it frequently in subsequent conversations: 'You showed me then that I could really bring anything to these conversations.'

Carl Rogers on counselling

The psychologist Carl Rogers has promoted person-centred counselling in a way that can be inspiring for the coach. Rogers tends towards an extreme position, in which the coach contributes and directs as little as possible. In his view, the coach in the first instance should provide the conditions that enable the coachee to design and undergo a personal process of growth or learning. The coach can do this primarily by offering empathy, respect, warmth and genuineness in his or her relationship with the coachee (Rogers, 1957).

In Rogers' person-centred approach, the following beliefs are central:[1]

1. Rogers' ideas about counselling appear in many publications. We particularly recommend *On Becoming A Person* (1961), about individual counselling, and *Carl Rogers On Encounter Groups* (1970), about team counselling.

- Confidence in the *self-actualisation* of the coachee: Rogers assumes this self-actualisation to be a fundamental, driving force of personality. If all circumstances are favourable and there is nothing to obstruct the personality, it will grow into an 'optimal individual form': an ever-increasing development and refinement of personal capabilities. Rogers therefore has a deep and unshakeable confidence in every personality and in its ability to develop ever-greater balance and health.
- In order to create the favourable conditions referred to above, the coach must accept the coachee unconditionally. Outside the counselling relationship, unconditional acceptance by another person who has no wish to influence them is relatively rare. Within the counselling relationship, this attitude on the part of the coach is essential for the coachee's development.
- The coachee is the focal point of the counselling. This is made possible by approaching the coachee with as much empathy as possible. By 'empathy', Rogers means the ability to take on board the coachee's perceptions, experiences and concerns as if they were the coach's own. Empathy means identifying your own perspective completely to that of the coachee and also demonstrating the extent to which you have succeeded (however imperfectly) in understanding him or her from the inside, thereby seeking even greater understanding.
- It is asking a lot of the coach to meet the coachee with unconditional acceptance and empathy. According to Rogers, the coach can do this only if (s)he also accepts him- or herself unconditionally and is therefore free of differences between the way (s)he 'is' and the way (s)he 'should be or would like to be' in his or her own eyes. Rogers calls these differences *incongruences*. What is therefore required of the coach is to be congruent. A congruent coach is above all genuine, especially with respect to him- or herself, and so accepts all of the internal feelings – positive and negative – with respect to the coachee. Whether or not all of those feelings are expressed depends on the contribution that this would make towards offering safety and unconditional acceptance. Congruence combined with empathy does call for a great deal of openness on the part of the coach with regard to what is going on in his or her own mind. Rogers called this *transparency*: showing what is going on in yourself in response to issues of the coachee.

An example

A manager in a large organisation is deadlocked in a number of relationships. He is a bright and keen to be coached, but the sessions vary in their success. He is very open and seeks feedback, but then rejects the feedback. He wants contact, but then cuts himself off. He doesn't want to discuss his family relationships, but actually he'd quite like that. He doesn't know what he wants to talk about, but comes to the session anyway. After one session, the coach is left with a big 'hangover'. The coachee makes her feel that she is not good enough as a coach, that she is not able to get through to this coachee. She decides to try an intervention she hasn't used before: she writes the coachee an email. In it, she reflects on her feeling of 'not being good enough' for this coachee. She writes that she doesn't know how much of it has to do with the coachee, but that this is how she felt after the session. She asks if the coachee has ever received similar feedback before. After initially dodging the question, the coachee starts to address it and talks to some of those around him. His behaviour is recognised, and this gets the coachee thinking about what he does and why he does it. All of this leads to an enlightening session and real contact between coach and coachee: a breakthrough in the coaching.

Techniques of the counsellor

Structuring techniques

The coach finds diary space for the coachee and draws up a type of contract in which the coachee states learning objectives for the coaching process. The coachee determines the number and frequency of meetings. During the coaching process the coach reflects the coachee's contribution regularly by summarising and referring to links in the material submitted.

Directive techniques

All directive techniques which involve structuring the conversation, making suggestions, or giving feedback, advice, assignments or instructions are quite out of place here. The aim is that the coachee should work on personal issues at his or her own pace and in his or her own way. The only direction from the coach serves to ensure that this comes about – in other words, the initiative in the conversation is left to the coachee. Rogers was well aware that the complete

Figure 7.1 The counsellor approaches the coachee with an unconditionally positive regard

avoidance of directive tendencies is not feasible in practice and is in
itself a sort of direction. Using himself as an example, he writes that
he is generally interested in emotions and deeper personal convictions, such as standards and values (Rogers, 1961). He is not
surprised, therefore, that his own counselling conversations were
often concerned with those more personal layers of the communication However, Rogers does go so far as to avoid giving any form of
feedback. Feedback, or opinions offered by the coach, which always
have an element of appreciation or rejection about them, would be
too directive because the viewpoint from which the feedback is given
(the 'locus of evaluation' – Raskin, 1952) is an external one. For
Rogers, appreciation and rejection act as conditional acceptance of
the coachee, and are consequently quite inappropriate.

Non-directive techniques
Counselling makes particular use of techniques involving an accepting presence, a listening, relaxed attitude and a minimum of 'initiat-
ing' behaviour. The primary aim here is to observe closely – and

'from the inside', as it were – the words, opinions, behaviours and emotions of the coachee. The coach attempts, so to speak, to look together with the coachee and through the coachee's eyes. Other non-directive interventions are those which communicate safety and acceptance within the counselling relationship, such as a sympathetic smile, eye contact, relaxed movements and gestures that emphasise proximity. The coach says little about him- or herself, usually only in response to a direct question from the coachee. When the coach does so, (s)he tries to be as genuine and truthful as possible – in accordance with the principle of transparency.

It is important to point out that these techniques for counselling provide a sound basis for any form of coaching. In coaching, coach and coachee consider the coachee's issue together, so it is always important for the coach to observe issues carefully and to understand them from the personal perspective of the coachee. In counselling these observational techniques are in fact the only techniques that are recommended, and any other intervention by the coach, such as direction or analysis, is disruptive to the coachee. The coach adopts a receptive attitude and need not add anything new, original or helpful. Indeed, counselling benefits greatly if the coach can control any selfish inclination to be helpful or inventive.

Approach to counselling

When we see counsellors at work or watch videos featuring Carl Rogers,[2] we can identify a number of non-directive interventions:

- *Invitations* to speak, in complete openness and without pressure to do so in any specific way.
- *Deepening* by attention, summaries and reflecting feelings. Sometimes the coach uses a single, non-directional, open question, but not often. Usually, time and space is given as well as summaries, often almost word-for-word, and reflections of feelings. In addition, some summaries are deepening because they also summarise what can be read between the lines.
- *Reinforcing contact* by encouragement, gestures and words which increase contact, as well as self-disclosure, primarily relating to how the coach is feeling here and now.

2.   See, for example, *Carl Rogers Counsels an Individual on Hurt and Anger*, or *The Right To Be Desperate*, both available from Concord Film, Ipswich.

In the appendices to this book we provide two instruments which may help you to become more proficient as a counsellor. Appendix C contains a 'sliding scale of push and pull', to demonstrate that you have both directing and facilitating alternatives at any moment in a conversation. In our view, pure 'pulling' behaviour is an extremely valuable skill for a coach (see also Chapter 12, where we summarise the associated interventions in terms of the styles 'exploring' and 'supporting', which we consider to be the most pure coaching styles). Appendix D contains the 'person-centred reflection form', an instrument which enables you to look back at a coaching conversation and identify the many obstacles to a non-directive or person-centred approach to coaching within yourself.

Summary: person-centred coaching

Counselling is a form of coaching in which:

- The coachee is, as far as possible, at the centre of attention.
- Coach and coachee work from the coachee's perspective and at the coachee's pace.
- The coachee can develop as autonomously as possible.

Basic principles of counselling:

- Self-actualisation of the coachee: the coachee has genuine freedom to develop in the right direction by him/herself.
- Unconditional acceptance and an unconditional positive regard.
- The coach seeks as much personal empathy with the coachee as possible.
- The coach's behaviour is as congruent and as genuine as possible.
- The coach is transparent about his or her own feelings and convictions.

The following basic principles result in a counselling approach that is as non-directive as possible:

- Give the coachee as much space and acceptance as possible.
- Understand the coachee as much as possible on his or her own terms.
- Reinforce contact by encouragement, proximity and self-disclosure.
- Let observation, evaluation and monitoring take place from the coachee's perspective as far as possible ('internal locus of evaluation').
- Structure and summarise, but without interpreting or analysing the material.

8
Analytic coaching:
In search of insight

There are a thousand unnoticed openings, continued my
father, which let a penetrating eye at once into a man's soul;
and I maintain it, added he, that a man of sense does not lay
down his hat in coming into a room – or take it up in going
out of it, but something escapes, which discovers him.

Laurence Sterne, *The Life and Opinions of
Tristram Shandy Gentleman*

Introduction: psychoanalysis and analytic coaching

In analytic coaching, 'understanding from the inside' is central, in
the form of a joint journey of discovery by coach and coachee. The
aim is to increase the coachee's insight into his or her own issues and
problems. The coach does not pose as an 'expert', or even as someone who has acquired a large measure of self-knowledge or insight
into human nature. The coach's position is rather that of an 'empiri-
cist' – someone who has already trodden this path of insight and
understanding – and of a 'companion' on the journey of discovery.
Preparation for analytic coaching consists mainly of acquiring deep
understanding of your own coaching issues from the inside.[1]

Why is 'insight into your own issues' considered so important? For
the following four reasons in particular:

- Because you can only change yourself, or that which you yourself contribute to difficult situations.

1. There are many introductions to the analytic or psychodynamic approach.
   We refer in the text to Freud, its founder, and have also used Brown and
   Pedder (1979), Symington (1986) and Malan (1995), among others.

- Because 'insight' as such can bring a healthy form of relief – painful feelings often *dissolve*[2] when you know where they come from.
- Because obtaining insight is a first necessary step towards *expressing* your feelings, which brings more of that same kind of relief.
- Because insight and expression contribute to the realisation that things are not as 'terrible' as you may have thought before.

Surprisingly, 'learning' is not central in this approach, despite the emphasis on 'insight' and 'understanding'. The aim here is not to 'learn about yourself'...indeed, as we will see later, this form of learning is considered suspect by analysts. Rather, the aim is to 'learn in yourself': by examining your actions and feelings, identifying the barriers to insight within yourself and reflecting on the effect that enhanced insight has on you.

What is it that we are trying to understand in analytic coaching? To answer this, it is useful to go back to the coachee's initial position, or the problem as it is presented at the outset. That initial position always concerns either:

- something that the coachee has but does not want, or
- something that the coachee does not have but would like.

To put it briefly, in this initial position there is always a degree of conflict. As coaches we start with a *conflict* as often as we start with a new issue, and when we dig deeper we usually find...a conflict! Conflicts pile on top of each other and exist on several levels:

- To start with, there are often conflicts between myself and my circumstances, or between myself and others.
- Below that level, I often note a conflict within myself, in the form of inconsistencies between opposing needs and tendencies – for example, between 'what I want now' and 'what is good for me', or between my actions and my reasoning.
- Below that level, I note conflicts within deeper layers of myself. What do I actually want? Am I myself working to achieve what I really want? Are there internal barriers preventing me from doing so?

2. In 'dissolve' the two meanings of the English word 'solution' come surprisingly close together, as Freud (1900) also points out with reference to the German words 'lösung' and 'auflösung' ('resolution' and 'solution').

The analytic coach attempts to explore these conflicts between opposing forces; hence *psychodynamic coaching* as an alternative name for analytic coaching, derived from the dynamics of opposing force fields.

The assumption of conflicts within and between layers of our personalities point to contributions from an unconscious part of ourselves, according to the founding fathers of psychoanalysis. This position is debatable, because it assumes the existence of deeper layers that we cannot apprehend – so how do we know that those layers do indeed exist? It is difficult to demonstrate something that we cannot apprehend.[3]

Phenomena

The analytic approach focuses on everything that can produce deeper insight, as well as on all of the barriers to greater insight. Over the years, various people have listed the psychological phenomena that we may encounter in this approach. Many of these are also mentioned in other approaches, thereby testifying to their debt to the psychoanalytic approach.

Transference

In the relationship between coachee and coach, things happen that also happen between the coachee and others, and between the coach and others. With the coach, the coachee repeats patterns of interaction which (s)he has played out previously with others. These patterns of interaction may shed light on the coachee's expressed problem. This phenomenon of the repetition of patterns originating outside the coaching situation itself was referred to by Freud as *transference* (*Übertragung*). More specifically, when it occurs in the coachee it is known as *transference* and when it occurs in the coach it is known as *counter-transference*.

Transference can often be recognised in disproportionate responses, or in responses which do not seem to bear any relation to what has just been said. It is worth the coach's effort to unravel carefully – and

---

3. Nevertheless, the books and articles in which Freud gathers together the different clues to the existence of an unconscious – in dreams (Freud, 1900), slips of the tongue, slips of the pen, mistakes, forgetfulness and clumsiness (Freud, 1904/1924), jokes (Freud, 1905), works of art (e.g. Freud, 1914b), humour (Freud, 1928), denials (Freud, 1925) and symptoms (Freud, 1926) – are among his most illuminating works.

sometimes together with the coachee – 'what' comes from 'whom'. In other words, 'What originates within myself?' and 'What does the other person trigger in me?'

An example

A friendly but introverted consultant comes for her second session. She wants to be more assertive at work, and to make contact more easily with others. This doesn't happen automatically because she is not very happy with herself. She believes that colleagues and especially managers within the organisation perform much better than she does, and in meetings often feels inhibited about contributing: if she says something, she wants to be sure it is worthwhile and properly expressed. She believes that other people judge her too positively. That she is nowhere near as good as they think. The coach suspects that the coachee is extremely critical of herself and that this paralyses her in work situations. So she compliments the coachee on a number of points in the hope that this will increase her self-confidence. The coachee expresses her disappointment with this approach: she would like the coach to be more critical and confrontational. The coach's initial reaction is one of surprise. Perfectionism and fear of failure are no strangers to him either. In good time he comes to realise that this is a repetition of the coachee's pattern: she is afraid that the coach is judging her too positively. The coach then brings this pattern up for discussion and it is acknowledged by the coachee.

In his early collaboration with Breuer, Freud realised how much insight these transference phenomena can give into the client's problem.[4] Freud and his followers connected transference with formative patterns in a person's life: in other words, patterns within the family in which a person is raised. Transference is therefore usually described as the repetition of patterns of interaction originally played out vis-à-vis parental figures. These days, we see more and more interpretations that refer to current patterns, for example to the coachee's present working relationships (Malan, 1995). Chapter 14 – on 'organisation coaching' – looks in more detail at transference originating in the coachee's organisation.

4. For information on waxing insight in transference, see Breuer and Freud (1895), and Freud (1912b) or (in the entertaining guise of a novel) Yalom (1992).

We see transference as a phenomenon that occurs in virtually every situation in which someone is talking about their own situations or experiences. It starts in fact when someone talks in an agitated manner about something that has led to anger, or gloomily about some disappointment. The coachee is not just talking about that situation but, in a way, also expressing him- or herself as if it were being relived. Chapter 11 of *Learning with Colleagues* – on 'reflections of there-and-then in here-and-now' – contains examples of transference in peer consultation groups: behaviour during the session that reflects behaviour from the situation described by the issue holder. Similar reflections occur very easily in coaching conversations.

There are clear indications that the discoverers of transference phenomena, Breuer and Freud, were greatly shocked at first by the power of the (sexually charged) transference that they experienced in the presence of 'Anna O.' and 'Dora' respectively (see, for example, Lear, 2003). Only gradually did Freud become aware of the high value that transference can have in terms of the beneficial impact of therapeutic conversations themselves. It enables coach and coachee to explore together what is happening with them in the present moment. From this, they can gain insight into what is going on within the coachee.

The value of counter-transference – or the feelings and response patterns that the coachee, during the conversation, triggers in the coach – was recognised explicitly only after Freud's death. The first generation of analysts usually saw counter-transference as something that the analyst keeps 'under control'. In these terms, a well-trained analyst continuously 'delivers' the same dispassionate and exploring behaviour, as a firm reminder of the task at hand and as a 'smooth mirror', and thereby to be as open as possible for transference phenomena originating with the client The usefulness of counter-transference in the coaching process itself was only appreciated subsequently. Paula Heimann (1950) was among the first to propose that counter-transference be viewed as a tool for understanding the client better. She suggests that feelings aroused in the therapist be used as a key to deeper understanding of the client, so that the therapist no longer regards the repression or communication of those feelings as the only two alternatives.[5] An analytic coach must be able

---

5. According to Heimann (1950), both of these alternatives have an adverse effect on the quality of the helping relationship. If counter-transference feelings are repressed the coach would greatly restrict his/her own scope for action; if counter-transference feelings are communicated, however,

to listen not only to the coachee, but also to internal reactions and feelings as they arise during the coaching process.

When looking into transference phenomena, it is often useful to consider the following patterns or scenarios:

1. Successful attribution to the other person of a part of oneself, also known as *projective identification* (Klein, 1946).[6] Here, the coachee attributes something to the coach with which the coach can identify. Conversely, the coach attributes something to the coachee with which the coachee can identify.
2. Attempts to influence the relationship and possibly to undermine the clear division of roles between coach and coachee. This can include:
   - the desire to experience earlier relationship patterns again and again (*re-enactment*)
   - the attempt to provoke another party into adopting a different position or a different role.
3. An addition to the process of exploration within the coaching: the transference phenomena add something to the joint verbal exploration (see Freud, 1914a and the examples in Chapter 11 of *Learning with Colleagues*).
4. An addition to the results of the coaching: 'trying out' or 'testing' with the coach of new or almost forgotten patterns of interaction. This often goes by the name of the *corrective emotional experience*, see for example Malan (1995).

The value of the addition of (counter-)transference to the exploration process is particularly hard to overestimate. As coach you can offer considerable added value if you are able to note the initially unconscious transference phenomena, draw attention to them and use them in the exploration with the client.

> *An example*
> The coachee and the coach have made a first appointment and the coachee arrives very early. The coachee later admits that she wanted to avoid arriving late at all costs. A revealing start, as

they would distract coach and coachee from the coaching itself, which should remain focused on the coachee.
6. Strictly speaking this definition of the Kleinian term projective identification came about slightly later, with W.F. Bion (1959). This newer definition, which is essentially more relational, is now the more common one."

it later emerges. The coachee always has the feeling that she is being asked to meet very high standards and is not up to it. She is so afraid of failure that she works away endlessly on reports which she thinks are never good enough. She lacks the nerve to ask colleagues for feedback on her ideas. This recurs in the coaching relationship as well. The coach has a tendency to behave in a similar manner to the coachee. Through her efforts to 'do the right thing', she reinforces the pre-existing pattern in the coachee. The latter feels that her coach is making demands on her and endeavours to meet those demands. She wants to do the right thing for the coach and wants to meet all of her (assumed) expectations. The coach feels that she is treading on eggshells and cannot give any feedback that may come across as overly critical. The coachee starts to talk less, in order to prompt fewer reactions. When the coach points out that relationships at work may be repeating themselves in the coaching relationship, this comes as an enormous relief to the coachee. She can now be herself in the coaching relationship and gradually learns to be a little easier on herself. And so does the coach!

Defences against emerging insight

The coachee is free, even without the coach, to gain a great deal of insight into his or her own issues. However, the coachee often fails to take up these opportunities and does not admit certain insights – or, according to Freud, represses the possibility of insight within the unconscious. It may be that certain insights are unpleasant or painful, that they bring conflicts too close to the surface, or that they stand in the way of certain ways of living and working. If such insights break through into the coaching situation the coachee may, instead of welcoming them, erect all sorts of barriers against them, just as (s)he does outside the coaching context. In the analytic literature, these barriers are known as *defences*.[7] Freud's daughter Anna listed all the defence mechanisms uncovered by her father (Freud, 1936):

1. *Repression*, in which we are unaware, or no longer aware, of unpleasant or unwelcome feelings or experiences. *Suppression* is a more active variant, in which we intentionally try not to think about something.

7. For the earliest discussion of defence or 'Abwehr', see Freud, 1894 and 1896.

2. *Regression:* withdrawal from painful situations and difficult responsibilities. In more extreme situations, this can quite literally give rise to a return to childhood behaviour. Harmless examples of this are sleep as regression from our waking existence and holidays as regression from the seriousness of our work. Dissociation and phobic avoidance of certain situations are more extreme variants, as are delusion and depersonalisation.

3. *Reaction formation:* feeling or behaving in a way that is diametrically opposed to the unpleasant fact and to one's own experience. Specific examples include:
   - active *denial* of unpleasant facts or perceptions
   - *rationalising*, by presenting current facts in an unrealistically positive light, or by dismissing them as irrelevant
   - *undoing*, by actually erasing traces of surviving memories, such as photographs and letters, or by changing the narrative when it is recounted
   - *obsessive-neurotic phenomena*, in which we permit ourselves all sorts of rituals and controlling behaviour.

4. *Isolation:* removing an impression or feeling from the context in which it arose.

5. *Projection:* externalising unacceptable feelings by attributing them to others. 'The pot calling the kettle black' is an expression of this.

6. *Introjection:* just as we can externalise unacceptable feelings (projection), we can also attribute positive qualities observed in others to ourselves. The combination of projection and introjection of positive and negative qualities is known as *splitting*.

7. *Displacement* as a way of dealing with unpleasant experiences. Instead of approaching directly a person who has offended us, we take it out on someone else. We may even take out our anger or other negative feelings on ourselves as the 'safest' target: turning against the self.

8. *Inversion* of a feeling into its opposite: for example, if we feel powerless we can lose ourselves in daydreams in which we are in control and all-powerful.

9. *Conversion*, in the form of a translation into a physical reaction. Examples can be found in all sorts of psychosomatic, and often stress-related, phenomena.

10. *Sublimation:* using the emotional energy released by frustration or unpleasant feelings towards 'higher ends', such as creative and altruistic work. This is a defence which is seen as very positive in a social context and may lead to positive results.

Clearly, these defences cannot be considered independently of each other, and basic defensive reactions such as repression and projection may give rise in a subsequent phase to other, more subtle defences[8] – especially when the pressure increases and new, unpleasant insights and feelings present themselves.

An example[9]

Coachees often talk about their relationships with their managers. For example, when a coachee expresses dislike of a boss, this is an unambiguous expression of an unpleasant feeling and so probably not a defence. Or perhaps it is after all a *displacement* of an inexpressible dislike of another, much more significant person in the coachee's life: (s)he might actually want to say: 'I don't know how to deal with my father and therefore I can't stand people in authority.'

A coachee may raise a dislike of the boss in another way, as a defence:

- *Repression:* 'I wonder why I often feel so tired and tense at work.'
- *Suppression:* 'I am irritated with my boss but I don't know why.'
- *Regression* (dissociation): 'I'm always telling my boss stupid jokes.'
- *Reaction formation* (denial): 'My boss is irrelevant to me.'
- *Reaction formation* (rationalisation): 'My boss still has a lot to learn about managing.'
- *Reaction formation* (acting out): 'Without thinking about what I was doing, I smashed my computer by throwing it on the floor.'
- *Isolation:* 'I don't agree with my boss's strategic plan.'
- *Projection:* 'My boss doesn't like me.'
- *Introjection:* 'Strange that it should be my boss who made me realise how well I'm actually doing.'

8. Within reaction formation in particular, there are many interesting and complicated defences, such as *acting out* (converting one's own impulses into behaviour without thinking), *intellectualising* (giving oneself over to abstract thinking) or *learning* (merely understanding what is happening without converting that understanding into a response). These are defences that we often encounter during coaching.

9. The idea for this example comes from Vaillant (1992).

- *Displacement:* 'I don't like that bootlicking colleague.'
- *Displacement* (turning against the self; passive aggression): 'I don't like myself"
- *Inversion:* 'I love my boss.'
- *Conversion:* 'Yesterday I spent another day with my boss (...) Later I went home with a fever.'
- *Sublimation:* 'I rewrote my boss's strategic plan and had it approved by him and the board of management.'
- *Sublimation* (to altruism): 'I have become the works council mediator for people who have trouble with the style of management in this organisation.'

Approaches to analytic coaching

Traditional approach

Historically, analysts have not been keen to prescribe or to follow fixed procedures. However, Freud wrote six 'technical papers' (Freud, 1912–15 inclusive) which we can draw on for advice on to

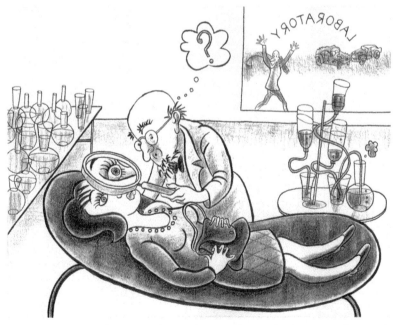

Figure 8.1 In analytic coaching the coachee submits to a thorough examination, and defends him or herself against it

how to proceed as an analytic coach. The papers start from the analyst's basic rule which states that coachees undertake to share everything that comes into their head, without censorship or selectivity. The coachee talks and associates freely and easily, so providing 'material' that can be analysed. The analytic coach reflects this basic rule with a receptivity that accepts all of the material, also without censoring or selecting. The coach practises an 'evenly hovering attention' ('gleichschwebende Aufmerksamkeit' – Freud, 1912c), which listens to everything without censure. The aim is to receive information without focusing one's own attention on specific points or being concerned, for example, about whether something that has already emerged is significant or needs to be analysed further. The coach trusts that insight will come of itself, from the coach's 'unconscious memory'. The intention is, therefore, that the 'giving unconscious' of the coachee should come into contact as closely as possible with the 'receiving unconscious' of the coach.

As the coach, you seek to disconnect yourself from your memory and your desires,[10] in order to be as fully present as possible in the here and now with the coachee. You end up with a negative capability (Bion, 1970) – the ability to be in situations where uncertainty, ambiguity and doubt prevail, without making laborious attempts to get out of them, for example via the route of statements of facts, interpretations and solutions.

An example

(The coachee is talking about a difficult client with whom she is just not making any headway) '... it's like walking through treacle. He is so ambitious but so quiet at the same time, almost timid, but not very aware of his own impact. He's not my type of person... he works on the trading floor, isn't really interested in people ...' 'Your type of person? What do you mean?' 'He has a tendency to be controlling, to keep a tight grip on everything, so we're unable to complete the project. It is unbelievably frustrating. I just feel confusion when I think about him... What am I to do with that man? In fact, I feel confused now as well.' 'What does his "type" remind you of?' 'What? What does he remind me of? Perhaps he reminds me most of my brother ...'

---

10. Bion (1970) refers to an active *elimination* of memory and desires, and even of sensory impressions and understanding, in order to be able to free attention for the emotional quality of the client's 'material'.

(Talks about her brother, and suddenly interrupts herself) '... perhaps I am avoiding something here. Maybe I have the same sort of rivalry with that client as I do with my brother? Phew... Isn't life difficult sometimes? There aren't many people as difficult as my brother ...' 'You said that you're feeling the same confusion in this conversation as well... ?'

Another attempt to sum up in a word what is expected of the coach in analytic coaching is *containment* (Bion, 1963). The aim is quite literally to act like a vessel to 'contain' the problem presented by the coachee, including the accompanying emotions, so that it becomes possible for the coachee to transform the emotions and gain new insight into their own defences. This containment helps the coachee to pause and reflect at precisely those moments when strong emotions or difficult issues are in the room. Containment offers space to think about these emotions and issues, and keeps boundaries around that thinking space to protect it from tendencies to move away to other, safer issues which are, again, defences to emerging insight.

Containment places great demands on the coach:

- not just remaining calm and neutral in an emotionally charged situation
- but also accepting the widest possible range of expressions and accompanying emotions
- while using one's own emotions, which are often triggered unconsciously by the coachee's emotions
- and intervening on the basis of one's own emotions, without actually expressing them as emotions (Heimann, 1950)
- and being able at the same time to offer clear and firm boundaries on the coaching relationship – the coach offers exceptional acceptance, but only within the limits of the coaching, outside which that availability disappears.

The coach usually finds indications of conflicts and defences in the coachee's material, which also express themselves in transference as *resistance* to the analysis and to the coach.[11] The difficult task of the

11. Freud (1912b) points out that in virtually every case where the basic rule becomes difficult for the coachee, and free association thus breaks down, there is something going on within the coachee that is connected with the person of the coach. This illustrates just how strong transference is.

coach is to bring these conflicts and resistances, and this transference, to the surface. This requires a considerable courage – not only to look for snags, omissions and discrepancies in the coachee's story, but also (and even more) to explore the coach's own relationship with the coachee out loud. This also requires a great deal of experience, and the ability to communicate possible insights into conflicts and hidden forms of resistance in a measured way that is manageable for the coachee.

The aim of analytic coaching is to shine the light of insight on what the coachee has repressed and kept to him- or herself and thereby to overcome internal defences and resistance (Freud, 1914a). Analysts have become fairly strict in terms of their methodology to achieve this. Freud, too, after an informal, exploratory start, made his own contribution. The now 'traditional' psychoanalysis is intensive and thorough, with four to six sessions a week taking place over a period of years, the arrangement with a couch where the coachee is unable to see the coach, and a long period of training for analysts as analysands and as physicians (although Freud himself was never keen to impose the latter obligation). Freud defended the spatial arrangement with the couch by saying, among other things, that he did not want to be stared at all day (Freud, 1913). Crucially, of course, this arrangement allows considerably more scope for free association and transference.

The ladder of inference
A tried and tested method to stimulate insight in a coaching conversation is described in Argyris (1990). It is designed to facilitate moving the coachee away from complaining and finding fault in others or in external causes and towards his or her own stake in the problem, Argyris is not, like Freud, looking for unconscious motivations. He starts with something that all of the defences described above have in common, and that their existence discloses: the fact that something unpleasant has been warded off or kept at a safe distance. The unpleasant feeling or problem has been 'dealt with' or 'processed' in a defensive manner. The experience with even the beginnings of increasing insight was experienced as unpleasant, disagreeable or even intolerable, and so was brushed aside. Conclusions have been arrived at and the defence is the result. In practice, this usually results in the coachee taking action on the basis of his or her own first impression, without first going over scenarios, alone or together with the coach. It is as if the coachee is climbing a ladder

Figure 8.2 The ladder of inference can expose new insights

very quickly, missing out the occasional rung: a ladder that runs from a specific event, to the impressions it makes, to the emotions, to the interpretations, to the conclusions, and finally to the actions.

In this analytic approach, coachee and coach slowly go back down the ladder of inference and attempt to return to the situation that preceded the defences: in other words, before the current situation in which everything appears to be 'resolved'. Put another way, the question is: 'How can we, nevertheless, gain insight from that first, painful event? How can we find other interpretations/draw other conclusions/prepare other courses of action?' Much too often, we assume that (Senge et al., 1994):

- our actions are well-founded in our convictions
- our convictions are *the* truth
- our convictions are based on real data
- the reality is clear
- the data that we select are the (only) real data.

A coach using the ladder of inference goes about it as follows. On the basis of a statement or question from the coachee, (s)he tries to identify the underlying conflict that generated the negative experience. The coach tries to adopt as independent a position as possible. The procedure is roughly as follows:[12]

1. The coachee presents a concern or problem – something (s)he is having trouble with or wants to resolve.
2. Together with the coachee, the coach looks at the way in which the concern or problem has been formulated – what sort of conclusions or assumptions are evident? For example, the coach looks at the descriptions of self and others. What does the coachee seem to emphasize, and what appears to have been left out?
3. The coach considers personally what these assumptions are based on. What are the observations or impressions that lead the coachee to draw these conclusions? In this step we sometimes come close to the source of the defences. If not – if no powerful, painful observations or impressions come to the fore – the coach can ask about associations, or about intuitions that support the assumptions. These may even be things that seem not directly relevant here. The more spontaneous, the better.
4. The coach endeavours to keep the conflict that has now emerged – the unpleasant impressions, the contradictions, the offences, the fragility of the coachee, and so on – the focus of the conversation. The coachee is often tempted to respond to this by releasing a new defence: a rationalisation perhaps, or a strongly intellectualising label, or perhaps a projection vis à vis the coach. But this is precisely the moment that can produce insight. However painful it may be, it is worth sticking with it and examining it a bit longer.
5. Finally, there is time for a critical review of the assumptions referred to above (Step 2). Often, the defences (generalisations, attributions, repressions, rationalisations, and so on) do not stand up to careful examination.

12. This procedure has similarities with the U METHOD from *Learning with colleagues* (Chapter 4) and with some RET approaches. One difference is that these two approaches attempt to replace the assumptions with other, more 'appropriate', 'rational' assumptions. This makes these methods much more directive.

Summary: analytic coaching

Analytic coaching is a form of coaching in which:

- Coach and coachee work towards increasing insight into the coachee's problem.
- Coach and coachee work with internal conflicts within the coachee and the resulting defences and resistance.
- The aim is to overcome defences and resistance, in order to gain insight into factors that were previously less obvious.

Psychological phenomena investigated in analytic coaching:

- Defences as barriers to enhanced insight, such as repression, regression, reaction formation, isolation, projection, introjection, displacement, inversion, conversion and sublimation.
- Transference as a carrier wave for defences to become visible as resistance to the coaching process and to the coach.

We introduce two different analytic approaches:

- Traditional analytic coaching, in which the basic rule is to share everything without censure or selection (coachee) and to receive everything without censure or selection (coach). Moreover, the coach offers evenly hovering attention and containment.
- More cognitive analytic coaching: the ladder of inference in which, in a more systematic, directive manner, statements are investigated with a view to identifying assumptions, perceptions and underlying conflicts.

9
Paradoxical coaching:
Moving with defences

> [Change does not exist, for] what would be in change changes neither in the shape it is in nor in the shape it is not in.
>
> Zeno of Elea, Fragment DK 29B4

Introduction: the 'difficult' coachee

The paradoxical approach is eminently suited to tricky coaching situations in which 'things are not going smoothly'; where, for example:

- The coachee does not appear to accept the coach whole-heartedly.
- Initiatives appear to get bogged down.
- In one way or another, the coach feels constantly challenged – to be a better coach or to give more, less, or cleverer advice.

When coaching is going well, there is harmony between coachee and coach. The coachee has a real problem or questions; the coach possesses real expertise and authority – also in the eyes of the coachee! – and there is a willingness on the part of the coachee to be coached and on the part of the coach to coach. When things are not going smoothly, invariably one or more of these conditions are not being met, though other conditions may well be – if this were not the case, then the coaching relationship would have been discontinued. Things may not go smoothly because the coach does not feel capable or motivated to coach, in which case it is time to refer the coachee to someone else. But it may also be because the coachee does not meet some of the conditions and is therefore sending out ambiguous messages. This can happen overtly or less overtly. Signs of this may include:

- 'I don't have a problem' (e.g. by referring to others who 'do have a problem').
- 'Nothing can be changed here' (e.g. by emphasising the extent and complexity of the situation, or by referring to one's own powerlessness).
- 'I doubt your expertise' (e.g. by saying that the coach doesn't understand, or doesn't understand well enough, or by suggesting that (s)he is not offering useful advice or appropriate interventions).

All of these signals are completely reasonable and understandable but, within the coaching relationship, they have a *paradoxical* significance: the coachee is evidently appealing to the coach to look at his or her concerns and problems, but simultaneously undermining that appeal. The paradoxical signal is that within an appeal for help and influence, there is simultaneously an undeniable appeal to leave the coachee alone or to let everything carry on as usual. In this situation, nothing the coach can do is ever good enough: helping is good but not all good, and not helping is good but not all good. In the literature this is known as the *double bind* (Watzlawick et al., 1967): the coachee double-binds the coach using contradictory requests and, simultaneously, exerting pressure (coming from the contract, an on-going relationship, or even a threat) to make progress. A confusing, frustrating and dispiriting dilemma, but one that we have all experienced as coaches at some time.

Ambiguous communication

The paradoxical approach claims to provide an answer to dilemmas of this type and says that it is necessary, in these situations, for the coach to start sending out ambiguous signals as well. The coach thereby puts the coachee under pressure to resolve the dilemma personally. The paradoxical approach is extremely *directive*: not only within the coaching, which employs directive interventions, but also within the coaching relationship, which the coach puts to the test. Another feature of the paradoxical approach is that it is above all *interactional*: it focuses less on the problem and its background than on the interaction between the coachee and others, specifically the coach. The aim is to influence this interaction in such a way that it becomes less ambiguous.

The main paradoxical technique is the 'utilisation technique' (Erickson, 1959): instead of persevering with a more or less overt conflict, the coach starts to (counter-intuitively!) utilise the specific characteristics of the difficult interaction, in such a way that the coach helps the coachee to:

• take more responsibility for her own behaviour, even if that behaviour consists of such 'negative' things like symptoms, moaning, ambiguities or resistance
• introduce and test alternatives to the coachee's current patterns of behaviour.

The utilisation technique does this by, first, inviting the coachee to continue doing the same, second, requesting more of the same, or third, suggesting the same thing in new guises. In fact, the coach puts the coachee in a paradoxical situation that cannot be resolved as long as the coachee continues to under mine a productive coaching relationship. All examples of 'utilisation technique' are ambiguous and paradoxical, because the coach accepts all of the coachee's resistance to the coaching relationship *while remaining present and available in that relationship as the coach.* The coach therefore reacts paradoxically to the coachee's paradoxical behaviour.

Paradoxical coaching approaches

Well-known applications of utilisation technique (Haley, 1963) include the the ones we will work through in the following example.

An example
A manager has received disappointing reactions from her own staff to the distribution of a 360° feedback form ('You don't spend enough time with us'; 'You're not in the department very much and seem more interested in the external, ceremonial aspects of being a manager', and so on). She takes this feedback very much to heart. She calls in a coach but, right from the outset, displays little confidence and is despondent about her own prospects: 'I'll never be a good manager'; 'This is going nowhere ...'

1. *Positive labelling* of symptoms and problems as well as of the resistant behaviour itself. A positive motive, and sometimes a positive result, is consistently attributed to the apparently nega-

tive behaviour. The coach emphasises the positive side of the problem and the advantages associated with the current situation. In fact, the coach accepts and confirms all of the coachee's behaviour, including the behaviour that is undermining the coaching itself.

Example, continued
The coach says that the manager is just showing that her heart is very much in it by representing the department so often, and that she is doing the right thing by treating her staff as independent adults and not trying to 'pamper' them too much. And that it is very professional of her to call in a coach. It is precisely by *not* always running after people that you can take time to be a great manager. Furthermore, the very fact that the manager is dispirited is interpreted by the coach as a sign that her heart is in it.

2. *Prescribing problems and resistance.* The coach suggests that the 'difficult' or 'problematic' behaviour be displayed more, even extended, and applied in more situations. Coach and coachee can also make agreements about planning and applying the same behaviour more frequently, so that the coachee can get an (even firmer) grip on it.

Example, continued
The coach says: 'In my view you would do best to be present even less, so as to become an even better manager. Moreover, they don't accept you anyway, so concentrate on the tasks that you prefer and that you do best.'

3. *Eliciting change through surprises.* The coach does not react 'congruently' to the behaviour presented, but incongruently: instead of going along with the usual patterns of interaction (for example by offering help, or wearing herself out), the coach opts for the unexpected. (S)he intervenes in surprising ways and introduces new situations and circumstances.

Example, continued
'Perhaps it would be a good idea to have your staff distribute a 360° survey of their own. Then you can tell them what you think of them!'

4. *Negotiating en route to the 'continuum of change'*. Knowing that a small step in the right direction sometimes makes a big difference, the coach makes a proposal for a minuscule change, usually as an experiment and often merely a change in an irrelevant aspect of the problem situation. Negotiating techniques can be used here: 'To what extent are you prepared to try something different?'; 'When would you be prepared to change?', and so on.

> *Example, continued*
> 'What's more, while you're still managing the department and before you're finally rejected by your staff, you can also experiment with 'attention', in preparation for your next job as a manager. I wonder if anything will change if, for example, you maintain eye contact for one second longer each time you meet someone. Do you think they will notice the difference?'

5. *Posing the counter-paradox*. The most powerful intervention, in which the coach him or herself poses a similar unsolvable dilemma for the coachee. The coach creates a situation which is unpleasant for the coachee, one from which (s)he can escape only with unambiguous behaviour. The most common application of this is the (apparently) realistic assertion that no change or improvement is likely, so that the coachee herself feels called upon to 'prove' that something better is indeed possible.

> *Example, continued*
> 'And perhaps we can extrapolate the experiment to this coaching situation, because this will come to an end too of course – there will come a day when I reject you as my coachee. How far could you take things with me? You could turn up late next time, or forget the appointment, or talk absent-mindedly as if your thoughts are elsewhere. And then ask me for feedback.'

Two variations: ironic and provocative

There are two further variations on this directive, ambiguous and interactional path, one of which is less severely manipulative and directive, while the other goes even further than the paradoxical approach. The gentler variation is the *ironic approach* (de Haan,

Figure 9.1 Paradoxical coaching sometimes finds completely unexpected, almost magical, answers to the coachee's questions

1999) and the more radical variation is the *provocative approach*
(Farrelly and Brandsma, 1974).

The *ironic approach* resembles ordinary directive coaching. The
coach offers frequent, honest and sound advice within the context of
the coachee's question while simultaneously *hinting* at quite different
advice outside that context. The advice is therefore communicated
ambiguously, with the suggestion that other kinds of advice might
also be given. This prompts the coachee to think carefully about
what 'the ironic coach' actually means. Due to its ambiguity, irony
provides a strong incentive to independent thought on the part of the
coachee. At the same time, it is a gentler intervention than the paradoxical approach because you do not encourage the coachee to do
something really unusual, such as repeating and amplifying sympto-
matic behaviour.

Example, continued
'It strikes me that your staff are only able to talk about you in a 360° feedback survey. Are they so intimidated by you that they can only say that they want to see more of you by means of a questionnaire? You must really keep them under your thumb! Or is something else going on?'

The *provocative approach*, on the other hand, is an exaggeration or enlargement of the paradoxical approach. The coach is now truly a Devil's advocate who provokes, challenges and derides the coachee in every possible way. The coach becomes a sort of court jester who uses gallows humour and applies a *reductio ad absurdum* to all the coachee's behaviour, making it appear more and more ridiculous. The intention behind this rather tormenting approach (coachees must first sign a document confirming that they agree to this provocative method!) is to mobilise as much of the coachee's resilience as possible. This approach toughens up and strengthens the coachee: if the coachee can stand up to the provocative coach, life in the work situation will no longer pose any problems either, so the thinking goes.
Provocative utilisation techniques include the following:

6. *Drawing out resistance.* In provocative coaching, the 'difficult' situation with ambiguous messages from the coachee is precisely the situation that is desired, so the coach attempts to engineer that situation as quickly as possible, for example by saying: 'There is an enormous problem here', 'I'm not really an expert' or 'Really everything needs to change here'. (Compare these statements with the three conditions for coaching at the start of this chapter).

Example, continued
'But that is terrible. The last time I "treated" a manager with such a feedback profile it led via the works council to a case before the senior management. The manager was sacked on the spot and hasn't worked since. I'm none too optimistic for you. What can you still do to conceal these feedback results from the rest of the organisation?'

7. *Jokes, anecdotes and associations.* The coach seizes the initiative in the conversation by talking animatedly about his or her own past and all sorts of interesting previous coachees. In addition,

the coach introduces a joke or a strange, exaggerated association each time the coachee makes a contribution to the conversation.

Example, continued
'This isn't great for me either. I can't always be associated with coachees who lose their jobs, unless I can attribute the dismissal to myself of course. What do you think about us drafting a letter of resignation for you together now, saying something like: "After carefully studying the feedback from my staff I decided that I was not up to the job of manager. My coach made me realise that, for my future career, I would do well to aspire to a purely ceremonial position."'

8. *Interrupting and frustrating* the coachee's story. In fact, the coach does not even allow the coachee to present a problem or initial question at the start of the conversation. Sometimes, the coachee doesn't get halfway through a sentence before the coach is shouting 'You look funny today!' or 'Did you brush your hair this morning?' Interruptions and discouragements of this type remain a permanent part of the coaching.

According to practitioners of these three coaching approaches, which are all *manipulative* in nature, all other coaching approaches are also manipulative, though their practitioners don't always admit it. The non-directive, person-centred opening, for example, which states explicitly that the coach will not influence the coachee (see Chapter 7), is in fact very paradoxical and manipulative because the coachee is specifically entering this relationship in order to request influence from the coach. Paradoxical coaches say that the most important ingredient of any effective coaching is the fact that the coachee does not gain control over the coach (see the marvellous epilogue about 'one-upmanship' in Haley, 1963).

An example
A female coachee, a manager in a government organisation, has had a number of sessions with staff due to a degree of agitation within the department. One thing her reports say is that they would like more attention from her as their manager. They comment that few compliments are given. The coachee, busy as usual, seeks a practical solution. She asks her secretary to e-mail all staff on her behalf, saying that she is very pleased

with the excellent results they have achieved as a department. She is proud to have acted quickly and now expects a compliment from the coach. The coach cannot help bursting out laughing and asks the coachee what she thinks happened next, following that e-mail. Are all of those bright people in her department now satisfied that their call has been answered? Or will they soon delete the e-mail because they see it more as a practical solution or gimmick than as evidence of actual, personal attention to individual contributions? The coachee can take the practical humour and joins in the coach's laughter: it had not crossed her mind that her email could be taken like that. This is followed by a genuine discussion about what the staff in her department is actually asking of the manager.

Summary: paradoxical coaching

Paradoxical coaching is a form of coaching in which:

- The ambiguity in the coachee's presentation of the problem is central.
- The coach answers that ambiguity with his or her own ambiguity vis-à-vis the coachee.
- The coach intentionally influences the patterns of interaction between coachee and coach.

The paradoxical coach approaches the coachee with utilisation techniques that utilise the coachee's difficult behaviour, such as:

- positive labelling of the coachee's symptoms and problems
- prescribing new problems and resistance
- eliciting changes by surprising assignments
- negotiating with the coachee about the extent to which (s)he is going to change
- posing the 'counter-paradox'.

An alternative, gentler form of paradoxical coaching is ironic coaching: the coach gives advice but also suggests that different advice is possible, or deliberately introduces doubt about the advice (s)he is giving.

An alternative, more radical form of paradoxical coaching is provocative coaching: the coach deliberately provokes resistance and frustrates the coachee's thought processes. Examples of provocative coaching techniques include:

- drawing out resistance by exaggerating the problem
- jokes, anecdotes and associations at the coachee's expense
- interrupting and frustrating the coachee's story.

10
Coaching methodologies

Every coach, consciously or unconsciously, uses certain *conversational models*, or established ways of developing a coaching conversation. In this chapter, the different approaches to coaching conversations introduced in the previous four chapters are summarised as conversational models in terms of specific methods for use in coaching conversations. Bear in mind that the non-directive approaches to coaching cannot be summarised in step-by-step methods – by definition, such conversations

Figure 10.1 A step-by-step coaching method gives the coach the opportunity to observe the coachee while she is hard at work

are structured not by the coach, but by the coachee. In two of the following methods, the ANALYTIC METHOD and the COUNSELLING METHOD, therefore, no formal steps are indicated. The suggested approaches are as specific as possible and can be used by the coach in facilitating the coachee. It is also advisable to work with one of the methods *explicitly*, putting it on the table during coaching: this creates a situation where coach and coachee regularly and explicitly reflect on their process in the here-and-now, which can be very effective.

The methods necessarily simplify the coaching approaches that we have described before. In principle, each method shows how to handle a single issue or problem, while coaching conversations generally involve the handling of several, intertwined issues on many levels. Moreover, we often set aside the last few minutes of every coaching conversation for a short review, something that does not feature in every method.

Two of the conversational models illustrated below have been published previously: the GROW METHOD in Whitmore (1992) and the IRONIC METHOD in de Haan (1999). Some methods display similarities with the consultation methods in *Learning with Colleagues* (Chapter 4). In particular, the SOLUTION-FOCUSED METHOD displays similarities with the LEARNING FROM SUCCESS METHOD and the LADDER METHOD – inspired by Argyris (1990) – shows some similarities with the U METHOD.

The GROW method

Step	Description	Time
Step 1	*Presentation of the problem* Coachee introduces his/her issue briefly.	1 min
Step 2	*G: Goal* Coach asks about the goal for the issue *and* for this session: • What do you want to achieve, and when? • What do you want to achieve with me now? • To what extent is that goal specific/challenging/attainable measurable? N.B.: avoid negatively-worded goals.	5 mins
Step 3	*R: Reality* Coach asks about the current state of affairs: • What have you done about it so far, and with what results? N.B.: do not ask any 'how' or 'why' questions at this stage.	5 mins
Step 4	*O: Options* Coach asks about the options open to the coachee: • What options do you have? • What are the pros and cons of the different options? N.B.: when you seem to have all the possible options, ask for just one more.	10 mins
Step 5	*W: Will* Coach asks about the option, or combination of options, that the coachee is going to put into practice: • What are you going to do, and when? • Does that meet your goal? And what about the goal of this conversation? • What obstacles do you expect and how are you going to overcome them? • What resources do you need and how are you going to get them? • Indicate on a scale from 1 to 10 how likely it is that you will carry out that action.	5 mins
	Time needed	26 mins

The solution-focused method[1]

Step	Description	Time
Step 1	*Presentation of the problem* Coachee briefly introduces his/her issue and what has already been tried. The coach asks in particular about what was useful, and what helped.	5 mins
Step 2	*Miracle question* Coach asks about indicators of improvement: how can the coachee check that an improvement has actually taken place? What exactly will be different at that moment?	5 mins
Step 3	*Exceptions* Coach asks about times when the problem does not arise: what are those times like? What happens then? What is the situation like exactly? *Option*: Coach asks for a rating of progress at the present time, on a scale from 0 (no change) to 10 (issue has been completely resolved).	10 mins
Step 4	*Suggestions* Coach gives positive feedback, and suggestions for creating more of that sort of 'exception'.	5 mins
Step 5	*Contracting* Coachee says what (s)he wants to do next and how. The coach assigns 'homework' and explains the rationale behind it. Coach and coachee make a new appointment to review the situation.	10 mins
	Time needed	35 mins

1. Within 'appreciative inquiry' there is a similar structure, the *4-D model* (Cooperrider and Whitney, 2002):

    - *Discover*: discovering in a structured way when the coachee is at his/her best.
    - *Dream*: a dream in which the situation from the first step ('discover') is the norm rather than an exception.
    - *Design*: together with the coach, working towards the realisation of the dream with specific plans.
    - *Deliver*: making arrangements about how to put the plans into practice.

    Discover corresponds to Step 1, Dream to Step 2, Design to Step 4 and Deliver to Step 5 of the SOLUTION-FOCUSED METHOD.

The counselling method

N.B.: this is not a step-by-step method in the usual sense. The scheme presented here merely indicates what types of intervention will be used by the coach. It is the coachee, rather than the coach, who determines what stage the process is at, at any given time. Nor can any indication of time be given, because the coachee decides when is the best time to move on.

Option	Description	Time
Option 1	*Introduction* The coachee starts the conversation, in the way (s)he wishes.	?
Option 2	*Invitation to explore* The coach adopts an inviting and available stance, but without applying pressure to say more or to explain any particular aspects.	?
Option 3	*Broadening* The coach broadens the issue by summarising and by reflecting feelings. The coach also tries to paraphrase 'between the lines' – stimulating awareness of attitudes, values, etc. – and asks the occasional open question.	?
Option 4	*Reinforcing contact* The coach increases the contact with the coachee by reflecting on the contact itself and by means of self-disclosure: how the coach feels at this moment and how (s)he is involved at this moment.	?
Option 5	*Review* Coach and coachee review the session together and try to describe how they feel following the conversation.	?
	Time needed	

The analytic and organisation coach method

N.B.: this is not a step-by-step method in the usual sense. The scheme presented here merely indicates what types of intervention can be used by the coach. It is the coachee, rather than the coach, who determines what stage the process is at, at any given time. Nor can any indication of time be given, because the coachee him-/herself decides how long to devote to any one subject – although the coach often monitors the overall length of the session when using this approach.

Option	Description	Time
Option 1	*Introduction* The coachee starts the conversation, in the way (s)he wishes, as far as possible using the basic rule that (s)he can voice anything, including fancies and thoughts that arise in the moment, without selection or criticism. The coach listens, also without selection or criticism. The coach asks him/herself: 'What sorts of signal am I picking up?'	?
Option 2	*Background* The coach looks out for what may lie behind the coachee's spoken words, as well as for assumptions implicit in the coachee's story. The coach is also sensitive to what the coachee leaves out. The coach asks him/herself: 'What is not being said?'	?
Option 3	*Obstacles to insight* The coach explores with the coachee what obstacles there are to incipient insight; what conflicts may be playing a role in the background; and how the coachee attempts to keep those conflicts and other unpleasant feelings out of his/her consciousness and out of the conversation. The coach asks him/herself: 'What conflict do I see?'	?
Option 4	*Transference* The coach explores with the coachee what obstacles there are to gaining fresh insight in the course of this conversation, and what conflicts and resistance are emerging in this conversation. The coach asks him/herself: 'What does the coachee want from me?'	?
	Time needed	Fixed

Extension for the organisation coach method

Option 4a	*Organisation transference* ? The coach explores with the coachee what barriers existing within the coachee's organisation might resist fresh insights, and what role the coachee 'automatically' takes on. The coach asks him/herself: 'How does the coachee's organisation want the coachee to feel now?'

The ladder method

Step	Description	Time
Step 1	*Presentation of the problem* The coachee presents an issue or problem and provides an explanation as necessary.	5–10 mins
Step 2	*Assumptions* Coach and coachee look together at this formulation: what conclusions or assumptions emerge? What attributions does the coachee make, what does (s)he take for granted?	5–10 mins
Step 3	*Motivation for the assumptions* Coach and coachee explore together the bases of these conclusions. What observations or experiences led the coachee to make these assumptions? *Alternative*: The coachee undertakes a free association in relation to the assumptions: what do they remind him/her of?	5–10 mins
Step 4	*Underlying conflict* Coach and coachee explore together what the 'issue behind the issue' is: what problem or deeper conflict lies behind the problem presented? To what extent do the identified assumptions play a role in creating the problem?	5–10 mins
Step 5	*Testing the assumptions* Coach and coachee consider what different assumptions they could make.	5–10 mins
Step 6	*Alternative presentation of the problem* Coach and coachee explore what this means for the nature of the problem.	5–10 mins
Step 7	*Review* Coach and coachee review this conversation together and try to describe what insights they have gained from it.	5–10 mins
	Time needed	35–65 mins

The ironic method

Step	Description	Time
Step 1	*Presentation of the problem* The coachee presents an issue or problem and explains it if necessary.	10 mins
Step 2	*Reformulation as a dilemma* The coach attempts to reformulate the issue as a dilemma, in which an internal contradiction or discrepancy comes to the surface: 'The coachee wants to ... but feels held back by ...'; or 'The coachee wants to put an end to ... but is aware that ...'	10 mins
Step 3	*The ironic intervention* The ironic communication itself. This can consist of a strong emphasis on an aspect of the dilemma that the coach wants to query. Alternatively, the coach can contribute his/her own point of view and place it in a different perspective at the same time. Example: 'Listening to your enthusiastic story, I am strangely reminded of something which went quite wrong last week. But I imagine that it is quite irrelevant in this situation.'	10 mins
Step 4	*Working through* The coach monitors the coachee's response attentively and tries to facilitate this response as much as possible, by means of invitations, open questions or summaries. The coach will summarise the coachee's response to the ironic intervention, without removing the ambiguity of the irony.	15 mins
	Time needed	45 mins

The paradoxical method

Step	Description	Time
Step 1	*Presentation of the problem* The coachee presents an issue or problem and explains it if necessary. The coach helps to make the problem as specific and verifiable as possible and attempts to reformulate the problem for him/herself in terms of a dilemma.	10 mins
Step 2	*Positive labelling* The coach looks for as many positive aspects and motives as possible in the coachee's behaviour in the problem situation. If there are any defences or resistance, the coach accepts and encourages them.	10 mins
Step 3	*Paradoxical instruction* The coach formulates an assignment for the coachee that also contains a dilemma. This new dilemma is designed in such a way that it reflects the initial dilemma, and thereby invites the coachee to persist with both aspects of the initial dilemma. N.B.: a break for reflection is often necessary before the coach can find a suitable paradoxical instruction; Step 3 then takes place in a subsequent coaching conversation.	10 mins
Step 4	*Contracting for the future* Coach and coachee look to the future and the completion of the paradoxical instruction, the coach providing further encouragement.	15 mins
	Time needed	45 mins

Summary: coaching methodologies

The following coaching methods are introduced:

- the GROW METHOD
- the SOLUTION-FOCUSED METHOD
- the COUNSELLING METHOD
- the ANALYTIC METHOD and the ORGANISATION COACH METHOD
- the LADDER METHOD
- the IRONIC METHOD
- the PARADOXICAL METHOD.

Together, these coaching methods cover the entire window of coaching, from exploring to suggesting and from supporting to confronting, including the four different approaches:

1. Problem-focused: GROW METHOD, PARADOXICAL METHOD and IRONIC METHOD.
2. Solution-focused: SOLUTION-FOCUSED METHOD.
3. Person-focused: COUNSELLING METHOD.
4. Insight-focused: ANALYTIC METHOD, ORGANISATION COACH METHOD and LADDER METHOD.

11
Choosing the right method

> The more the therapist is able to tolerate the anxiety of not knowing, the less need is there for the therapist to embrace orthodoxy. The creative members of an orthodoxy, any orthodoxy, ultimately outgrow their disciplines.
>
> Irvin Yalom, *Love's Executioner*

In this chapter we briefly review the 'coaching outcome' literature, and we offer suggestions for using the different approaches and methods and the conversations within which they can be applied. We start with a summary of conclusions from research into the effects of coaching and psychotherapy, which quickly refutes the myth that there is a single 'right' method for every coaching issue, or even for one specific issue. Then we take a look at the evidence from research and practical experience that argues for or against certain methods. This evidence gives rise to recommendations as to the choice of method. However, the main recommendation is to choose a method that fits as closely as possible with your own personality, and to keep exploring and developing that 'personal' method on an on-going basis.

What do we know about the effectiveness of coaching?

There is a small but increasing quantitative research literature into the effectiveness of coaching. For a more detailed summary of the literature, see De Haan and Duckworth (2013). Below we have grouped the existing, original research studies in coaching that we could find into four separate blocks of studies: evaluation studies, studies with independent outcome variables, studies with independent outcome variables and a control group, and studies that are designed to compare conditions and therefore cannot demonstrate overall effectiveness.

Overview of executive-coaching outcome research I: evaluation studies

Most empirical research into executive coaching is concerned with the value of coaching from the perspective of the client, with the research taking the form of an extensive evaluation of 'customer satisfaction'. On some occasions clients are asked to estimate how much their coaching has contributed financially to the bottom line of their organisation (e.g. McGovern et al., 2001). Levenson (2009) provides detailed information demonstrating the positive business impact of coaching in 12 case studies. Wasylyshyn et al. (2006) and Kombarakaran et al. (2008) both show high outcome ratings for in-company coaching programmes. Wasylyshyn et al. (2006) provide ratings for $N = 28$ clients and $N = 17$ 'others' (direct colleagues of clients) in a pharmaceutical company. Kombarakaran et al. (2008) provide ratings for $N = 104$ clients and $N = 29$ coaches. In both these studies the majority of those surveyed report high value or 'sustainability of learning' from coaching. Schlosser et al. (2006) measured the outcome of executive coaching across a range of variables and industries and from the perspectives of manager/sponsor ($N = 14$), client ($N = 56$), and coach ($N = 70$). Whilst a significant positive outcome was reported for all subjects, a significantly lower rating for the managers, in terms of return on investment, was reported.

In a different approach, taken by Grant and Cavanagh (2007), the results of a self-report measure of coaching skill (scored by $N = 218$ coaches) was correlated with $N = 38$ clients' assessment regarding outcome. This correlation was significantly positive ($r = 0.58$; $p<0.001$) thus providing a good indication that coaching skill can be inter-subjectively established.

Overview of executive-coaching outcome research II: incorporating independent outcome variables

The following studies explore the effectiveness of coaching by looking at independent variables over and above client, coach or manager satisfaction, but with no control group. Peterson (1993) studied $N = 370$ leaders from various organisations at three points in time (pre-coaching, post-coaching and follow-up) with outcome defined by their own coaching objectives and five standard 'control' items, rated by at least themselves, their manager and their coach (multi-source ratings). The coaching programme was intensive and long-term, with typically 50+ hours of individual coaching with a professional coach for over at least a year. Peterson found that clients, on average, achieved significant improvement on all measures of outcome related to coaching objectives (effect sizes $d > 1.5$). Olivero et al. (1997) studied managers who had taken part in a three-day educational training course followed by eight weeks of coaching. They found that both the training and the coaching increased productivity considerably, with most of the increase attributable to the coaching (increase of 22.4 per cent with training alone and of 88.0 per cent with training and coaching, i.e. almost fourfold; a difference which was significant at the $p<0.05$ level). In another study by Thach (2002), $N = 281$ managers participated in four one-hour sessions of coaching for over five months with a 360° (multisource) feedback process before and after the coaching. They found an average increase in 'leadership effectiveness' both as rated by the coaches and their co-workers (average increase 60 per cent but no significance reported). Bowles et al. (2007) looked at effectiveness in terms of increased productivity in army recruitment managers ($N = 30$) and executives ($N = 29$) who received coaching as compared to productivity changes in a non-random group of experienced recruitment managers over a similar, but not contemporaneous, time interval. The individuals who were coached showed greater productivity gains ($d = 0.43$ with $p<0.05$ for the middle managers and $d = 0.75$ with $p<0.01$ for the executives). Finally, Perkins (2009) studied the effectiveness of executive coaching on improving leadership behaviours in meetings, as rated by the coach. Using quantitative and qualitative methods with a small sample ($N = 21$), pre- and post-measurement of meeting behaviours were scored by the coach and author, with a clear improvement of behaviours reported (effect sizes $d > 0.95$ for 9 out of 11 behaviours measured, and $p<0.01$). There may of course have been researcher bias in these scores as coaches might understandably want their clients to do well.

Overview of executive-coaching outcome research III: employing control groups

We could find only three studies that employed a control group in their design. A significant impact of executive coaching when compared with a control group has been found by Smither et al.

(2003), Sue-Chan and Latham (2004) and Evers et al. (2006). Sue-Chan and Latham (2004) compared the impact of internal and external coaches with a wide difference in reputation in terms of (perceived) expertise and credibility. This outcome study involved MBA students in two countries (total $N = 53$) and compared the performance in terms of team playing and exam grades and found small but statistically significant differences at $p<0.05$, between faculty, peer and self-coaching with the first the most impactful. As in Perkins (2009) above, this study may suffer from researcher bias as the external coaches/tutors did the scoring of performance.

Evers et al. (2006) measured self-efficacy beliefs and outcome expectancies, on each of the three dimensions. Their study compared a pre-intervention and post-intervention measurement and also involved a (non-randomised) control group. The intervention was short with an average of only four coaching sessions. Although the sample was not very large (30 managers in both the experimental and the control group) they did find some objective evidence for a positive outcome of the coaching intervention. There was a significant increment for the coached group over the control group for one of the three dimensions in both self-efficacy beliefs ('setting one's own goals") and outcome expectancies ('acting in a balanced way') [$d \approx 0.5$ with $p<0.05$].

One of the most thorough studies on the impact of executive coaching was undertaken by Smither et al. (2003). This study worked with a (non-randomised) control group and conclusions were based on more objective criteria than evaluations by the clients. Smither et al. (2003) included evaluations by independent researchers together with clients' superiors, colleagues and staff (multisource feedback). This research involved 1202 senior managers in one multinational organisation with two consecutive years of 360° feedback. However, there were no more than 'two or three' coaching sessions per client (Smither et al., 2003; p. 29). The researchers found that managers who worked with an executive coach were significantly more likely than other managers to (1) set specific goals ($d=0.16$; $p<0.01$); (2) solicit ideas for improvements from their superiors ($d=0.36$; $p<0.01$); and (3) obtain higher ratings from direct-reports and superiors in the second year ($d=0.17$; $p<0.05$).

Brief overview of mentoring outcome research

The above findings are further supported in the more extensive *mentoring* outcome literature reviewed by Allen et al. (2004), through a meta-analysis comprising 43 outcome studies of mentoring in the organisational/workplace domain. Taking only the studies with control groups they found generally small, but significant effect sizes (e.g. 10 per cent explained proportion of variance for the mentoring effect on number of promotions and 4 per cent explained proportion of variance for the mentoring effect on career satisfaction; i.e., $d < 0.2$). They also found the criterion measuring the mentoring relationship ('satisfaction with mentor') to be the best predictor of career outcomes (14 per cent explained proportion of variance or $d \approx 0.2$ for career mentoring and 38 per cent explained proportion of variance or $d \approx 0.4$ for supportive or 'psychosocial' mentoring).

One thorough study of mentoring outcomes included by Allen et al. (2004) is Ragins et al. (2000) who studied a group of 1162 professionals from a wide variety of organisations and looked at the effect of formal/informal mentoring relationships on a range of work and career attitudes. Of the respondents, 44 per cent had an informal mentor, 9 per cent a formal mentor as part of a mentoring programme and 47 per cent had no mentor. This last group was used as the control, which was therefore not randomised. Their results show that the crucial factor in effectiveness is the client's satisfaction with the mentoring relationship. In the absence of that factor, there were no demonstrable differences between professionals who were mentored and those who were not. If client satisfaction with the relationship is present, however, professionals clearly demonstrate more positive attitudes towards themselves (self-confidence), their work, promotion prospects, their organisation and their career. The authors of Allen et al. (2004) later confirmed the results summarised above in a much larger meta-analysis, with $N > 10,000$ and including workplace, youth and academic domains (Eby et al., 2008).

Conclusions from coaching and mentoring outcome research

In summary, we note that outcome research in coaching is still in its infancy and that the holy grail of executive coaching – "Is executive coaching an effective intervention?" – is still there to be sought. In fact, no clear and agreed sense of what 'outcomes' should be or how outcome should be measured has yet emerged. There is no agreed research standard like the randomised controlled trials used in psychotherapy outcome research (Norcross, 2011). Also, the studies include a variety of processes which might themselves affect outcomes, such as explicit goal-setting, written development objectives, 360-degree feedback and other assessment tools, manager involvement, and even training programs and a presentation to senior executives to summarise achievements (e.g. Olivero et al., 1997). Treating this body of research as equivalent is too simplistic. That said, what is striking is that the first five research papers above (Peterson, 1993; Olivero et al., 1997; Thach, 2002, Bowles et al., 2007; Perkins, 2009), which did not make use of a contemporary control group, found large effects ($d>0.75$), generally larger than those found in psychotherapy. On the other hand, the more rigorous studies involving control groups (such as Allen et al., 2004; Smither et al., 2003; and Evers et al., 2006 and the work done in mentoring outcome studies) found only small effects, generally smaller than those found in psychotherapy ($d<0.5$; compare with average $d \approx 0.8$ in psychotherapy – see Wampold, 2001, and below). However, these are studies with mentors and internal coaches whilst many of the studies without control groups involve more significant coaching programmes with qualified professional coaches, and this is also a possible factor in the higher effects.

In conclusion, it appears that if the client alone is the focus of the study, the outcome tends to be very positive. However, when such common-methods bias is controlled for, the effect is much smaller, although still positive.

Overview of executive-coaching outcome research which compares conditions

The overview of effectiveness studies in coaching above has shown that there are some indications that executive coaching is an effective intervention. However, there is also another body of coaching research, to which our own most recent research study (De Haan et al., 2013) belongs. This newer body of research in coaching outcome assumes general effectiveness of coaching and then compares conditions to determine the degree to which various aspects of the coaching, of the coach or of the client impact on outcome. If one accepts the assumption of general effectiveness (e.g. as demonstrated by the studies quoted above) the experimental conditions of this type of research can be a lot less stringent. In particular, client, coach or sponsor satisfaction can be used as the outcome variable, and one does not need to employ randomised controlled groups, because the various conditions create proper comparison samples within the study.

We have found the following eight studies which explore the question of *what sort* of coaching is effective; in other words, *which* coaching models, personality matches, or coaching behaviours make a significant difference to clients?

Scoular and Linley (2006) looked at how both (1) a 'goal-setting' intervention at the beginning of the conversation and (2) personality (dis-)similarities between coach and client as measured by MBTI impact on perceived effectiveness. The sample size was $N = 117$ clients and $N = 14$ coaches. No statistically significant difference resulted for outcome measurements at two and eight weeks after the session between 'goal-setting' and 'no goal-setting'; but when the coach and client differed on particular aspects of the personality instrument (the MBTI 'temperaments') the outcome scores were significantly higher.

Stewart et al. (2008) looked at how both client personality and client self-efficacy correlate with coaching outcome. They measured so-called big-five personality factors (Digman, 1990) and general self-efficacy (see Schwarzer et al., 1999) for 110 clients and correlated these with coaching outcome. They found moderate positive effects for conscientiousness, openness, emotional stability and general self-efficacy, but warned that other factors are likely to play a role as well.

Boyce et al. (2010) studied 74 coach–client relationships in a U.S. military academy where clients were cadets and coaches were senior military leaders who had had some training in executive coaching. The study analysed the impact of relational aspects (rapport, trust and commitment) and matching criteria (demographic commonality, behavioural compatibility and coach credibility) on coaching outcome. Their main findings were that matching had no significant impact on outcome, whilst relationship, as assessed by both client (explained proportion of variance around 50 per cent) and coach (explained proportion of variance around 25 per cent), affected outcomes significantly.

With a sample of internal coaches working alongside a leadership development programme within a manufacturing company involving 30 coach–client pairs, Baron and Morin (2009 and 2012) were able to show that coaching clients' rating of the *working alliance*[1] as a measure of the coaching relationship correlated with coaching

1.   Working alliance, as originally defined by Greenson (1965), is a measure for the strength of the coaching relationship. Bordin (1979) suggested that the working alliance can be thought of as a combination of agreement on tasks, agreement on goals and strength of bonds. Based on

outcomes (measured in terms of changes in client self-efficacy, explained proportion of variance around 25 per cent) whilst coaches' ratings of the working alliance did not correlate with outcomes significantly.

De Haan et al. (2011) examine how various executive coaching interventions make a difference to clients. Seventy-one coaching clients, from as many organisations, reported on the various interventions of their coaches and these ratings were compared with their evaluations. In that work, De Haan et al. found no distinction among specific coach interventions, leading to the conclusion that effectiveness is much less correlated with technique or intervention than by factors common to all coaching, such as the relationship, empathic understanding, positive expectations etc.

De Haan et al. (2013) build on the previous study to research the relative impact and importance of various common factors for 156 new executive coaching clients and 34 experienced coaches. The purpose of this research was to look at various elements common to *all* coaching approaches (the 'common factors') and to measure which of these are likely to have the highest positive impact on clients. The study showed that client perceptions of the outcome of coaching were significantly related to their perceptions of the working alliance, client self-efficacy and perceptions of coaching interventions ('generalised techniques') of the coach. The client–coach relationship strongly mediated the impact of self-efficacy and the majority of techniques on coaching outcomes (except for perceived explicit focus on goals and helping the client to make discoveries), suggesting that the relationship is the key factor in coaching outcome.

One final article stands out in particular as it is the only quantitative study we have found analysing executive coaching outcome on the basis of genuine interaction data from videotaping initial coaching sessions (Ianiro et al., 2012). Ianiro, Schermuly and Kauffeld analysed the full interchange within 33 first coaching sessions with trainee psychologists as coaches and young professions as clients, in terms of both the client's and the coach's interpersonal behaviour, over two basic dimensions: affiliation and dominance. Findings

Bordin's (1979) model, Horvath and Greenberg (1986) designed the Working Alliance Inventory with three sub-variables: tasks, goals and bonds, which is now the most widely used of many well-validated tools to measure working alliance.

suggest that both (1) the coach's dominance behaviour and (2) similarity of dominance and affiliation behaviour between coach and client predict positive client ratings of goal-attainment after five sessions; whilst (2) also predicts positive client ratings of the relationship quality after five sessions.

The above studies constitute an emerging trend pointing at the importance of common factors as manifested through the coaching relationship. There are various helpful taxonomies of 'common factors' (e.g. Grencavage and Norcross, 1990; De Haan, 2008), focusing on relationship-, client-, coach-, change- and structure-related factors. The factors that have been studied so far include coach personality, client personality, generalised technique, relationship and self-efficacy. There are other factors of possible relevance, such as coach allegiance, client expectancy ('hope' or placebo-related factors) and 'client's life circumstances' that we hope will be opened up to quantitative research in the near future.

An excursion into psychotherapy outcome research

As also argued by McKenna and Davis (2009), executive coaches can learn from the fact that in the older and more established profession of psychotherapy these same questions of effectiveness have been studied since at least the 1930s (Rosenzweig, 1936). In this tradition, rigorous research findings which seemed initially unclear and contradictory have begun to yield convincing results (starting with Smith and Glass, 1977), so that the demonstration of generally high effectiveness of psychotherapy is now near universally accepted amongst professional practitioners.

In summary the answers to our initial questions, when applied to psychotherapy, are as follows:

- **Does psychotherapy work?** Yes, in fact, it has been demonstrated that the average psychotherapy client achieves a higher effect on the relevant scales than 80 per cent of the people in the control group ($d \approx 0.8$; Smith and Glass, 1977; Wampold, 2001). This is considered a large effect size in both psychology and medicine.
- **What aspects of psychotherapy work?** Different interventions, approaches, models and protocols don't appear to make any difference in effectiveness. The aspects that dominate are *common* to all approaches, e.g. client context (what happens outside the therapeutic relationship); therapist characteristics (including

empathy, understanding, respect, warmth and authenticity, being attractive; inspiring confidence and appearing confident, the therapist's own mental health and the ability to tailor the therapy to the patient); and the relationship between client and therapist during the session (Cooper, 2008; Norcross, 2011). Common factors[2] are therefore central to effectiveness in psychotherapy.

- **Under what circumstances do we find differential effects?** Not a lot is known yet but there are strong indications that motivational factors such as the therapist's *allegiance* to their approach and the client's *expectations* are more important than was previously thought (Wampold, 2001). These are also common factors.

For a more detailed appreciation of psychotherapy outcome research and its relevance in the executive-coaching profession, see De Haan (2008) and McKenna and Davis (2009).

One can always argue that these intriguing and convincing findings from psychotherapy are not relevant for coaching, because the investigations were conducted with professional therapists working clinically with clients suffering from mental health problems such as depression and anxiety, which is markedly different from the needs and issues typically addressed in executive coaching. On the other hand, these are convincing results based on meta-analysis of multiple rigorous studies, of a rigour we are not likely to achieve in coaching.

A number of other curious facts from research into the effectiveness of psychotherapy:

- For large groups of patients, it is possible to show that 'therapy' is more effective than 'no therapy', and indeed more effective than 'placebo therapy', but the differences compared with the latter are minimal (Lambert and Bergin, 1994).
- Therapists' approaches in the therapy sessions themselves seem to have more in common than their theoretical approaches would lead one to believe (Corsini and Wedding, 1989).

2. The idea of *common factors* was already introduced by Rosenzweig (1936). He argues that if all professional therapies are equally effective, there is a good chance that the ingredients they have in common will determine the effectiveness of therapy – and not the specific interventions of an individual school of therapy. The active ingredients of therapy must therefore be common to all approaches. Examples are the relationship, the setting, the expectations, the personalities of coach and client, the presence of an ideology or approach, etc.

- Some therapists are successful in every technique, others are unsuccessful in every technique (Lambert, 1989).
- Experience, education and length of supervision are poor indicators of success (Beutler et al., 1986). Indeed, inexperienced and non-professional therapists sometimes turn out to be more effective than experienced and trained colleagues (Dumont, 1991).
- Within the generally influential variable of the personality of the therapist, the following aspects appear to have a positive effect on outcome:
  - Empathy, respect, warmth and genuineness – the criteria emphasised by Carl Rogers (Rogers, 1957; Goldfried et al., 1990).
  - Creating an attractive (!), trustworthy and expert impression, in that order (McNeal et al., 1987).
  - The emotional well-being of the therapist (Beutler et al., 1986).
  - The ability to let go of one's own value system and to communicate within that of the client (see Beutler et al., 1994; also Chapter 12 of this book).

What works for whom?

The question which naturally concerns us most as a coach is: what will work for this coachee? Which approach and which method can I apply in order to best help *this* coachee, with *this* problem, in *this* coaching session? Clearly, there is no obvious answer to this question, if only because:

- In principle, any approach can be applied to any coaching issue.
- Research shows that effectiveness may be relatively independent of the approach adopted (Lambert, 1989).
- Problems are multi-layered: coachees often ask for a certain type of 'treatment' but, at a deeper level, they need something quite different (consider, for example, the coachee who seeks advice because she is afraid of giving herself advice).
- Coaches themselves have preferences and talents that fit in with one of the approaches: for example, if you as a coach are blessed with really good listening skills, why deny yourself the person-centred approach?

However, something can be said about the effectiveness of each method; moreover, there are also some research results (see, for example, Roth and Fonagy, 1996). Most of the suggestions below are no more than conjectures, resulting from research and our own experiences as coaches and coachees. The four approaches are discussed in the order in which they have been raised previously in this book.

An example

She's a woman in a 'macho' organisation with an abrasive business culture. She didn't have the chance to go to university – her parents thought it unnecessary – but she is clever and has progressed from administrative worker to insurance specialist. Her husband has been unable to keep up with her progress. He trivialises what she does and would prefer that she stay at home with the children. She feels little understood by those around her, including her boss. Her boss notices that sometimes she freezes completely when they are discussing her work. At those times she feels undervalued by him, but doesn't dare to say so. They are unable to work it out together and he refers her to a coach. The coach might have chosen a provocative approach by trivialising her contributions even more, which could have helped the coachee find her strength through anger. The coach opts for a different, more person-centred approach, however. The coachee talks about her work a lot and slowly her feelings, which fluctuated from feeling superior to feeling injured, develop into a growing self-confidence. The coach helps her to prepare for a performance appraisal with her boss, in which she stands up for herself and says what is bothering her. She asks explicitly for more appreciation for her work, and for a raise in salary. It works: she gains greater recognition from her boss – though the boss didn't refer anyone to that coach again.

1. The directive approach

While the directive approach is the one that emerges best from quantitative research this is partly because this approach, which focuses on measurable results, simply lends itself best to research of this nature (Roth and Fonagy, 1996). Directive approaches are particularly successful in clinical cases of depression and phobias. In these areas, directive approaches are almost 'unbeatable' when compared to other approaches: coachees start to believe in the future again and

Figure 11.1 Because we still know so little about the effectiveness of
coaching, choosing the right coach and the right approach
is often still mainly a matter of taste and following adver-
tising slogans

work systematically on different, more effective behaviours. If we
look at the directive coaching methods in this book, we can see that
the GROW METHOD and the SOLUTION-FOCUSED METHOD are the easiest and quickest to apply, due to their step-by-step, coach-directed
nature, and often provide a solution in short and informal coaching
conversations as well.

- A step-by-step model such as the GROW METHOD can be learned
  quickly and easily. The coachee always takes something away
  from the session: (s)he brainstorms about possible approaches,
  lists those approaches and makes a considered decision personally. Moreover, this method helps to structure thinking, and to
  examine: 'What was our goal again?'
  (*Special use:*) We prefer to use the GROW METHOD when a
  coaching conversation becomes aimless or 'plodding'. Asking
  about the 'goal' and following up with a systematic exploration

of subsequent steps can restore dynamism to the coaching, and a focus on results.

(*Contra-indication:*) The GROW METHOD is not recommended where strong emotions are involved: it is a highly practical method that completely skims over emotions, and this can result in the coachee feeling completely misunderstood. This method can also reinforce unworkable solutions, because it does not even pretend to investigate the underlying 'issue behind the issue'.

- The SOLUTION-FOCUSED METHOD is suited to coachees who are anxious about the future and have lost heart somewhat. This method often increases the coachee's enthusiasm and belief in the future. Moreover, this approach encourages the coachee to draw on reserves that are already present but are hidden from or inaccessible to them.

(*Special use:*) This type of coaching is especially applicable where the coachee has already fretted a lot about his or her problem and accompanying difficulties, and is somewhat 'stuck' in the past and in previous, unsuccessful approaches.

(*Contra-indication:*) Some solution-focused therapy manuals classify coachees as 'visitors', 'complainers' and 'customers' (De Jong and Berg, 2001) and express a clear preference for the latter – in other words, for coachees who see themselves as part of their problem and are prepared to work on themselves (see Chapter 6). Clearly, this method is therefore less suitable for 'difficult' coachees who do not want to change and who tend to blame others, perhaps even their own coach.

2. The person-centred approach

The person-centred approach offers a helpful basis for any coaching. Being open to the person of the coachee is very valuable in any coaching situation. The counsellor is concerned almost exclusively with 'being open'. As in the analytic approach, the quality of person-centred counselling usually increases with increasing experience and supervision, because these refine and train listening skills. Because the counsellor adds far fewer personal interpretations to the coachee's story, the risk of the coaching breaking down due to its careless application is greatly reduced.

- Our COUNSELLING METHOD is in fact hardly a method, more a compact reminder of the main aspects of person-centred coaching.

(*Special use:*) In our experience, the COUNSELLING METHOD is particularly applicable where there is a lack of self-confidence and assertiveness, because this method devotes constant attention to the coachee: how (s)he feels at this moment and sees his or her problems.

(*Contra-indication:*) Where the coachee asks for or needs – and is strong enough for! – a critical 'sparring partner', who sees through excuses and highlights weaknesses, the COUNSELLING METHOD is less suitable because it is primarily supportive and uncritical.

3. The analytic approach

The analytic approach is the most meticulous when it comes to exploring the problem, and is exceptionally powerful in that it subjects the interaction between coach and coachee to explicit discussion. The analytic approach prides itself on being better able than other approaches to handle multi-layered problems and coachees who do not (yet) see themselves as part of their problems. There is clear evidence that psychoanalytic therapy achieves good results in cases of depression and personality disorder (Roth and Fonagy, 1996). This is perhaps the most 'thorough' coaching approach, where coach and coachee look at possible courses of action only once the current issue has been exhaustively explored. Even then, when the coachee has mapped out a course of action and wants to proceed, the coach continues to ask questions and draw attention to alternative assumptions and courses of action. As a consequence, analytic coaching is not always quick or easy to put into action.

• The ANALYTIC METHOD and ORGANISATION COACH METHOD. Like the COUNSELLING METHOD, these methods provide a sound basis for any coaching: listening properly to the problem is central, in such a way that new, previously unseen aspects of that problem come into view.

(*Special use:*) The ANALYTIC METHOD starts where the directive approach leaves off: with coachees who have a strong emotional involvement in their own issue and do not at first (want to) acknowledge their own part in their problem, or the issues underlying their explicit issue. Instead of looking only at the 'customer' in the coachee, the ANALYTIC METHOD endeavours to expose the 'visitor' or 'complainer' in the coachee.

(*Contra-indication:*) Effective analytic coaching calls for a great deal of training and supervision to develop the sensitivity of the coach and teach him or her how to handle transference. This method is not recommended for inexperienced coaches. The analytic method is also not recommended in short-term, results-oriented coaching, and where the coachee lacks the self-confidence needed to cope with challenging interpretations.

- The LADDER METHOD is primarily a way of applying the analytic approach in less intensive or frequent coaching. The LADDER METHOD is a specific translation of analytic principles, which can thereby be applied to more specific issues.

  (*Special use:*) This method is suitable where a coachee wants to think about his or her own assumptions systematically and is prepared to subject personal plans and emotions to a critical and strict examination.

  (*Contra-indication:*) The LADDER METHOD is less suitable for non-specific issues, or where strong emotions are involved.

4. The paradoxical approach

This fourth approach is manipulative in nature. For that reason alone, many coaches never want to apply it in practice. The paradoxical approach does not combine well with the person-centred approach, because of the coach's lack of transparency when using the former. If coachees are in a particular defence that is interfering with the coaching itself, and if the coach lacks the time or skill to analyse that defence, paradoxical coaching can be used as an alternative to the directive and analytic approaches. We ourselves use this approach only on a short-term basis and only if the coachee, in our view, is manipulating us or sending out strongly ambiguous messages. The IRONIC METHOD is used more frequently, and is easier to use, than the more radical PARADOXICAL METHOD. Although it makes sense in most cases to use a certain approach consistently, this is much less true for the paradoxical approach: we can use it once, to stir things up or to influence the coaching relationship in some way. After that, we can continue with one of the other approaches, preferably a directive approach.

- The IRONIC METHOD is particularly useful where:
  - the coachee asks for advice, but the coach does not think that advice will help much ; or

– where the coach wants to give advice, but encounters resistance in giving it.

For example (De Haan, 1999):

– When a price has to be paid for accepting the advice: irony continues to point to other approaches even when a particular course has already been embarked upon.
– When advice cannot be understood at face value: irony creates an opportunity for a deeper, more integrated understanding.
– When the advice is too painful or disappointing: irony raises no obstacles, but provides scope for other ideas.
– When the advice repeats something that was dismissed earlier: repetition only prompts more resistance, whereas irony places the same advice in a different perspective.

(*Special use:*) When the coachee finds it difficult to take responsibility for his or her own situation: the IRONIC METHOD places the responsibility on the coachee. When a more 'reflective approach' is required (in other words, when we want to make

Figure 11.2 Sometimes, after a lot of searching, we finally end up with the right coach

the other person think more) irony offers ambiguity, and thus scope for reflection.

(*Contra-indication:*) This method is risky if the coachee lacks self-confidence, or lacks confidence in the coaching. Take care not to apply an ironic approach as an 'excuse'. In a situation where it is hard for a coach to give a specific piece of advice directly because (s)he fears coachee resistance, irony can be an unhelpful 'easy way' of 'saying it anyway'.

In conclusion, we recommend that coaches should:

• choose a coaching style that fits in with their own personality;
• broaden their coaching style by trying out other methods;
• continue to develop general coaching skills, such as empathy, sensitivity and dealing with resistance, by (for example) receiving coaching themselves in the form of supervision (Hawkins and Shohet, 2000) or peer consultation (De Haan, 2004).

For more information on the use of various methods, see the following chapter, where we discuss the use of more specific interventions.

Summary: choosing the right method

There is no single best method of coaching and no single method of coaching is equally effective in every situation. The sensitivity and personality of the coach, the issue and personality of the coachee, the goals of the coaching, and the context in which it is taking place are all factors that influence the effectiveness of the methods described here. What works for whom? depends not only on the problem and the coachee, but also on the objective, the context and the personality of the coach. Assumptions for correct application of the different coaching methods:

Method	When can it be used?	Recommended where there is/are	Not recommended where there is/are
GROW METHOD	Broadly applicable, even to short, specific issues	High motivation, but little idea of possible ways to move forward	Emotional issues; non-specific issues; double meanings
SOLUTION-FOCUSED METHOD	Broadly applicable, especially to practical issues	Discouragement, anxiety about the future	'Visitors' and 'complainers', i.e. those not prepared to consider their own share in the problem
COUNSELLING METHOD	Broadly applicable, especially in a longer-term coaching relationship	Lack of self-confidence or self-motivation	Need for a critical sparring partner
ANALYTIC METHOD ORGANISATION COACH METHOD	Broadly applicable, especially to multilayered and emotional problems	'Visitors' and 'complainers'; multi-layered issues	Need to achieve quick results and find solutions; low self-confidence
LADDER METHOD	Multilayered problems, including short, specific issues	Willingness and ability to consider their own assumptions	Non-specific issues, highly emotional issues
IRONIC METHOD	Broadly applicable	Those that ask for advice; those that do not take responsibility	Low self-confidence; lack of confidence in coaching
PARADOXICAL METHOD	In the case of ambiguous, internally contradictory questions to the coach	Strongly ambiguous messages and unclear motivation for coaching	No strong and absolutely necessary reasons for using it

NB: These suggestions are merely indications and are generally not, or at most barely, substantiated by independent research.
Conclusion: be genuine and stick with an approach that suits you!

Part III

Reflection on coaching

Introduction:
'Individuality'

'Helping' conversations are generally conversations in which someone thinks *with* you, but not *for* you. Ironically, therefore, they are often conversations in which someone is deeply involved and absorbed in your story, while at the same time remaining detached, avoiding total immersion. We have all had experiences that remind us that a truly objective and independent perspective is often more valuable than input from a compassionate colleague who 'suffers with you'. As a final reflection on 'helping' conversations, this part of the book contains four chapters which are intended to help to preserve the independence of coach and coachee. This simultaneous independence and helpfulness is often a matter of setting boundaries: boundaries between the coachee and the coach, as well as boundaries between the coachee and his or her organisation, boundaries between the coach and the other facets of the coach's personal and working life, and boundaries within the coaching relationship. We hope that these chapters can help strengthen the individuality and fortitude of the coach, who knows that (s)he can fall back on:

- the anchoring of his or her work in personal skills and qualifications (Chapter 12);
- the autonomous learning process that the coachee goes through, which takes place largely outside the coaching context (Chapter 13);
- organisational structures in the context of the coachee as a support for his/her interpretations (Chapter 14); and
- the boundaries of internal or external coaching, which are protected by clear codes of conduct (Chapter 15).

The four chapters go together in pairs, as in Part I.

1. Chapter 12 contains a list of *skills of the coach*, ranging from values and ethics, attitude, knowledge and relational skills to specific styles and interventions.

2. Chapter 13 concerns the development of the *skills of the coachee* and so examines the coachee's learning styles, both during coaching and during his/her career more generally. Finally we consider the limits of learning as a coachee, when referral and solutions other than coaching are indicated.

3. Chapter 14 demonstrates how difficult it is to *monitor boundaries in coaching conversations* properly, because both coach and coachee bring different aspects of their personalities with them to the coaching process, while the coachee's organisation also plays a significant role in the sessions.

4. Finally, Chapter 15 examines the *boundaries between internal and external coaching* – i.e. the pros and cons of both – and outlines ethical boundaries in the coaching relationship, in the form of 'rules of conduct' for coaching.

12

The capabilities of the coach

There is a wide range of literature on the skills of the coach. Most books and articles about coaching contain directions and practical recommendations described from the basis of a single perspective or preferred style, such as the GROW model, Rational Emotive Therapy or Transactional Analysis. In our view, there is no single best method of coaching and different coaching styles are effective in different situations. Chapter 5 contains a broad overview of four basic approaches for coaches: *insight-focused*, *coachee-focused*, *problem-focused* and *solution-focused*. The talents and personality of the coach, the issues and personality of the coachee, the goals of the coaching and the context in which it is taking place all determine the effectiveness of any approach. An experienced coach is aware of his or her own preferred approach or approaches, and is able to deviate from them if something different appears to be more effective. *Flexibility* in choosing a personal coaching approach is perhaps the most important skill a coach can have.

However, in a general sense, there are many things to be said about the attitudes and values, knowledge, methodical skills and behavioural techniques displayed by 'good' coaches. The following pages contain some suggestions regarding the skills of the coach, based on different layers of the 'coach personality'. Ideally, those different layers should fit together well and support each other, resulting in an 'integrated coach'. Our personality structure starts with a relatively stable core and moves towards a more changeable outside: from convictions, values and ethics, to attitudes, knowledge, relational skills and specific styles, and lastly, to behaviour.

The convictions and values of the coach

The convictions and values of coaches can be as diverse as those of different family backgrounds and cultures. We do often find that

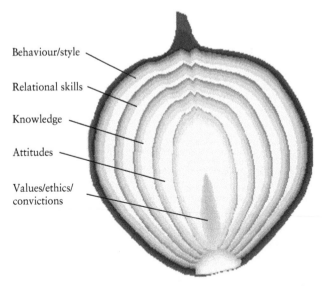

Behaviour/style

Relational skills

Knowledge

Attitudes

Values/ethics/
convictions

Figure 12.1 The coach as 'onion': structure of the personality of the
coach in five nested layers

coaches have a high regard for personal or cultural achievements and
a certain openness to convictions other than their own.

Downey (1999) challenges coaches to consider the following basic
convictions, which can underpin their effectiveness even when they
are personally in doubt about the best way forward:

- Coachees have huge potential.
- Coachees have a unique map of reality – not to be confused with
  reality itself.
- Coachees have good intentions, for themselves and for others.
- Coachees achieve their own objectives – perfectly – at all times!

Because coaching often concerns very personal problems, where one
person takes the role of client and the other the role of helper, there is a
risk that the coachee will see the coach too much as a 'leader' or 'guide'
and attach excessive importance to individual comments or signals. We
have often been confronted in our own practice with coachees who
could still remember certain comments years after the event. A good
coach is well aware of the impact that coaching can have on the coachee
and weighs his or her words and gestures carefully. The coach is continually aware that the coaching is for the coachee's benefit, not for the

Figure 12.2 The coach has many different layers, and they must all fit
            together properly

greater glory of the coach, and should therefore focus exclusively on the
interests of the coachee. The coach should therefore refer the coachee
elsewhere if (s)he feels unable to help further, and has a reliable referral
network of fellow coaches and therapists. These ethical aspects of coaching are examined in more detail in Chapter 15, where we consider codes
of conduct.

The attitudes of the coach

As far as we are concerned, the attitude of a coach is characterised by:

- empathy, respect, warmth and authenticity in relation to the
  coachee (see also Chapter 7)
- tolerance and openness to different values and opinions
- availability – calm and space for the coachee
- an appropriate balance between detachment and involvement
- an encouraging and gentle approach towards the coachee
- readiness to let the other person take initiative and responsibility

- an attitude of service towards the coachee, helping him/her to (learn how to) do it in person
- an inclination to give as little advice as possible (even if that is requested), based on the conviction that giving advice is often an insult to the other person, who has already spent a long time thinking about the issue and can give the best advice to him/ herself
- a confrontational approach only if the coachee can take it and will benefit from it, otherwise a preference for supportive interventions
- humour and an ability to put things into perspective.

The knowledge of the coach

What knowledge does a good coach have? This depends partly on the coachee's question (see also Chapter 1). Where the coaching concerns questions that centre on content and specialist knowledge ('what' and 'how' questions) the coach should also have that specialist knowledge. Yet many questions asked by coachees are more personal in nature, with a link to their work ('who' questions). For example, these are questions about how the coachee holds his or her own in the organisation, how (s)he works with others or acts with respect to his or her managers. When addressing this type of question specialist knowledge is less important, and can even be an impediment (the coach might switch from coaching to giving expert advice). What knowledge, then, is relevant to addressing these 'who' questions?

- In the first place, *self-knowledge:* the coach is aware of the way in which (s)he tends to view problems, and is able to look at the coachee from multiple perspectives. The coach knows the patterns and traps lying in wait for the unwary coach (for example, being quick to give advice, asking suspicious questions, or emphasising only the positive in the coachee's account); and is aware of the emotions (s)he experiences during sessions and how to manage them professionally. The coach is also aware of his or her main qualities, which are relevant because the biggest coaching pitfalls are often associated with them.
- Good coaches have knowledge about the development of individuals and groups. They know which problems are associated with particular life stages and what patterns may emerge in them.
- Because coaching is always work-related, coaches also have knowledge about the development of organisations. This includes

a sound understanding of management and change. Context-less coaching is doomed to failure (see also Chapter 14).

- Coaching is not therapy. Nevertheless, a basic knowledge of psychodynamics and psychotherapy is necessary to enable the coach to choose the right interventions, to keep a watchful eye on the boundary between coaching and psychotherapy, and to make timely referrals.
- As stated above, no single coaching style is always effective. Knowledge of different approaches to coaching, interventions and levels of intervention, as well as of your own preferred styles and interventions, is necessary in order to be able to tailor your approach to the coachee in his or her context. It is also necessary in order for you to be aware what your own contribution is at any moment in the coaching conversation.
- Coaches have extensive knowledge of communication techniques (conversational techniques, influencing styles) – in order to be effective personally in directing the conversation and to make the coachee aware of his or her effectiveness in communication and in using influence.

The strategic skills of the coach

- The coach needs a number of skills in order to mould his or her approach consistently over a longer period and so create a context for constructive interventions within coaching sessions:
- Coaches are able to engage in and maintain diverse types of *relationship*: they have the ability to build up and wind down relationships with a wide range of coachees, to create the working alliances in which coaching becomes possible. It helps in this respect to be clear, unambiguous and consistent, and to be able to tolerate a wide range of feelings, both within oneself and in others.
- An effective coach is able to use the different areas of knowledge outlined above effectively in the coaching context. This starts with *effective management of expectations*, an issue that comes up afresh in every session. The coach is transparent and checks regularly that the goals of the coaching are clear and attainable.
- An effective coach *can work consistently with different approaches* – for example, insight-focused, coachee-focused, problem-focused and solution-focused – and makes a considered choice, depending on the question, the coachee and his/her context.
- Irrespective of the approach adopted, a coach is good at *recognising patterns and mental models*. The coach is on the lookout

during the sessions for possible links between the 'here and now' and the coachee's issue as presented.

- Perhaps most importantly, a coach is able to manage his or her own many painful experiences in coaching conversations, as in the case of:
  - ambiguity, 'not understanding' and 'not knowing'
  - managing his/her own emerging 'stuff', in the form of personal judgements, recollections and expectations
  - handling criticism, unrealistic expectations and transference.

Along the lines of the list of ten defences in Chapter 8, to which the coach as well as the coachee must not fall prey, the coach would do well to develop an *eleventh defence*, namely a buffer between stimulus and response – staying calm and attentive in a situation marked by painful stimuli.[1]

The specific interventions of the coach

A useful model for the different specific skills that the coach can use at any moment in a coaching conversation is provided by John Heron (1975). The six styles proposed by Heron can be represented effectively (Figure 12.3) in our 'window onto the coach' from Chapter 2.[2]

Three of these styles are relatively directive (challenging, directing and informing) and three are more facilitative (releasing, discovering, supporting). The styles can also be viewed in complementary pairs, as follows:

- *Discovering* and *directing* are both strongly directional, one from the coachee and the other from the coach.
- *Releasing* and *challenging* are both confrontational, although the former is much less critical of the coachee than the latter.
- *Supporting* and *informing* are both supportive, the former on the basis of feelings and the latter on the basis of content.

In the application of the different coaching approaches from Part II, it is clear that each of those approaches relies particularly on a subset of the six styles. For example, the COUNSELLING METHOD makes use almost

1. This strategic skill is sometimes referred to as a *negative capability* (Bion, 1970).
2. We have renamed Heron's 'six categories of counselling intervention' as follows: prescriptive–directing, cathartic–releasing, confronting–chal-

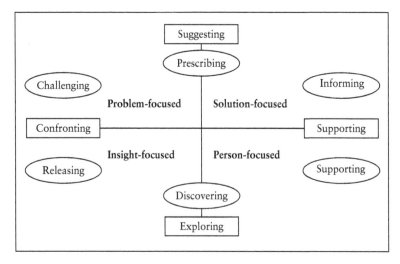

Figure 12.3 The window onto the coach: six specific behavioural
styles of coaches

exclusively of *discovering* and *supporting* – even *releasing* would shift
the perspective too much towards the coach and weaken the internal
'locus of evaluation'. Similarly, *discovering* and *releasing* are the main
styles for the ANALYTIC METHOD, while *directing, informing* and *challenging* are the main styles of the PARADOXICAL METHOD. In the SOLUTION-
FOCUSED METHOD, *directing* and *informing* are the main styles used by
the coach, who uses a lot of *discovering* and *supporting* within those
styles at a more content-related level, while the GROW METHOD can also
use *challenging* in addition to those styles.

The following tables contain more detailed information on the different coaching styles. Before you read these tables in detail, it is recommended that you inquire about your own dominant coaching styles.
In Appendix E we present the Coaching Behaviours Questionnaire, a
tool with which to explore your own coaching styles.

lenging, supportive– supporting, informative–informing, catalytic–discovering. We adopt Heron's definitions in terms of skills here, but their
placement in the 'window onto the coach' is ours.

Figure 12.4 Coaching can be a very enjoyable activity

Directive coaching styles

1. Directing

Specific behaviours:	• Giving directions, advice, recommendations, suggestions • Contributing to alternatives and suggestions of the coachee • Insisting on a specific approach • Motivating with clear instructions
Examples of interventions:	• 'Have you also thought of ...?' • 'I think it would be good for you to ...' • 'My approach is ...' • 'I suggest ...'
Traps to avoid:	• Giving unsolicited advice • Taking over and imposing solutions • Directing the conversation too much • Creating dependence on the part of the coachee • Weak application by doubting, hesitating or undermining your own advice – or by being over-controlling
When to use:	• When the coachee lacks self-confidence • When the coachee is unable to direct own learning • When (ethical, legal, safety, professional) guidelines are imposed

2. Informing

Specific behaviours:	• Imparting information and knowledge • Presenting new perspectives • Adding interpretations and summaries • Checking understanding • Answering questions
Examples of interventions:	• 'That book contains further information on ...' • 'To my knowledge the most important approaches are ...' • 'That seems (il-)logical, because ...' • 'My own answer to that is as follows ...'
Traps to avoid:	• Overloading with information • Too much jargon • Too little underlying structure • Too little linking with the directing style: unclear why information is given

- Too much emphasis on coach as 'teacher': teaching versus learning focus

When to use:
- If asked to explain something
- Adding missing information
- Describing one's own experiences
- Structuring the coachee's story

3. Challenging

Specific behaviours:
- Giving feedback
- Posing direct questions
- Testing (underlying) assumptions
- Challenging possible defences, excuses and evasions
- Encouraging (self-)reflection

Examples of interventions:
- 'That's not how you come across to me.'
- 'Do you realise that you are not making use of important talents?'
- 'I am not sure you are very clear on this.'
- 'Are you assuming that it is the same problem as last year?'
- 'One could also look at that quite differently ...'
- 'I have just heard a lot of positive things about your report.'

Traps to avoid:
- All of the traps associated with the giving of feedback[3]
- Too much emphasis on the coach as 'independent assessor'
- External 'locus of evaluation'[4]
- Putting relationship to the test over a 'trivial' matter
- Escalation to competition between coach and coachee

When to use:
- To increase the (self-)insight of the coachee
- To increase insight into perceptions of others, or into the possible consequences of actions
- To challenge the coachee to reconsider automatic assumptions
- To reinforce self-confidence by providing positive feedback

3.   See also Chapter 10 of *Learning with Colleagues*.
4.   See also Chapter 7 of this book.

Facilitative coaching styles

1. Discovering

Specific behaviours:	• Asking questions and listening • Reflecting back statements or feelings of the coachee • Paraphrasing and summarising • Inviting new perspectives from the coachee
Examples of interventions:	• 'How would you like to start?' • 'What do you mean by ...?' • '...?' • 'What advice would you offer someone else in your situation?' • 'What do you think about it yourself?' • 'What would you do differently?'
Traps to avoid:	• Too many questions • Asking closed questions • Suggestions concealed in questions • Structuring too soon • Being led by your own curiosity instead of that of the coachee • Contributing your own experiences and allowing them to dominate • Not clarifying – by asking! – the objectives
When to use:	• Good basis for *any* coaching conversation! • To foster deeper understanding, especially in the coachee • To help the coachee assume more responsibility • To promote commitment, self-motivation, self-evaluation and self-confidence

2. Supporting

Specific behaviours:	• Expressing appreciation • Displaying confidence • Displaying availability, involvement, concern • Explicitly increasing self-confidence • Expressing shared feelings
Examples of interventions:	• 'You did that well' • 'I can imagine that you're worried about that.' • 'I'll be here again tomorrow morning if you need me' • 'I am confident that you will make this a success' • 'Don't worry if all of the details have not been worked out.'

Traps to avoid:
- Flattery, false compliments and exaggeration
- Against all odds: 'yes, but ...'-type support
- Exaggerated protection; patronising the coachee
- Being held back by own inhibitions
- Giving mixed signals
- Levelling off using 'plusses' and 'minuses'

When to use:
- To build morale and self-confidence
- To offer support in taking risks
- As an approach to 'withdrawn' coachees
- To encourage learning from success

3. Releasing

Specific behaviours:
- Active and focused listening
- Asking follow-through questions
- Asking about what 'seems to be hard to say', or 'what is left unsaid'
- Self-disclosure, empathy and sharing own feelings
- Reflections on the coachee's feelings at this moment
- Inviting underlying and different perspectives

Examples of interventions:
- 'Why do you lack self-confidence?'
- 'What is going on here?'
- 'By the way in which you talk about it you seem to be saying ...'
- 'What exactly?'
- 'What you seem to be talking about less this time is ...'
- 'Is it difficult to talk about that here?'
- 'But you don't seem to feel confident about that.'
- 'That leaves me feeling rather lost.'

Traps to avoid:
- Filling in too much for the coachee
- Psychologising; going too deep
- Making a mountain out of a molehill
- Showing sympathy too easily
- Losing own independence by feedback or support
- Denying or criticising coachee's feelings (unintentionally)
- Putting up barriers for the coachee

When to use:
- To deepen insight
- To make space for new perspectives
- When the coachee feels blocked or incompetent
- When the coachee is frustrated, demotivated or angry
- When the coachee is afraid to take risks

Finally, we give a list of common and more elaborate coaching interventions which are not so easy to classify in terms of Heron's coaching styles:

Interventions	Matching coaching approaches	Matching coaching styles
Reflection on the coachee's use of language, e.g.: • talking without using the first person: 'you', 'people', 'everyone' • talking in terms of impossibilities • indirect allusions which may refer to this conversation or the coach, for example.	Analytic	Depending on directive or facilitative intervention: *informing* or *discovering*
Pattern recognition, such as reflection on: • links with what was said in a previous session • repetition of certain words or expressions • use of certain types of imagery and associations.	Analytic	Depending on directive or facilitative intervention: *releasing* or *challenging*
Converting objections into opportunities, e.g.: • by using the question 'How could it be done?' if the coachee keeps pointing out why something cannot be done • by the 'miracle question' (see Chapter 6).	Directive Solution focused	Depending on directive or facilitative intervention: *directing* or *discovering*
Research in the form of questionnaires, e.g. concerning personality, stress indicators, learning styles, leadership styles, team roles etc.	Directive Analytic	Combination of *directing* (handing out questionnaires) and *discovering* (about the coachee)
Homework in the form of diary, biography, logbook, coaching conversation report, mind map, story, drawing, etc.	Directive	*Directing*
Exercises in the form of role-play with the coach or with the aid of a video camera in the workplace.	Directive	*Directing, informing* and *challenging*

Summary: the capabilities of the coach

The convictions held by different coaches can vary widely, but good coaches are transparent about them and open to alternatives.

The most important attitude is one of respect for the coachee and involvement in the coachee's learning process.

A successful coach has self-knowledge, knows his or her own style and is able to deviate from it if a different style appears to be more effective. In addition, (s)he has knowledge of:

- development of individuals and groups
- organisation and change management
- psychodynamics and psychotherapy
- approaches to coaching, interventions and levels of intervention
- communication techniques.

An effective coach is skilled at:

- maintaining relationships with a wide variety of coachees
- managing expectations
- working with different methods
- recognising patterns and mental models
- utilising painful impressions and experiences.

The behaviour of an effective coach can be characterised as focusing on the following six central coaching styles:

- directing or giving directions, advice and recommendations
- informing or giving information, knowledge and summaries
- challenging or increasing (self-)awareness and exploring assumptions
- discovering or deepening insight by facilitating self-exploration
- supporting or raising self-confidence and self-esteem
- releasing or exploring emotions which are blocking progress.

13
Learning through coaching

Coaching is a form of individual learning which helps people to progress in their professional development – their 'career'.[1] In this chapter we examine how coaching fits in with individual learning styles and individual careers. We also explore situations when coaching is perhaps not the best answer. As a coach, reflecting on the coachee's learning can help you emphasise the autonomy of the coachee and so avoid becoming too involved yourself. Finally, the role of the coach is to encourage the coachee's autonomous learning process. The coachee remains the owner of that process: (s)he will have to go through it in person!

An example
A female coachee is a manager in a government department. She has a chance to move up a level but her line manager has told her that, if she does, she will need to be able to delegate more effectively. She recounts her life story to the coach. Both her parents died when she was very young and she was raised by her stepfather. A kind-hearted man, he was on the road a lot in order to keep the family going financially and often came home late in the evening. She made a bargain with him that she, as a ten-year-old, would cook and put her little sisters to bed. She could do it, she argued, because she was very intelligent and caring and had a great sense of responsibility. In her adult life,

---

1. Earlier, in Chapter 8, we wrote about 'learning' as a possible defence for the coachee against new insight. In this chapter, we write about the opposite: learning not as a method of masking repression but as an expression of authentic progress and change.

she continues to organise a lot for others. So much in fact that it sometimes gets her into scrapes and now may even start to limit her next career move. It helps her hugely to make the connection between the events in her youth and her current position. In effect, she has continued to do what she once felt was necessary, something she was very successful at doing. Slowly but surely, she learns to set boundaries more effectively and to prioritise. It helps to become more and more aware of what she actually wants now, and what she considers important in her life. In the end, the sessions help her to become aware of the individual contribution she wants to make to society and she decides on a new move, outside the organisation.

Coaching and individual learning styles

Being coached is a very personal and completely unique experience. Mindful of Rogers' well-known words,[2] however, we can still perhaps make some general comments about this personal and unique experience. What is the impact of coaching, and how can a coach reinforce that impact? Coachees report that coaching can have an impact on many fronts – sometimes even apparently opposing ones – through (for example):

- facilitating reflection on one's day-to-day practice
- facilitating reflection on one's own role at work, and on one's own career
- providing a haven and support when going through transitions at work
- offering challenge and inspiration in breaking out of periods of stagnation at work
- helping find new answers and untapped potential
- allowing preparation and practice of a new attitude or new behaviour at work.

Learning is personal, and different professionals differ with regard to how they would prefer to learn (see *Learning with Colleagues*, Part III). In his book *Experiential Learning* (1984), Kolb describes four different learning styles. If we think of coaching as stimulating individual learning processes, it is important for a coach to know which learning style best suits the coachee. To this end Kolb drew up the

2 'The most personal is the most universal' – see Chapter 7.

learning style inventory, which we included in *Learning with Colleagues* as Appendix D. Kolb identifies the following learning styles:

Divergent
In this learning style you consider specific situations from many different perspectives and establish links between different aspects and approaches. Besides listening and looking carefully, your imagination and powers of observation help you to consider events, issues or problems from a variety of angles. This is a *divergent* learning style because you keep seeing new aspects, which keep leading to new meanings and values. It is especially suited to the appropriation of new experiences and the generation of new ideas. Interest in, and sensitivity to, personal and interpersonal aspects often go hand-in-hand with this learning style.

Assimilative
In this learning style you move from diverse observations and reflections to an integrated explanation or to theoretical models. Using precision and sharp logic, you judge information and models on their merits. This is an *assimilative* learning style, because you assimilate diverse ideas and information or adapt them to an encompassing theoretical framework. This learning style is especially suited to the inclusion of data in models, and when testing whether these models are complete and offer a basis for generalisation. The learner's interest lies mainly in the beauty and completeness of the models themselves, at the expense of interest in people or in practical matters.

Convergent
In this learning style you combine theory and practice in usable and achievable solutions. Using selective attention, problem-solving capability and progress-oriented decision-making, you adapt and apply models in order to provide new answers and solutions to practical questions. This is a *convergent* learning style, because the style helps you get to grips with complex and ambiguous experiences and transform them into a single experiment or defensible approach. This learning style is therefore eminently suited to situations where a single hypothesis or solution is necessary and possible. Concentrated attention and the nerve to break new ground and take decisions often go hand-in-hand with this learning style.

Accommodative
In this learning style you can achieve practical results by rolling up your sleeves, trying things out and seeking out new experiences. Using adaptability, commitment and entrepreneurship, you take steps to follow up choices and try out solutions. This is an *accommodative* learning style, because you react and adapt to changing circumstances. It is particularly suited to complex situations in which progress is required, and where 'trial-and-error' offers a good approach. The learner's interest here is often intuitive and implicit, directed towards action, influence, mastery and new experiences.

A coach can act within each of a number of facilitative roles (compare Chapter 16 of *Learning with Colleagues*), serving as:

- a developer within divergent learning, encouraging reflection and different ways of looking at things
- a teacher within assimilative learning, encouraging reading and research, linking with theory and literature and helping to structure divergent learning
- a process manager within convergent learning, preparing and testing new approaches
- a trainer within accommodative learning, giving support, looking for opportunities to practise and encourage actual application of skills and learning
- a sparring partner between the learning styles, encouraging balance and approaches other than the usual, preferred style
- a meta-teacher between the learning styles, inviting the coachee to look at the quality of the learning itself and at his or her own way of learning (in other words, inviting meta-learning).

Coaching may therefore facilitate learning processes in all of the different learning styles. Due to its conversational nature, however, and because it occurs away from the workplace, it is geared primarily towards divergent learning, just like the 'coaches' or 'consultants' in peer consultation (see Chapter 19 of *Learning with Colleagues*).

Coaching and individual careers

If we take a longer-term perspective, then coaching is located somewhere within the coachee's 'individual career' and aims to enrich and facilitate that career by raising his or her relationship with certain experiences, ambitions and issues for discussion The extent to which the longer term – and hence the coachee's career trajectory – is a subject of coaching depends, of course, on the objective of the coaching, and differs for each unique coaching relationship. If coaching has an impact, however, it will certainly have an impact on the coachee's future career as well. This is why we also consider its effects on professional careers.

Combining the insights within influential articles by Kanter (1989) and Arthur (1994), we can assume four different generic careers or 'career scripts':

- The *bureaucratic career* entails moves from rank to rank and job to job in a succession of hierarchical positions. In this pattern, people are not particularly attached to specific tasks or colleagues, but are often very loyal to the organisation as a whole. Progress in this career is vertical – the only way is up! If progress stagnates it is usually because the person concerned does not understand the rules of the game, or does not apply them properly.
- The *entrepreneurial career* is focused on entrepreneurship. In this script, professionals are entrepreneurial, creative, innovative and competitive. Once they have found their niche, they stay there. The more commercial success, the more income. Progress in this career is strongly linked to the extent to which someone is able to create new products or services. Progress stagnates when the business is not prepared to (continue to) grow.
- The *professional career* is a career based on expertise. The person concerned acquires status and reputation by excelling in professional knowledge and skills, for example in academia. The professional is very loyal to his or her specialism, but less so to the organisation. Progress is assessed in terms of an individual's response to increasingly demanding assignments. It stagnates when the professional notices, too late, that his or her specialism is no longer necessary and fails to develop a new specialism in time.
- The *boundaryless career* has no standardised script. Professionals write their own script while working on projects – often in a self-employed capacity or in temporary networks. They create progress by continually developing new things, both in terms of form and content, and by renewing their own network. Each new project brings a new challenge. Progress in this career takes place when the person concerned feels ready to take on increasingly complex and uncertain assignments. Progress stagnates if (s)he makes choices without carefully considering his or her own

interests, or lacks market discipline, resilience and/or powers of recovery.

These four types of career entail different sorts of learning issues. The following barriers can be identified:

- In the *bureaucratic career* there is a risk of passive, risk-averse learning behaviour and it is particularly difficult to develop accommodative learning.
- In the *entrepreneurial career*, the usual focus on action and objectives is at odds with the calm and reflection of divergent learning, in particular.
- In the *professional career*, there are already so many intrinsic, content challenges that these 'knowledge workers' sometimes do not take on extrinsic challenges and may have difficulty with application-oriented, convergent learning.
- In the *boundaryless career* there is a lot of experience of meta-learning, but professionals may be so exposed to fragmentation, discontinuity and an excess of information that confusion results, and systematic assimilative learning in particular becomes difficult.

Coaches can, as usual, point out what is missing and what appears to be going badly. They can help more generally by, on the one hand, helping the coachee to break out of periods of stagnation and, on the other, helping bring calm to periods of transition.[3] Professionals can go through substantial transitions, for example by acquiring new responsibilities in new jobs, new contacts with clients, and new sorts of assignments. These transitions call for new knowledge, skills and behaviour, which are themselves essential components of their learning processes. If a professional does not handle a transition well (s)he may be uncertain and unproductive for a while, and might even burn out. The dominant career thinking often associates difficulties in transitions with individuals 'not fitting in', 'not managing' or 'not being strong enough'. We prefer to describe problems of this sort as *relevant learning opportunities* that call, above all, for solid coaching.

Limits on coaching

So far we have considered a range of indicators for coaching and a variety of individual learning styles and careers to which coaches, in

---

3. Similar to the *confronting* of 'what could be done differently' versus the *supporting* of 'what is going well' in our 'window onto the coach' (Chapter 2).

our view, can make a useful contribution. However, when is coaching not the right answer? When would it be sensible to initiate a different learning activity or to refer the coachee to others? We believe that the limits of effective coaching have been reached in any situation where one of the following three statements applies.

The coachee presents puzzles instead of problems

The difference between *puzzles* and *problems* is that puzzles have a single, optimal solution that can be found with the right expertise, while problems have many solutions, but are never really completely resolved. A work-related problem that the coachee can solve using the Internet, or by looking up certain information inside the organisation is, in our view, not 'interesting' enough to bring to a coach. In more general terms it is useful, in the case of 'one-off' coaching issues, to consider whether coaching is necessarily the best answer or if it would be better just to call in an expert, as in the example below.

An example

A director of a small charity has placed an advertisement for an office manager, who will be only the third full-time employee of the organisation. He realises that this is an important expansion of the team and that he himself has little experience of taking on staff. He therefore asks his coach to coach him in the recruitment and hiring of staff. The coach suggests that he attend a number of job interviews himself, instead of focusing on the way in which the director handles this issue during coaching conversations. This is what happens and the outcome is to everyone's satisfaction.

The coachee presents organisational rather than personal problems

Coaching, in the first instance, looks at the coachee's own stake in a problem, and the way in which (s)he can strengthen and develop his or her personal contribution towards its resolution. Where organisational problems or 'team problems' are concerned, therefore, it is debatable whether coaching is appropriate. Coaching can certainly reinforce individuals in their handling of team and organisational issues, and so reinforce individuals' effectiveness in teams, but it can also reinforce a mistaken belief within an organisation that an individual coachee plays a key role in a problem of some kind. Coaching can therefore reinforce an 'individualising' tendency in the organisa-

Figure 13.1 Sometimes the advice to enter into coaching is not the best advice

tion, and may (unintentionally) aggravate problems if it feeds a habit of placing too much emphasis on the individual's contribution to wider problems and to their resolution. In the following chapter we look in more detail at the role of the organisation in coaching issues. When considering issues involving the dynamic between groups of colleagues, *Learning with Colleagues* (de Haan, 2004) is usually a more appropriate source of information. In the case of organisational issues, it sometimes helps to call in an external organisational development consultant to look at the broader organisational system, and to work in a learning manner with the organisation as a whole.

The coachee presents all-pervading problems, extending far beyond work-related issues
If the issues for which the coachee is seeking coaching extend over many areas of his or her working and private life, coaching may not provide the right answer. If the problem is of all-pervading personal significance, and so has a constant hold on the coachee, it is

important to refer him or her to a physician and psychotherapist. There are several indicators that such an all-pervading problem might be present, such as:

- disturbances and major exaggerations in the coachee's self-image or images of others
- major anxiety, expressed as anxious, attacking or controlling reactions
- insensitivity, alienation or strongly dependent behaviour.

An important indicator when deciding if coaching is appropriate is the coachee's resilience. Is the coachee able to undergo and use the sometimes painful learning experiences in the coaching?

Often, the coach realises soon enough that there is something 'fishy' going on, or that the coaching is not working. At such times it is a good idea to make a referral, to summarise your own impressions objectively and decisively, and to have recourse to names and telephone numbers of other professionals who may be able to help.

An example

The coachee is a young family man with three children. His wife is seriously ill. He works full time and does everything around the house. He has no time at all for himself. In a training course, he talks about himself and his situation. He receives feedback that he comes across as cold and clinical in the way he talks about his situation, and the trainer recommends that he go and talk to a coach. He arrives for his first session. The coach doesn't fully recognise the trainer's feedback but does get the impression the coachee wants to keep everything under control. Not just at home but also at work, and that this takes a huge amount of energy. To the coach, this seems to be a logical strategy given the situation, but she is still concerned about the boundary between coaching and therapy and rings a psychotherapist from her network for advice. What would be appropriate for this coachee? According to the therapist, the coachee is displaying a normal reaction to abnormal circumstances and coaching is therefore a good opportunity for reflection. Based on her experience as a therapist, she advises the coach regarding the direction the coaching might take and the coach gratefully follows her advice.

Summary: learning through coaching

Coaching is a form of individual learning in which coachees explore their own relationship with issues in their professional development - in other words, addressing specific concerns but also with regard to the broader context of their 'career'.
  Kolb (1984) identifies the following learning styles:

- divergent (concrete experience)
- assimilative (reflective observation)
- convergent (abstract conceptualisation)
- accommodative (active experimentation)

Different sorts of careers may benefit from emphasising different sorts of learning issues:

- the 'bureaucratic' career, in which accommodation in particular is difficult
- the 'entrepreneurial' career, in which divergence in particular is difficult
- the 'professional' career, in which convergence in particular is difficult
- the 'boundaryless' career, in which assimilation in particular is difficult.

The coach can support the coachee in tackling these learning issues, offering assistance in going though and balancing periods of stagnation and transition in career development.

Sometimes coaching is not the right answer to an individual problem, for example:

- when dealing with puzzles instead of problems
- when an issue is more truly an organisational than an individual one
- when severe or complex personal issues on the part of the coachee are in play.

14
The organisation coach

Every coach is an organisation coach. All coaching described in this book is coaching not only of a coachee, but also of an organisation, because the coachee's organisation is present in and through every coachee. This is the main difference between coaching and psychotherapy: coaching is work- and organisation-oriented, while therapy is more remote from the working organisation – the organisation being only one dominant system of which the coachee forms part.

This chapter is concerned with the 'use' of the organisation in coaching conversations. It therefore focuses on external coaching slightly more than other chapters. We assume that the coach here is not part of the coachee's organisation. However, internal coaches can also find something for themselves here: the word 'organisation' is a broad and vague concept. For example, if the coach is part of a corporate services department and the coachee's position is deep within a division or business unit, we can safely assume that the coach is not part of the coachee's relevant organisation. The coach is therefore 'external' enough to apply the principles outlined in this chapter. For the limitations of internal coaching, see also Chapter 15.

This chapter looks primarily at the struggles, shortcomings and conflicts within the coach/coachee and coach/coachee/organisation relationships. We therefore concentrate to some extent on negative or imperfect aspects of organisation coaching. However, in our view the positive and constructive thing about coaching is precisely that the coach can draw attention to, examine and perhaps resolve these aspects. We provide only brief descriptions of the different ways of looking at the dynamics of the coach/coachee/organisation triad, but references to relevant literature are also given.

The psychodynamics of organisations

We cannot cover the whole of the theory of organisation in this book, of course – not even what has been said about it from a psychodynamic perspective – but we can raise some relevant aspects regarding working in an organisational context and discuss how those aspects can come into play in coaching conversations.

We are all members of different groups and organisations, and we all have some degree of ambivalence about working and living in groups. In short, groups are hard to live with, but also hard to live without. We have great difficulty in giving up parts of our individuality in order to fit into an organisation yet we find it hard, if not impossible, to live or work without connections. For the sake of convenience, we view organisations here in terms of activities of sensemaking (Weick, 1995) and adjustment (De Board, 1978) with regard to a variety of processes and activities. In *Learning with Colleagues* (Chapter 22), the following three, fairly general, processes in organisations were distinguished:

- *Working*, which includes the primary process of the organisation, but also a variety of jobs and tasks that employees take on for various reasons.
- *Controlling* or *managing*, which includes the management of the organisation, but also a range of local management tasks such as the development of a departmental strategy, annual departmental plans, a planning and control cycle, meetings, daily planning, and so on.
- *Learning:* all efforts to acquire knowledge in order to bring about improvements in the other two processes.

All members of organisations have to keep defining and re-defining their own positions in relation to these 'organising processes', *via* sensemaking and adjustment. Most coaching conversations concern doing this as effectively as possible: in other words, they concern boundaries, authority and taking responsibility (Czander, 1993). Coaching is about *boundaries to*, *authority within*, and *responsibility for* the role adopted by the coachee in the organisation.

Often, the aim of a professional within an organisation is to connect his or her own thoughts and feelings to processes that are of personal relevance, in the form of *role behaviour*. Role behaviour means the ability (Reed, 2000):

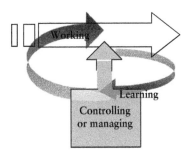

Figure 14.1 Working, managing and learning processes in organisations

- to find a role (finding a suitable work process or function; analysing the state of that process)
- to make a role (flexibility and authority in creating a suitable role)
- to take a role (assuming responsibility for and authority within one's own role).

Right from the start of coaching, it is important to think in terms of roles. If we simply look at the coachee's issue and disregard the coachee's organisation, we initially ask ourselves the question: 'Why is this dysfunctional?' If we consider the issue from the perspective of the psychodynamics of organisations, however, we ask ourselves the completely different question: 'Why is this issue thought to be dysfunctional?' We follow up with another question: 'And how does this issue, which may have a negative significance for the coachee in his or her own environment, impinge upon the functioning of the greater whole?'

As the coach, it is therefore helpful to ask yourself regularly during coaching conversations: 'How does this problem contribute to the functioning of a greater whole? What is the function of this problem? Why did it arise, and what role does it play in the continuation of the *status quo?*'

An example
The coachee is a female manager of a division of a large company. She hasn't been in the post for very long but has noticed that she needs to start setting boundaries more effectively – to learn to say 'no' – or she won't last long. She is young, enthusiastic, and brimming with good ideas. As a result,

she is asked to do all kinds of things – not only by fellow managers and the Board, but also by clients – and she says 'yes' to everything. Mainly because she doesn't want to offend people; she believes it is important to her that people like her. But in fact she doesn't show much respect for other people's time: every week her diary is crammed with appointments and she tries to wriggle out of her commitments, by turning up late or getting her secretary to ring up and cancel. She is always able to gloss over it afterwards. Because she does so in a very charming and courteous manner, it works every time: people don't get openly angry with her. At the same time, she is gradually losing her credibility and getting more and more stressed herself by this behaviour, and people are starting to count on her less. She discusses it with her coach and also displays the same behaviour with regard to her sessions: she shows up late for appointments, gets her secretary to cancel and glosses over it by turning on the charm. This gives the coach a good opportunity to bring up this behaviour and its background, and also to explore its effects further with the coachee. They explore how the coachee's behaviour is connected with the surrounding organisational culture and the pressures she experiences in her role. They discover parallels between her needs to be liked and the larger organisational issues, such as the vain attempts by her company to improve its quality of service

The coach in the role of coach

The coaching conversation, too, involves two clearly different roles, to which the two parties adjust to a greater or lesser extent: the role of coach and the role of coachee. In the previous chapters we discussed many characteristics of – and hence boundaries to – the role of coach. See, for example, Chapter 12 on the coach's capabilities, or the role choices in the different approaches in Part II. Many of the boundaries concern the coach's availability to focus on the coachee and the 'material' of the coachee:

- As the coach, you confine yourself largely to observation and exploration: seeing and saying what you see.
- As the coach, you dissociate yourself as far as possible from your own memory and desires (Bion, 1970), in order to be present here and now in this situation as far as possible.

- As the coach, you also have a 'negative' capability (Bion, 1970): the ability to be in situations where uncertainty, ambiguity and doubt prevail, without making laborious attempts to get out of them, for example by means of observations, interpretations and solutions.

Perception has its own limitations and is subject to distortion. In fact, much of perception is a magnificent *illusion* that we conjure up ourselves (de Haan, 1994). Yet illusions, while they subtly deceive us, also frequently enable us to explore our surroundings better. It is these illusions that enable us to take in the 'right' information. Consider a television set. If we were to see it as it is – as a distorted, multi-coloured, changing series of flat images – we could no longer take in the content of the programmes. Illusions come about by *filtering and aggregating*, removing from our consciousness the unimaginable amount of information that is available to us but that we do not need in order to act. Illusions are the result of collecting the 'raw' information on a higher aggregation level. Whether or not illusions are a by-product of that process is a question that remains unanswered. Perhaps it is precisely *thanks to* our illusions that we can use our perceptions in order to act! Illusions often relate, therefore, to our own generalisations, and to the things that we ourselves 'take for granted'.

Selective attention also contributes to a distorted view of reality and enables us to expand our scope for action and, more importantly, to choose what we want to perceive.

Finally, there are the *distortions*: the things that we do not see or see poorly because we have not developed any sensitivity to them, or because we have (often unconsciously) developed barriers or prejudices against them as a result of our own experience.

The aspects of perception outlined above are difficult to apply in coaching because they would no longer be illusions, selections or distortions if we were fully aware of them. They would become different perspectives, ways of looking at things that we could use as we choose. Especially when confronted with confusion and ambiguity, we often feel we do not have control over our perceptions, and feel ourselves inadequate. We then sometimes feel frustrated and think that we need more information, more perceptions. However, we may be deceiving ourselves by our own – not entirely conscious – realisation that more accurate perception might give rise to all sorts of painful feelings. The art is sometimes to convert 'not being able to perceive' into 'perceiving what is not there': something that is missing, that does not fit in, that is incongruous…

It is therefore helpful, as the coach, to ask yourself regularly during coaching conversations: 'What am I not perceiving?' What is missing from the coachee's story? What aspects of the story do I find hard to make sense of? What 'colour' are my own (metaphorical) glasses at this moment? It is difficult but, with training, not impossible, to perceive one's own 'perspective', or way of perceiving!

The coachee in the role of coachee

The tensions in the coachee – in terms of 'being' coachee – have already been discussed, in Chapters 8 and 9 among others.

Coachees frequently come to the coach not in order to change, but as a last resort in order to stay the same. Consequently, the initial question is often at best a symptom of an underlying question that the coachee is initially unable or afraid to raise.[1] The initial question then acts to divert attention away from, and to hide, the actual problem. It is difficult to underestimate how painful change is, or the lengths to which coachees and organisations will go in order to avoid it. They often prefer to live with a 'symptom': a painful inconvenience that simply will not go away, and over which they have limited influence. The coachee's initial question often translates as: 'Help me without taking my symptom away'; or 'Just take my symptom away and don't change anything else'; or 'Change me without changing me!'

The coach's basic principle is generally: 'In order to change you will have to learn.' However, 'learning' can also be used to avoid change: it can act as a last line of defence (see the list of defences in Chapter 8) for the coachee. Learning is not the same as 'becoming' or 'growing'. Learning can mean understanding what is going on and leaving it at that. Learning can easily become a goal in itself.

If the issue is worth the trouble of entering into a coaching relationship, there are usually powerful emotions at stake. These emotions will be connected with the issue, the problem and failed attempts to resolve it to date, but also with entering into the coaching relationship itself. The latter feelings occur both in the coachee and in the coach.

Much of the emotional charge of a coaching relationship, especially at the start (see also Chapter 4), is still unprocessed and so is partly unconscious. Unprocessed emotional charge can be expressed

1. The original Greek word *symptoma* means literally 'accident' or 'discomfort'.

in a variety of ways: resisting behaviour, controlling behaviour, attributions to others in the form of projections, and so on.

For the coachee, coaching is a process which begins with a cocktail of emotions, and moves first towards contemplation of those emotions and then to action – instead of acting immediately on the basis of those emotions. This process can be seen as the transformation of emotional experience into new opportunities for action (see Bion, 1965). 'Acting' in this context means making use of the thinking – not in the first instance to learn, but rather to become and to grow.

It is therefore helpful, as the coach, regularly to ask yourself: 'How does this coachee want me to feel?' In other words: what impact does my coachee's story have on me? What aspect of the story do I find hard to make out? How does it feel to be in conversation with the coachee at this moment?

The coachee in the role of coachee and of professional in the organisation

The coachee is the person who translates and applies the outcome of coaching conversations in his or her own practice. With the aid of coaching, (s)he makes renewed sense of the situation, and prepares to adapt accordingly. The coachee is the link between the coaching relationship and organisational practice. In fact, for the coachee, entering into a relationship with a coach means an additional adjustment and finding a new role, namely that of coachee of this coach. Because it is a role that is situated partly outside of his or her ordinary working practice, it offers greater opportunities for gaining insight and for experimenting. However, it is sometimes useful to look at your coachee as a *translator* or intermediary between coach and organisation. This is particularly true if it emerges that certain actions planned during the coaching conversation are not carried out in the coachee's refractory day-to-day practice – in other words, when the coachee experiences (in the view of the coach) a 'relapse'.

The coachee attempts to develop within a role provided by his or her organisation. The coachee develops him/herself and a personal role at the same time. On the basis of life experience, the coachee brings along all sorts of (behavioural) patterns, which are visible in his or her role-behaviour. After some time in the role, moreover, the coachee carries the organisation internally, as in a hologram.[2] A hologram has the amazing property that a fragment still contains the entire original image. Like a hologram, the coachee reflects elements of his or her entire emotional experience in an organisation in every fragment of conversation. Like a fragment of the hologram, the coachee presents a complete and personal image of the organisation. The coachee's problems and emotions can often be related to the problems and emotions prevailing within the organisation. It is as if the organisation is contained within the coachee, just as the coachee is contained within the organisation. Coaching may start from either angle.

It is possible to carry out a *role analysis:* in other words, to explore with the coachee his or her available roles, and the choice of roles that may be open (Reed, 2000). The following distinctions can be made in this respect:

- *Role biography* focused on the coachee: what roles has the coachee played in this and in other work processes, and what experiences are associated with those roles?
- *Role history* focused on the organisation: what roles has the organisation traditionally offered and nurtured?

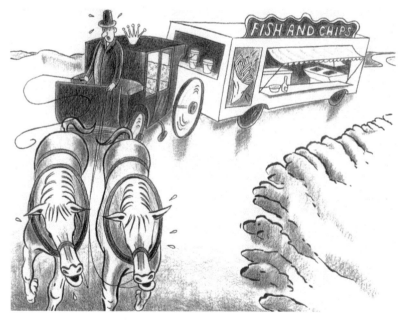

Figure 14.2 The coachee's entire organisation is present during a coaching conversation

2. This phenomenon of representing in oneself the emotional experience within the organisation is also known as the 'organisation in the mind' (see Armstrong, 1997).

- *Role dialogue* focused on both: what conversation or negotiation takes place – partly unconsciously – between organisation and coachee, in order to arrive at the most appropriate role interpretation?

Pay attention during the coaching to the coachee within yourself: be aware of what the coachee and what (*via* the coachee) the organisation triggers in you.[3] This can tell you a great deal about the less conscious aspects of the organisation in the experience of the coachee. Pay attention too to the coach within yourself. What needs, unprocessed emotions, uncertainties, change issues and other factors do you bring to this coaching relationship yourself?

Why did you actually choose the role of coach in the first place?

It is helpful, as coach, to ask yourself regularly during coaching conversations: 'How does this coachee's organisation want me to feel?' In other words, what sort of function do I fulfil as a coach in the coachee's organisation? For what stories and emotions am I a 'safety valve'?

This question can also be put to the coachee: 'How does your organisation want you to feel?' What is the emotional 'value' of your role in the organisation? What is it that you are taking on for this organisation, as a coachee? This may put you on the track of phenomena known as *valencies* (see Bion, 1961, or *Learning with Colleagues*, Chapter 12): susceptibilities of certain people and roles in organisations to particular emotional charges, which express themselves most – or even exclusively – in that person and role. Valency can therefore relate to an individual susceptibility, but also to a susceptibility associated with a certain role in the organisation.

An example

There is a preliminary meeting with the coachee, the director of a consultancy, and his manager, the majority shareholder in the consultancy. Strikingly, the coachee asks the coach for 'positive support' and 'a constructive approach' and even warns of the risk of 'burnout'.

In the first coaching conversation a few weeks later, the coachee says how ridiculously hard he has worked in recent years and how he is not accustomed to complaining about it: 'I

---

3. Compare the utilisation of *counter-transference* as described in Chapter 8. See also the *organisation coach step* in the ANALYTIC METHOD in Chapter 10.

don't know where my limits lie.' The image of 'burning' recurs, now in the form of 'fire-fighting'. This is his most frequent activity at work, but a change has occurred: recently he has been confronted on a daily basis with his own limitations and with failure.

He talks a lot about the majority shareholder, whom he experiences as negative, undermining and intimidating. He himself realises how, after his last promotion, the shareholder started to see him as a threat for the first time. In recent months he has therefore combined the valencies of 'protegee' and 'scapegoat' and it is starting to become too much for him. The coach feels paternal, concerned, caring. It is as if he is being called on to supply all of the behaviour not shown by the majority shareholder and the other consultants in the firm...

Figure 14.3 The coach and coachee

Behind the coach stands the emotional experience of the coach, who is sensitive to what the coachee triggers in him or her. Behind that are the reserves of the coach: other aspects of his or her personality that may be brought to this coaching conversation.

Behind the coachee stands the organisation in the emotional experience of the coachee, traces of the coachee in his or her role in the organisation. Behind that are the reserves of the coachee, other roles, life experiences, that are present both in that role, and in this coaching conversation.

Summary: the organisation coach

Every coach is an organisation coach: the coachee's organisation is just as present as the coachee personally. The coachee continues to be part of the organisation and the coachee has built up an internal representation of the organisation of which (s)he is part, so all coaching is organisation coaching.

Questions to ask yourself regularly as a coach:

- How does the coachee's (negative) problem contribute towards the (positive) functioning of the coachee or the (positive) functioning of the coachee's organisation?
- What am I seeing here and now? But also – what am I not seeing here and now?
- How does this coachee want me to feel?
- How does the coachee's organisation want the coachee to feel?
- How does the coachee's organisation want me to feel?

Struggles of the coach in the role of coach:

- influences based on his/her own memory and desires
- distorted perception due to illusions – filtering and generalisations
- distorted perception due to selective attention – his or her own interest, concentration and choices
- distorted perception due to distortions – distorting glasses and blind spots.

Struggles of the coachee in the role of coachee:

- emotions, including those connected with entering into the coaching relationship
- attachment to symptoms
- symptoms masking problems
- defences
- resistance.

Struggles of the coachee in the role of professional in his or her organisation:

- finding a role
- making a role
- taking a role
- valencies for emotions related to his/her own role.

15

Boundaries on Coaching
with Colleagues

Coaching with colleagues is a broad concept. As discussed earlier in this book, both colleagues from outside the organisation (external coaches) and colleagues from within the coachee's organisation (internal coaches) can play a helping role. There are also managers who use a coaching style of management but at the same time remain hierarchically responsible for their staff, with inevitable consequences in terms of what can and cannot be discussed during a coaching session. This book is not concerned with coaching leadership, though we find that leaders are able to use most coaching styles very effectively. In the relationship between manager and 'coachee', the coachee cannot really be at the centre: the manager's task is to represent the interests of the organisation and the department, and those interests do not always coincide with the interests of the coachee.

In recent decades the perception of coaching within organisations has changed radically (Frisch, 2001). The negative status and stigma that was previously attached to managers who needed a coach to support their professional development appear to have been replaced by a particularly positive status – the manager is apparently important enough to the organisation to warrant the investment in coaching. At the same time, coaching within organisations is being viewed less as a way to put derailed career paths back on track, and more as an investment in future careers. These developments have been accompanied by the phenomenon of internal coaches, which has developed into a formal staff discipline in a growing number of large organisations.

In this chapter we examine characteristics of internal coaches; the advantages and limitations of working with internal or external coaches; the application of the various styles by internal coaches;

and some ethical guidelines which we consider important in that respect. We also provide some practice in the form of ten specific and real-life ethical dilemmas to wrestle with, plus some reflection on those dilemmas.

Characteristics of internal coaches

Internal coaches differ from coaches coming from outside the organisation in two respects (Twijnstra and Keuning, 1988):

1. First, the internal coach is not truly independent with respect to the organisation. The coach has a personal role to play in it, and also has his or her own (emotional) experience of the organisation. This sometimes makes it difficult for the coach to 'empty his/her mind' and listen with complete objectivity to what the coachee is saying.
2. Second, the internal coach has more knowledge of the organisation and therefore a clear idea of the context within which the coachee is operating. This can be an important advantage over some external coaches who are unable to assess that context properly, with possible adverse consequences. However, it can also impede a fresh and independent assessment of the organisational context (see Chapter 14).

There are several reasons why an organisation might choose to work with internal coaches. Those reasons may derive from convictions within the organisation regarding how people should be managed. For example:

• The organisation sees coaching as an effective form of learning and wants to acquire relevant knowledge and experience of it, to enable the organisation to gain maximum benefit.
• The organisation sees regular coaching of staff as relevant to the effectiveness of the organisation and therefore wants to invest in it.

But there may also be entirely practical reasons for working with internal coaches. For example:

• The organisation wants to have constant access to coaching expertise and not to be dependent on outsiders.

- The organisation wants to keep the costs of coaching under control or offer it to broader target groups: external coaches may have to charge considerable fees.

Internal coaching can take a variety of forms. Some organisations decide to ask senior professionals to take on the role of coach on an occasional basis, in addition to their other responsibilities. This often occurs within consultancies. Other organisations decide to work with internal coaches who take on that role for the entire organisation, or they may even assemble a 'pool' of internal coaches.

> *An example*
> A back-office staff member in a consultancy organisation works as a sports coach in the weekends and is very curious about executive coaching. He takes his manager's advice of finding a mentor and approaches his colleague, an external coach. Because they know each other from work, some formal boundaries seem appropriate. They agree on four sessions over the course of six months, with specified objectives. The sessions always seem to circle around the same ambivalence: a huge ambition so vague that it borders on a pipe dream, together with insufficient discipline necessary to change the status quo. The coach is painfully aware that the coachee is a direct colleague. It is true that he is helping to make the dilemma explicit, but at the same time he is not switching to the more confrontational style that serves him well with external clients. The sessions start to repeat themselves and the four-session contract is not extended. The coach advises his coachee to continue with a mentor from outside the narrow workplace.

Advantages of internal coaches

There are a number of advantages to working with internal coaches:[1]

- The internal coach has wide knowledge of the organisation, the sector and sometimes the coachee's discipline. This gives the coach an idea of the context within which the coachee is

1. We refer to Frisch's article (2001) about internal coaches and also use the advantages of working with internal consultants mentioned by Twijnstra and Keuning (1988).

operating and enables him or her to make progress more quickly, especially in the early stages.

- The internal coach knows something about the power relationships, culture and problems within the organisation. This sometimes gives the coachee a sense of safety and confidence.
- For coachees, the barrier to the internal coach is often lower. The advantage in terms of cost may play a role in this respect, but also the greater familiarity and proximity.
- The internal coach can often be contacted quickly and easily. It is easier to pop in to visit, if necessary, than it is with an external coach.
- The internal coach has more opportunity to observe what the coachee does in the organisation and can bring those observations to the coaching conversations.
- Working with internal coaches means working towards a more 'learning organisation' (Senge et al., 1994), if only because then internal professionals are more explicitly involved with their colleagues' learning.

Limitations of internal coaches – advantages of external coaches

Besides the advantages, the use of internal coaches also has a number of limitations.[2] Of course, these are also advantages in external coaching.

1. The internal coach is less free with respect to the coachee's organisation:
   - The internal coach's knowledge of an organisation can also result in a 'corporate blind spot' which prevents him or her from seeing certain (power) patterns and mechanisms, or from raising them for discussion.
   - The internal coach has a personal history within the organisation. As a result, (s)he may be more tempted to become unhelpfully directive, as in: 'what was good for the coach is good for the coachee'.
   - The internal coach is dependent upon the organisation – being on the payroll personally, (s)he has managers and is part of the system within which the coachee is operating. This can be experienced as very limiting and less confidential, both by the coach and by the coachee.

2. Again, see Twijnstra and Keuning (1988) and Frisch (2001).

- The internal coach often has a reputation with the coachee already, which can sometimes get in the way of the coaching.[3]
- The internal coach may be contractually committed to management objectives, and see the senior management of the organisation as his or her first and foremost client. Just as in coaching leadership, this means that the coach cannot truly serve the coachee. We do not recommend such a contract for coaching, but realise that it is sometimes unavoidable for coaches operating from within the Human Resources function.
- The internal coach may be prone to choose an approach that is customary within the organisation (e.g. solution-focused coaching in a solution-focused culture), while the coachee would sometimes be better served by a completely different approach: perhaps a person-centred approach, for example.
- Internal coaching can raise internal costs, such as administration, training, use of office space and so on.

2. The internal coach has a less clear and well-defined relationship to the coachee:
    - Because the internal coach is part of the hierarchy, it is sometimes unclear who his or her client is for the coaching: his/her own boss, the coachee's boss or the coachee personally? To whom is the coach accountable, and for what? What happens, for example, if a valued coachee, after a successful coaching journey, decides on the basis of this work to leave the organisation?
    - The internal coach often quickly develops an informal, 'amicable' relationship with the coachee. Limits on the coaching conversations, and on containment of the coaching within the sessions (see Chapter 8), may suffer as a result. A temptation may arise to carry on coaching conversations 'as you go along', neglecting the monitoring of start and finish times and the importance of avoiding disruptive interruptions.

3. Sue-Chan and Latham (2004) compare internal and external coaches with a wide difference in reputation in terms of (perceived) expertise and credibility. The outcome study was performed among MBA students and compared the performances of these students under three conditions: tutors as coaches, peers as coaches, and 'self-coaching' (with instructions). The internal coaches score much lower than the external coaches, and sometimes even lower than 'self-coaching'.

Limitations of external coaches

Every new coaching issue raises the question of whether the coachee would be better served by an internal or an external coach. The summary of advantages and limitations above may help this decision. The question should also be considered carefully before adopting one of the coaching approaches mentioned. On the basis of our own experience, as both internal and external coaches, we consider that every approach can, in principle, be applied by internal and external coaches. We do believe that certain coaching approaches may be more appropriate than others in particular organisational contexts. This is mainly to do with the fact that some approaches require stronger protection or 'containment', which may be hard to build up given, for example, the limited organisational distance between the internal coach and the coachee (especially in smaller organisations) or the type of issues that are brought to internal coaching. Not surprisingly, we have concluded that the directive approaches are often more suitable for internal coaching than the person-centred and analytic approaches. The latter in particular call for a proper contract, a high level of confidentiality, a clear framework and an adequate time frame.

The profession of 'coach' is still probably one of the most unregulated professions in current business practice. We now have internationally accredited training programmes, some generally recognised codes of conduct, and a considerable number of generally trusted and recognised professional associations. It is still hard to say anything definite about the background and professionalism of external coaches in the field. We note that external coaches often have a background in psychotherapy, external management consultancy or management – or a combination of the three. Each background and each individual brings with them their own qualities and limitations as coaches. As pointed out already (see, for example, Chapter 11), other factors that come into play include the person of the coachee, the nature of the coaching issues, the type of coaching relationship that develops, and the objectives and context of coaching. What we have noticed is that:

- Coaching *management consultants* are often troubled by the possible presence of psychological health issues and problematic personal circumstances when dealing with coachees; they are generally aware of the need to have reference criteria (see, for example, our suggestions in Chapter 13) and to build up a network among psychotherapists.

- Coaching *psychotherapists* often have trouble with the organisational context, and with both the organisation's impact on the coaching and the coaching's impact on the organisation. They tend to overlook the context to some extent and focus primarily on the thinking, feelings and actions of the individual coachee.
- Coaching *managers* often find it difficult to create the right coaching relationship, in terms of providing service and advice. They sometimes find it hard to put the coachee and his/her issues truly at the centre and to intervene in a way that respects the autonomy of the coachee.

Beyond these three fairly general comments, we find it difficult to make any broad statements about the limitations of external coaching, if only due to the great diversity of that professional field. It remains important to emphasise how important it is that all coaching should take place within a safe and trusted relationship between

Figure 15.1 Sometimes it is difficult to open yourself up as a coach. Practical experience and knowledge, however useful, can form an obstacle to effectiveness!

coach and coachee, a clear and explicit coaching contract, looked after by regular professional supervision.

Ashridge's Code of Conduct for coaches

One of the risks of internal coaching is that it is fitted in amongst normal day-to-day activities, and that internal coaches may overlook a number of rules of conduct that external professional coaches tend to adopt more explicitly. Many different codes of conduct for coaches are in use. We have based the Ashridge Code of Conduct for Coaches on the standards for professional conduct of the British Association of Counselling Practitioners (BACP) and on the ethical codes of the Dutch organisation of professional coaches (NOBCO) and of the International Coach Federation (ICF). We believe this provides a framework which is relevant to both internal and external coaches. These documents are available for reference on the Internet (see www. bacp.org.uk, www.nobco.nl and www.coachfederation.org).

The purpose of this Code of Conduct is to establish and maintain standards for coaches and to inform and protect members of the public, their individual clients and organisations seeking their services.

Ethical standards embody such values as integrity, competence, confidentiality and responsibility. Ashridge coaches, in assenting to this Code, accept their responsibility to clients, colleagues and Ashridge. The client's interest is paramount, but where coaches sense a conflict of responsibilities they have to use their considered judgement. Therefore the Code of Conduct is a framework within which to work rather than a set of instructions.

General principles
Firstly, we maintain that:

1. Coach and client enter into an equal relationship which is used intentionally for the benefit of the client.
2. Clients ultimately know best what is best for them and can decide for themselves what they do or do not want, both in their private and in their professional lives; clients are therefore also responsible for the choices that they make and accountable for their actions.
3. The responsibility of the coach is to give the client an opportunity to explore, discover and clarify ways of living and working more satisfyingly and resourcefully.

4. During coaching the goals, resources and choices of the client have priority over those of the coach.

Code of ethics
ISSUES OF RESPONSIBILITY

*   Coaches are responsible for observing the principles embodied in this Code of Conduct.
*   Coaches accept responsibility for encouraging and facilitating the self-development of the client within the client's own network of relationships.
*   The coach takes account of the developmental level, abilities and needs of the client.
*   The coach is aware of his/her own cultural identity and that of the client and of the possible implications of any similarities and differences for the coaching.
*   Coaches are responsible for ensuring that they are not dependent upon relationships with their clients for satisfying their own emotional and other needs.
*   During coaching, the coach will not engage in non-coaching relationships, such as friendship, business or sexual relationships with coachees. Coaches are responsible for setting and monitoring the boundaries between working and other relationships, and for making the boundaries as explicit as possible to the client.
*   The coach will cooperate in the handling of a complaints procedure if one is brought against him/her, and makes sure that reasonable arrangements have been made for professional liability.

ISSUES OF COMPETENCE

*   Coaches recognise the power inherent in their position: they realise that they can exert considerable influence, both consciously and unconsciously, on their clients and possibly also on third parties.
*   Coaches are aware of the limitations both of their coaching and their personal skills and take care not to exceed either. They refer a client to a colleague, if necessary, and maintain a professional network to that end.
*   Coaches commit themselves to training in coaching and undertake further training at intervals during their careers.

- Coaches seek ways of increasing their professional development and self-awareness.
- Coaches monitor their coaching work through regular supervision by professionally competent supervisors, and are able to account to individual clients, colleagues and client organisations for what they do and why.
- Coaches monitor the limits of their own competence.
- Coaches, along with their employers and organisation clients, have a responsibility to themselves and their clients to maintain their own effectiveness, resilience and ability to help clients. They must be able to identify any situation in which their personal resources have become depleted to the extent that they must seek help and/or withdraw from coaching, whether temporarily or permanently.

Code of Practice
This Code of Practice is intended to provide more specific information and guidance in the implementation of the principles embodied in the Code of Ethics.

MANAGEMENT OF THE WORK

- Coaches should inform clients as appropriate about their training and qualifications, and the methods they use.
- Coaches should clarify with clients the number and duration of sessions and fees. They should also explore a client's own expectations of what is involved in coaching with him/her.
- Coaches should gain the client's permission before conferring with other people about the client.
- Coaches should abstain from using any of the information that they have obtained during coaching for their own personal gain or benefit, except in the context of their own development as a coach.
- If there is another internal client (e.g. a manager), coaches must ensure before the coaching starts that all parties have the same information concerning the goal and structure of the coaching and the intended working method. The coaching can progress only if there is agreement between them with respect to its goals and structure. If there is any change in the situation or the assignment, the coach formally revises the arrangements with all parties.

- Coaches who become aware of a conflict between their obligations to a client and their obligation to an organisation employing them will make explicit the nature of the loyalties and responsibilities involved.
- In situations where coaches have a difference of opinion with the client or other involved parties, they will maintain a reasonable attitude and keep dialogue open.
- Coaches work with clients to terminate coaching when the clients have received the help they sought, or when it is apparent that coaching is no longer helping them.

CONFIDENTIALITY

- Coaches regard all information concerning the client – received directly, indirectly or from any other source – as confidential. They protect their clients against use of personal information, and against its publication unless this is authorised by the client or required by law.
- Treating information 'in confidence' means not revealing it to any other person or through any public medium, except to those whom coaches rely on for support and supervision.
- If coaches believe that a client could cause danger to others, they will advise the client that they may break confidentiality and take appropriate action to warn individuals or the authorities.

ADVERTISING/PUBLIC STATEMENTS

- The coach obtains the agreement of the client before using the name of the client's organisation or other information that can identify the client as a reference, e.g. for potential clients.
- Coaches do not advertise or display an affiliation with an organisation in a manner that falsely implies the sponsorship or verification by that organisation.
- Coaches do not make false, exaggerated or unfounded claims about what coaching will achieve.

Application: working with ethical dilemmas

All coaches by nature aim for the good. They want to help their clients, they want to support growth and development. Unfortunately it is not always straightforward what 'good' is; for them, for their clients, and for those that depend on their clients. Interests may differ, different 'moral imperatives' may point into different directions, and their clients' requests may not be the same as their needs. At unpredictable points in their careers, coaches will come across insoluble ethical dilemmas, quagmires, issues that cannot be avoided nor resolved without hurt to someone or some of the people involved. This is where their 'ethics' gets tested, and where coaches need to reflect on what an 'ethical stance' or 'ethical decision making' means in a very particular situation and relationship.

As supervisors and coach developers we have been committed to help coaches prepare for ethical decision making and strengthen their ability to confront ethical dilemmas. We have found that no amount of preparation can fully prepare a coach for a 'tricky' situation. So when an 'ethical' situation arrives the best coaches do not stumble on in splendid isolation, nor do they just apply whatever they have learned in their training. At such points they involve others with their decision making. The best way to do that, given the need for confidentiality, is to ask their supervisor, coach or therapist.

In preparing coaches somewhat for the unknown ethical dilemmas they may encounter, we ask them about the ethical dilemmas they have experienced so far, and how have they resolved those. Equally, we invite them to consider real-life ethical dilemmas of other coaches, and ask them how they would have responded in the same situations. This approach is sometimes called quandary ethics (Appiah, 2008), that is, looking at ethics through the lens of specific moral dilemmas.

Through quandary ethics you learn how to advice others but you may still not know what to do if you are in the dilemma yourself. This is because if you deal with real-life ethical dilemmas yourself, you are in an intimate relationship with the partners involved. This makes a big difference from an ethical perspective. Ethics revolve around relationships and not just principles; so what you might advise someone in their dilemmas could very well change if you were the actual coach in that situation. In training with ethical dilemmas you are looking in from the outside and thinking in the abstract. This fine-tunes ethical thinking but does not replace it in the least. Carroll and Shaw (2008, p. 102) write, 'We love the "problem-pages" in our magazines and newspapers. Many of our "Agony Aunts" are almost as famous as film stars. Even serious journals have problem sections where an issue or dilemma is presented and experienced practitioners respond. The history of ethics has become famous for what has been called "Trolleyology" (the ethical dilemma of what to do if a trolley is out of control and about to kill five people), where "stylised scenarios" of a prepared ethical problem are presented and discussed. (...) While this approach helps to sensitise people to ethical issues and to play with possible resolutions, the concern is that we can begin to see ethics as simply resolving a problem. From this place, problems are "out-there' issues about which we can be dispassionate and rational. We are "outside the problem", like the Agony Aunts. The people involved are not known to us, do not have a relationship with us, and so we have to deal with what Appiah (2008) calls the "umpire fantasy" – that we are judges searching for the right answer. "To turn to them for guidance in the arena of ethics", writes Appiah, "is like trying to find your way around at night with a laser pointer" (p. 194). (...) Most of us make ethical decisions that take relationships into consideration. It is precisely because we are in relationship with individuals, groups, and organisations that we think and act the way we do. A man is faithful to his wife, even when opportunities not to be so present themselves and the chances of him being found out are low, because he knows her, sees her, realises the pain his action would cause her, because he loves her and cherishes his relationship with her. Whether to be faithful to her is not a problem to be solved, but rather a relationship to be considered.'

Here are nevertheless ten examples of real-life ethical dilemmas that our colleagues at the Ashridge Centre for Coaching have come across over the years. Read them through and think which principle(s) of your Code of Conduct would apply, which questions you would ask and how you would advise the coach in those very circumstances. Also, think what you would do if you were an internal coach who had to somehow respond to the case. Make some notes for every dilemma, so that you can compare notes with ours starting on page 195.

Brief examples of coaching dilemmas

Example of an ethical dilemma 1

An executive coach has been working in a company for some time now. She has been coaching an executive who shares with her that she is having real problems with her immediate boss.

That same boss has now asked this coach also to coach him and she feels she can do that and hold the boundaries between the two relationships even though she is aware of a growing tension between the two.

Example of an ethical dilemma 2
The coaching client is the number two of a global trade organisation. Between sessions two and three of a six-session contract, the client is suspended from work. A month later he is dismissed for gross misconduct, something which he and his lawyers are challenging. The issues could not have been foreseen when the coaching contract was drawn up, neither do they have anything to do with the coaching. The coaching contract was approved by his boss, the CEO. The organisation has paid four sessions in advance and the coachee is keen to continue the coaching.

Example of an ethical dilemma 3
The HR director introduces you to a number of coaching clients. The contract with the organisation is the development of management skills. A confidentiality contract is made with each individual. You discover that one of your clients is drinking to excess and you believe it is affecting his behaviour towards his subordinates. At a review meeting, the HR director asks if there is any general feedback.

Example of an ethical dilemma 4
A relatively new executive coach talks to you about one of her coachees. He keeps messing her about: cancelling his session at short notice, being busy when she arrives for his coaching session (which takes place in his office at work) and often having to wait while he finishes something. He is also prone to interrupt the session by taking phone calls and even making some. She has tentatively challenged him on this but his rather sharp retort was that she was being paid for the full time, whether he used it or not, so what was the problem? The coach is thinking of discontinuing the contract.

Example of an ethical dilemma 5
You are part of a coaching team that works within a wider consulting initiative. One of your coaching clients is using his

sessions to focus on his operational problems. However, during your work with senior management you have learned that if this particular client does not improve his strategic thinking he is going to be made redundant.

Example of an ethical dilemma 6
An executive coach has got somewhat entangled in a coaching relationship with an executive. The executive has made no secret of the fact that he finds her attractive. She finds him attractive, though unlike him, she has not shared what she feels with him. She thinks, on reflection, that she was somewhat indiscreet in agreeing to go to dinner with him after one of their coaching sessions. At their last session, two days ago, he gave her a 'small present': tickets for Wimbledon as he has found out that she enjoys playing tennis.

Example of an ethical dilemma 7
An executive coach worked four years ago in a coaching relationship with a Managing Director, paid for by his company. The coaching contract lasted six months. From all perspectives the coaching, focused as it was on his leadership qualities, went well. It was clear at that stage that he was having some problems with his immediate boss even though this was hardly a direct focus in coaching. Now, more than four years on, the coach has been asked by the company lawyers to provide his notes on the coaching sessions. His previous coaching client is in the process of a grievance procedure against the employer. The coach is unsure about his legal and ethical responsibilities regarding the request just made. He still has his session notes and post-session logbook from that time and notes that he has written some comments he would not like anyone to read (e.g. 'he looked depressed today' and 'I understand why some see him as a difficult character to get on with' and 'abrasive in his management style'). He is very nervous about being asked as a witness for the company.

Example of an ethical dilemma 8
In the course of your coaching your client describes sleeping badly, feeling miserable most of the time and feeling unable to concentrate on his work. He is anxious about his competence to carry out the role into which he has just been promoted.

Example of an ethical dilemma 9
Following a merger there is only one director required for a
particular function. Both the two previous directors apply for
the job. One is a man who gets the job – alongside a male team
of senior directors. The other, your client who is a woman,
believes that she was much more competent for the job, and
you agree. Rather than bother with Employment Tribunals, she
has decided to redress the balance by making some money
through insider trading.

Example of an ethical dilemma 10
You have been paid in advance for eight sessions of coaching
with a number of people. The coaching is to be aimed at
grooming managers for promotion. However, it emerges in the
first session that one of your clients intends to hand in his
notice at the end of the year (a month away) in order to move
to a farm in France. He has no need for nor interest in the
coaching.

Some suggestions for how to approach the dilemmas

Here are some personal ideas about how to approach these ethical
dilemmas. In most cases there are no hard and fast answers, and one
can argue a number of different responses which would all be strictly
ethical. It was Potter Stewart at the U.S. Supreme Court who said
that ethics is knowing the difference between what you have a right
to do and what is right to do. That applies to coaching ethical dilemmas as well: the number of routes you are entitled to take is much
larger than the ethically mature things you might do.

As a reader you are invited to compare notes and to use our
responses to develop your own ethical stance with regard to the
questions, tensions and dilemmas above. Dilemmas such as these are
more common than you may imagine in the coaching profession, and
we hope you will find it helpful to come more prepared by having
considered them now.

(Case example 1) A case that merits more exploration and consideration. If the coach would begin working with the senior client this
is likely to affect the coaching relationship with the earlier client,
even if only subliminally. We would imagine that here there are 'ethical rights of way', in other words the older relationship has a natural
primacy because it was established first and thus has acquired

primary importance. It is always good to look at possible clashes in terms of loyalty, confidentiality or trust when a second coaching relationship is suggested in the same organisational setting. Similarly the coach is likely to struggle with what she has heard about the executive before starting the work. It appears therefore to be more ethical and less risky if the coach would just recommend a colleague to do the second assignment, as that would give the senior client the same neutral starting point as the first client.

(Case example 2) This is clearly a contract with the global organisation, in that they are paying the bills. The circumstances of the contract have now changed and the coach therefore has a duty to contact the organisation before coach and coachee meet again. At the very worst if this goes to a tribunal, the coaching could be used by the coachee's lawyers to show that the organisation is implying that they recognise that they are in the wrong by continuing to pay for the coaching. As some of the sessions have been prepaid, the coaching organisation is required to contact the CEO and get her permission before proceeding, and if necessary to offer a credit note. The coaching could of course continue with the coachee paying himself which is what actually happened.

(Case example 3) The confidentiality agreement in the Code of Conduct suggests that we cannot tell the HR Director what we know about our client, and certainly not before notifying the client. Drinking to excess is not illegal in most jobs, so we are not justified in breaking the confidentiality agreement. What you can do is be very firm with the client. For example, you could refuse to engage in further coaching sessions unless he gets himself into treatment and gives you regular updates. At times though a 'duty of care' for the client could mean breaking confidentiality if you felt their lives were in danger or there was a high risk. Some coaching arrangements build in clauses about breaking confidentiality; for example, if someone was drinking on the oil rigs or as a commercial airline pilot.

(Case example 4) The main ethical issue here is that unilaterally discontinuing a coaching contract can be unethical, particularly if it is done only because the coach is out of her depth. It is a common occurrence in coaching that new coaches only gradually learn to challenge and to apply fearlessness in the interest of their clients' learning. This seems to be a case in point. A client in these circumstances would probably benefit from either some reflection on what he is doing with the coach and what this might say about his other (subordinate) relationships; or (and) a firm statement about boundaries that apply in order to deliver on a coaching contract. It may even be unethical to continue in a contract where the coach does not feel free to speak their mind or is unable to raise that very fact. There are times in coaching relationships, especially with top executives, when they find it difficult to not be 'in control' and directing operations. Confrontation rarely helps but sometimes sharing one's own reactions (in the form of self-disclosure) can help the coachee understand the impact of his/her behaviour on others.

(Case example 5) There are no ethical boundaries broken by this case. A three-way meeting would probably clarify the coaching agenda. Ethically, it's always difficult to be caught 'in-between' parties where each can fantasise about your relationship with the other and what you are sharing with them. Also, there are two relationships here in which to consider what would be an 'ethical' response. The first is your response to 'senior management' when you hear about the possible grounds for dismissal. You can raise their relationship with your coachee: have they told him this? In no uncertain terms? Might it be a good idea to reiterate this communication and tell your client again, particularly if management's aim is for him to change? Etc. Second, the coach needs to think about his next session with the coachee – and in particular in the circumstance that for some reason no word has gone out from senior management regarding the need to improve his strategic thinking. Sadly, coaches often come across circumstances where senior management finds it hard – or risky – to be open and direct with employees. Regarding the coaching conversations it is perhaps good to remember that normally there is no strict confidentiality agreement in place for conversations with sponsors of coaching, so that the coach does have the option of raising the issue of strategic thinking and strategic abilities with the client. This would have to be done with some caution, as you wouldn't want to worsen the simmering conflicts between these managerial levels. The coach might ask, 'What has been told to you?' and suggest that the client go back and ask his manager what should be his coaching focus.

(Case example 6) Erotic transference is notoriously common in intimate helping conversations, so the fact that there is this 'entanglement' is no surprise. Many a client is unfamiliar with or unaccustomed to the level of empathic and focussed attention they get in coaching, and may associate this intimacy with the erotic. It is however unethical and detrimental to the coaching contract to act on such feelings. Equally a substantial present is not something a coach can accept without being compromised in her work. Some organisations nowadays have very strict guidelines on presents which we believe are relevant to the rather intimate coaching relationship as well. Both the personal interest and the generous present are (already!) in breach of the principle in the Code of Conduct that tells coaches to refrain from non-coaching relationships. There is a line to be held here, and a supervisor would endeavour to help the coach to return the present and work towards an ending of the formal coaching contract. Generally speaking erotic transference from the side of the client is something that can in principle be worked through in helping relationships, but that requires intensive individual supervision (of a similar frequency as the coaching conversations, with a supervisor who is a trained therapist) and it requires the coach not to reciprocate the feelings of the client. Working through erotic transference will normally uncover defensive manoeuvers and resistance (the coaching relationship is perverted into something which is distinctly unlike coaching), and it will also normally lead into issues that are way beyond strictly coaching material, pertaining to the client's personal relationships (see Chapter 13 in the section Limits of Coaching). This is what makes working through erotic transference even more tricky for a coach. Part of the work for the coach will be to clarify boundaries and the nature of relationships involved in – and excluded by – coaching. Client safety means looking at possible double messages, for example, what message would it give to the client if the gift is accepted?

(Case example 7) Being asked as a witness to an employment tribunal is a very rare occurrence, but it is possible as both companies and former employees might refer to coaching. Employers could reference a coaching assignment as demonstrating enlightened and generous development opportunities. Employees might quote their coach and the conversations with an executive coach in the presence of their boss as an example of having had nothing but positive appraisals. Executive coaches are in no way exempt from legal obligations and have to bring their notes to a tribunal if they are subpoenaed to do so. In this case, the vignette shows the importance of proper note-keeping, where we avoid tendentious labelling and any derogatory terms that we would not want to have out in the open. It is important to make sure that we have notes from every session that we are engaged in (which means that we make a short log if we don't take any notes during a session), and also to make sure that at any time our client or even their employer can see the notes without the work or the partners in the work (coach and coachee) being compromised in any way. This means in practice that coaches need to write their notes as if they will be seen by clients and others. Our advice would be to stick to literal quotes taken from the coachee during the sessions. Such notes may be complemented by 'notes to self', containing interpretation or ideas for the next session, in such a way that the client and the sponsoring organisation are not compromised.

(Case example 8) This seems to be a situation similar to the circumstances that Chapter 13 covers, where one approaches the 'limits' of coaching. If your client is not coping well and brings a lot of tension home, struggling to find enough space and support to recover from the stresses of work, it may be time to gently refer the client to a doctor who could explore a wider range of issues with the client. The way in which this suggestion is presented is crucial, however, as one wouldn't want to compound the issues by a more or less subtle rejection on the part of the coach. In some cases and when the coach feels sufficiently experienced and is regularly supervised by a reliable and well-trained supervisor, it could be beneficial to just temporarily increase the frequency of the coaching, in order to find a way with the client to deal with the issues which after all are also work-related.

(Case example 9) This is a rather clear-cut case of the (threat of) malversation, in this case potentially fraudulent behaviour. It is important for the coach to raise the issues first with the client and see if fraud can be avoided. If this isn't the case and damage has already been done, the coach has no other choice but to report to the appropriate channels, in most cases primarily the sponsor of the coaching work. As any witness to crime, a coach may come under severe criticism if he or she does not report the incident. The law may be broken and the coach can therefore become an accessory by being told. It is worthwhile of course in a case like this to explore how much this is an angry response or threat and how much is really intended.

(Case Example 10) Here there seems to be some tension between the overall conflict with the organisation and the individual and confidential contract with the coachee. The same kind of conflict is very common in a milder form: many coaches begin to feel uncomfortable at the very moment a coachee discusses a topic which is not related to their role in the organisation, or even in some cases when a coachee raises a query which is outside of the limited scope of an overall coaching contract. There is always a tension between centrally imposed goals for a development activity and the need to address the issues in front of us to support or develop the individual client where she is now. In this case example the most problematic response would be to start refunding or in another way to let the sponsoring organisation know that your client has the intention to leave. This is a confidential piece of information and your client has the right to choose the time of announcing their departure, so it would clearly be a breach of ethical principles. If the client has no interest or motivation to use coaching then it would be unethical to pretend to continue and to charge the company. Most coaches would agree that an ethical response in this case would be to subtract the time investment with this client from the budget, and then to refund the remainder by the time the client has taken his leave from the organisation.

Summary: boundaries on coaching with colleagues

Two characteristics distinguish internal coaches from external ones:

- The internal coach is not truly independent with respect to the organisation.
- The internal coach has greater knowledge of the organisation within which (s)he practises.

There are different reasons – both fundamental and practical – for choosing internal or external coaches. There are also different possible ways of organising internal coaching, for example using a pool of coaches, or as an organisational function.

Opting for internal coaches has both advantages and limitations. These can be weighed up when choosing a coach in a specific situation.

Internal coaches can use all of the coaching approaches described in this book. In general, a directive approach appears to be quicker to apply in this context, especially in short-term coaching.

Internal coaches can make use of the codes of conduct for external coaches. They can use the same ethical framework with regard to:

- respect
- integrity and confidentiality
- responsibility
- professional conduct and conflicts of interest.

A good example of such an ethical framework is the Ashridge Code of Conduct for Coaches, which we quote in full and apply in this chapter.

Appendix A

Personal coaching profile

This form can be completed after a coaching conversation, by you in the position of coach, but also by your coachee for you.

It is interesting to compare the two approaches – by completing the form yourself as the coach, for example, and asking your coachee to fill it in as well. Once the form has been completed you can consider together with your coachee:

- On what dimension did the coachee experience the best interventions?
- What are the coachee's expectations? Do they coincide with the coach's profile?

Indicate the coach's position on each dimension:

Directive	←————————————→	Non-directive
Serious	←————————————→	Playful
Focused on issues/content	←————————————→	Focused on emotions/process
Unambiguous	←————————————→	Ambiguous/ironic
Solution-focused	←————————————→	Development-focused
Accepting	←————————————→	Changing
Analytic	←————————————→	Intuitive
Detached	←————————————→	Involved
Focused on past	←————————————→	Focused on future
Open-minded	←————————————→	Informed

Appendix B

Verbatim exercise for the coach

One of the best ways to increase your professionalism as a coach is to reflect on how you are doing it now. It is difficult to gain an unbiased view of your own style of coaching. The following tool can help here, because it is based on the most literal representation of part of a coaching conversation. The exercise involves the verbatim – or word for word – exploration of a coaching session and comprises the following steps:

1. Record the first five to 15 minutes of a coaching conversation. Both video and audio recordings can be used.
2. Within a few days of the event, transcribe the tape recordings in the right-hand column using the following format:

Left hand column	Right hand column
....	....
....	....
....	....
....	....
....	....
....	....
....	....
	(literal text, including 'ums and ers')

This will quickly give you several pages of text.

3. In the left-hand column, write down thoughts and feelings of which you were aware during the conversation, as literally as possible.

4. Check the right-hand column text in terms of the following ingredients:
   a. Identify your own 'most-used' words; pay special attention to the use of words such as 'but', 'though', 'because', 'so', which – although short – express a clear intention.
   b. Decide where on the scale of 'push' and 'pull' (see Appendix C) your own contributions are located.
   c. Look at your own focus: what appears to be your primary concern here as the coach? (Examples: making contact, continuing to ask questions, applying structure, supporting, challenging, finding solutions …)
   d. What was the atmosphere like during the conversation and what indications of that atmosphere are there in the 'verbatim' text?

5. Have your own coach or supervisor read and comment on the 'verbatim' text. Look together at the links and tensions between left- and right-hand columns. How much did you use your own internal responses (in your left-hand column) to inform your interventions? In the book *Relational Coaching* (De Haan, 2008), you can find an annotated example of this verbatim exercise (in Appendix D).

Appendix C
The sliding scale of 'push' and 'pull'

Coaching is really only possible with a strong and personal contact between yourself and the other person. You vary in the extent to which you as the coach or the other person as the coachee are at the centre. It is useful to be aware of this sliding scale between yourself and the other person, which runs from strict and clearly 'directive' to warm, attentive and 'non-directive' or, in other words, from 'push' to 'pull'.

Pull ▬▬▬ Push	Making clear what you want and what you want to talk about. *Example:* 'Listen, I would like to discuss your latest results.'
Pull ▬▬▬ Push	Giving the other person an opinion or personal feedback. *Example:* 'I think you're good at meeting almost impossible deadlines. I'm also pleased to see you so enthusiastic.'
Pull ▬▬▬ Push	Associating with the other person's input, and revealing something of yourself that is triggered by that input. *Example:* 'That makes me think of my time at Planning and Control, two years ago ...'
Pull ▬▬▬ Push	Continuing with closed questions, or leading questions. *Example:* 'Yes, but I am curious about what you did exactly. Did you or didn't you go to the manager?'

Pull   Push   Continuing with directive open questions.
                          Example: 'And what did you do once all of the figures
                          were in?'

Pull   Push   Continuing with clarifying, 'pulling', open questions.
                          Example: 'Could you say more about what you mean
                          by "analysing"?'

Pull   Push   'Reflecting' the other person: contributing your own
                          here-and-now experience.
                          Example: 'Do you know, the way in which you talk
                          about it is giving me a feeling of powerlessness now
                          myself.'

Pull   Push   Giving a summary of content and meaning for the other
                          person.
                          Example: 'You say that you would like to start all over
                          again, and I notice that you're disappointed with the
                          way things have turned out.'

Pull   Push   Giving a summary by literally repeating what the other
                          person says.
                          Example: 'Think it through again ...?'

Pull   Push   Listening with concentration, and occasionally encour-
                          aging the other person to continue with a gesture or
                          'mmm'.
                          Example: ' ... '

Appendix D

Person-centred reflection form[1]

This form can be used just after a counselling conversation. It can help to deepen your contact with your coachee and to put your coachee more at the centre of the coaching conversation.

1. Contact

- Did you have contact with the coachee?
- Did you feel connected with the coachee?
- If not, was that because of you? Your coachee? The situation? Or ...?

2. Being accepted

- Were you accepted by your coachee?
- What evidence of that did you see in the coachee?
- What evidence of that did you perceive in yourself?
- How could you become more accepted?

3. Unconditional positive regard

- What associations did you have with regard to this coachee?
- Did you make assumptions about the coachee?
- Did you give the coachee directions or guidance?
- Was there any particular issue or situation that led you to feel less confidence in the coachee?
- Did you have the feeling that the coachee expected something of you? If so, what? What was your response?

1. Inspired by a feedback form used by Maggie Ridgewell and Jonathan Rosen of the Metanoia Institute, London.

4. Empathy

- Did you manage to move within your coachee's frame of reference?
- How do you think the coachee felt during the conversation?
- Did you interpret the coachee's question or want to solve the problem?
- Did you stay in strong contact with yourself?

5. Congruence

- What were the things that you did not say? That you found difficult to say?
- What did you find difficult to do?
- Was there something preventing you from just being yourself?
- What physical sensations did you notice in yourself? What emotions?
- What did you criticise in yourself?
- Did you disclose anything about yourself? If so, what was your coachee's response?

Appendix E

Coaching behaviours questionnaire[1]

This is the coach's version of the Ashridge Coaching Behaviours Survey, presented as a self-assessment exercise.

Introduction
This questionnaire has been designed to help you to assess your interventions as a coach. It lists a number of different ways in which you might act towards people, and asks you to think about how often you act in each of these ways.

Instructions
Listed below are many different ways in which you might act towards people in a coaching role. For each item, please indicate your perception of how often you act in that way in the right-hand box. None of these behaviours are good or bad in themselves – there are no 'right' or 'wrong' answers. You will get the most value from this exercise by being completely honest with yourself. Don't spend too long considering your replies: your immediate spontaneous answer is likely to be the most appropriate one.

If you find it difficult to give just one answer to a question (perhaps because you consider that you act differently towards different people) we suggest that you try to give an 'average answer' on this form. You may then want to raise this issue for discussion at a review with your own coach or supervisor.

When answering the questions:
0 – Not at all (or 'not applicable')
1 – Rarely

---

1. This questionnaire has been developed by Richard Phillips at Ashridge, based on the six categories of counselling intervention that John Heron (1975) has proposed. We are grateful for Richard's help in publishing his questionnaire.

2 – Sometimes, but not often
3 – Moderately often
4 – Often
5 – Very often

'When working with people as a coach, I tend to do the following':

Question		Your reply
0	Example answer: please fill in your replies in this box ⟶	1 – 5
1	advise them of the appropriate action to take	
2	explain the purpose of a task	
3	raise their awareness of their own learning needs	
4	ask them to tell me about a negative incident which they have experienced	
5	encourage them to set their own learning goals	
6	show my respect for them as individuals	
7	give them feedback about the impact of their behaviour	
8	invite them to talk about a difficult personal experience of theirs	
9	help them to reflect on their experiences	
10	express my concern to help them	
11	suggest that they choose a particular solution	
12	inform them about a learning opportunity	
13	ask them what they have learnt from a particular incident	
14	acknowledge the value of their ideas, beliefs, opinions	
15	persuade them to take a particular approach	
16	interpret their experiences or behaviour	
17	ask questions to uncover what they are hiding or avoiding	
18	encourage them to express their emotions	
19	apologise for anything I do which is unfair, forgetful, hurtful	
20	ask them how they can apply what they have learnt	
21	help them to recognise their own emotions	
22	challenge their denials or defensiveness	
23	make them aware of the choices open to them	
24	ask that they change their behaviour	
25	ask them how they feel about a success which they achieved	
26	make them aware of their mistakes	
27	offer them an explanation of what has happened	
28	inform them about the criteria for measuring success in performing a task	
29	ask open questions to promote discovery	

30	praise them for a job well done	
31	encourage them to find their own solutions and answers	
32	ask them why they are upset or angry	
33	offer them emotional support in difficult times	
34	present facts which contradict their opinions	
35	demonstrate skills or actions that I want them to copy	
36	give them information which they need to achieve a task	
37	draw their attention to facts which they have missed	
38	reflect their feelings by describing what I see in their behaviour	
39	make them feel welcome when they visit me	
40	recommend the best way to do something	
41	challenge their assumptions	
42	ask them to evaluate their own performance	
43	give them feedback about their results	
44	propose the best course of action for them to take	
45	ask them to express feelings which are blocking their progress	
46	show them the consequences of their actions	
47	ask them to set their own work objectives and targets	
48	make myself accessible to them when needed	
49	help them 'with my hands in my pockets': i.e. without interfering	
50	ask them how they feel about a current difficulty	
51	encourage them to feel good about themselves	
52	tell them where to go to find information and help	
53	show them how to correct their mistakes	
54	confront issues of poor performance	
55	tell them how to get started on a new task	
56	reveal information about my own experiences	
57	affirm positive qualities or actions of theirs which they are denying	
58	help them to express their insights after an emotional experience	
59	help them to map out their present understanding	
60	share information about my own failures and weaknesses	

Record the score corresponding to the item number (1–60) in the appropriate spaces indicated below. Total each row to get your final score for each of the six behavioural styles of coaches.

1.:	2.:	3.:	4.:	5.:	6.: ......
11.:	12.:	7.:	8.:	9.:	10.: ......
15.:	16.:	17.:	18.:	13.:	14.: ......
24.:	23.:	22.:	21.:	20.:	19.: ......
28.:	27.:	26.:	25.:	29.:	30.: ......
35.:	36.:	34.:	32.:	31.:	33.: ......
40.:	37.:	41.:	38.:	42.:	39.: ......
44.:	43.:	46.:	45.:	47.:	48.: ......
53.:	52.:	54.:	50.:	49.:	51.: ......
55.:	56.:	57.:	58.:	59.:	60.: ......
DR:	IN:	CH:	RE:	DI:	SU: ......

DR   directing (Heron's prescriptive interventions)
IN   informing (Heron's informative interventions)
CH   challenging (Heron's confronting interventions)
RE   releasing (Heron's cathartic interventions)
DI   discovering (Heron's catalytic interventions)
SU   supporting (Heron's supportive interventions)

Like the Personal Coaching Profile in Appendix A, this is an excellent tool for comparing your own scores with those of your coachee. You can then ask your coachee to complete the Coaching Behaviour Feedback Questionnaire (Appendix F) with regard to yourself, both in terms of your most prominent behavioural styles and of what the coachee would like to see more or less of. At Ashridge Consulting we have available appropriate questionnaires for coachees, as well as interpretation software and a database of 600 coaches with which to make comparisons.

Appendix F

Coaching behaviours feedback questionnaire

This is the coachee version of the Ashridge Coaching Behaviours Survey, presented as a peer-assessment exercise

Introduction

You have been asked to complete this questionnaire to give some feedback to the person named below on their approach to Coaching. It lists a number of different ways in which they (the 'Coach') might act, and asks you to indicate **how often** you see them acting in each of these ways

Coach's Name: _____

Date: _____

Instructions

Listed below are many different ways in which the Coach might act towards you. For each item, please indicate **how often** you see them acting in that way. When you have finished all the questions, please transfer your answers to the Score Sheet on the last page.

None of these behaviours are good or bad in themselves. So there are no "right" or "wrong" answers.

Don't spend too long considering your replies: a quick spontaneous answer is likely to be the most valuable. Both you and the Coach will get the most benefit from this exercise if you are completely honest.[1]

---

1. Similar to Appendix D, this questionnaire was based on a tool developed by Richard Phillips at Ashridge. We are grateful to Richard for his help in publishing this questionnaire.

Answering the Questions

"WHEN WORKING WITH ME(*), THIS PERSON TENDS TO
DO THE FOLLOWING:"

0   –   Not at all (or 'not applicable')
1   –   Rarely
2   –   Sometimes, but not often
3   –   Moderately often
4   –   Often
5   –   Very often

(*) if they are not acting as **your** Coach, please respond according to
how you see them Coaching **other people**.

1 ____   advise me of the appropriate action to take
2 ____   explain the purpose of a task
3 ____   raise my awareness of my own learning needs
4 ____   ask me to tell him/her about a negative incident which
           I have experienced
5 ____   encourage me to set my own learning goals
6 ____   show his/her respect for me as an individual
7 ____   give me feedback about the impact of my behaviour
8 ____   invite me to talk about a difficult personal experience
           of mine
9 ____   help me to reflect on my experiences
10 ____   express his/her concern to help me
11 ____   suggest that I choose a particular solution
12 ____   inform me about a learning opportunity
13 ____   ask me what I have learnt from a particular incident
14 ____   acknowledge the value of my ideas, beliefs, opinions
15 ____   persuade me to take a particular approach
16 ____   interpret my experiences or behaviour
17 ____   ask questions to uncover what I am hiding or avoiding
18 ____   encourage me to express my emotions
19 ____   apologise for anything he/she does which is unfair,
           forgetful, hurtful
20 ____   ask me how I can apply what I have learnt
21 ____   help me to recognise my own emotions
22 ____   challenge my denials or defensiveness
23 ____   make me aware of the choices open to me
24 ____   ask that I change my behaviour
25 ____   ask me how I feel about a success which I achieved

26 ____   make me aware of my mistakes
27 ____   offer me an explanation of what has happened
28 ____   inform me about the success criteria for a task
29 ____   ask open questions to promote discovery
30 ____   praise me for a job well done
31 ____   encourage me to find my own solutions and answers
32 ____   ask me why I am upset or angry
33 ____   offer me emotional support in difficult times
34 ____   present facts which contradict my opinions
35 ____   demonstrate skills or actions which he/she wants me
        to copy
36 ____   give me information which I need to achieve a task
37 ____   draw my attention to facts which I have missed
38 ____   reflect my feelings by describing what he/she sees in my
        behaviour
39 ____   make me feel welcome when I visit him/her
40 ____   recommend the best way to do something
41 ____   challenge my assumptions
42 ____   ask me to evaluate my own performance
43 ____   he/she gives me feedback about my results
44 ____   propose the best course of action for me to take
45 ____   ask me to express feelings which are blocking my
        progress
46 ____   show me the consequences of my actions
47 ____   ask me to set my own work objectives and targets
48 ____   make himself/herself accessible to me when needed
49 ____   help me "with their hands in their pockets": i.e.
        without interfering
50 ____   ask me how I feel about a current difficulty
51 ____   encourage me to feel good about myself
52 ____   tell me where to go to find information and help
53 ____   show me how to correct my mistakes
54 ____   confront issues of poor performance
55 ____   tell me how to get started on a new task
56 ____   reveal information about his/her own experiences
57 ____   affirm positive qualities or actions of mine which
        I am denying
58 ____   help me to express my insights after an emotional
        experience
59 ____   help me to map out my present understanding
60 ____   share information about his/her own failures and
        weaknesses

Score Sheet

For each question, please transfer your score to the appropriate box below. *Please note that the question numbers in this table do NOT flow from left to right in their "correct" sequence!*
Then please add up the totals for each column.

Question	Your Score	Question	Your Score	Question	Your Score	Question	Your Score	Question	Your Score	Question	Your Score
1		2		3		4		5		6	
11		12		7		8		9		10	
15		16		17		18		13		14	
24		23		22		21		20		19	
28		27		26		25		29		30	
35		36		34		32		31		33	
40		37		41		38		42		39	
44		43		46		45		47		48	
53		52		54		50		49		51	
55		56		57		58		59		60	
TOTALS FOR EACH COLUMN:											
DR:		IN:		CH:		RE:		DI:		SU:	

Appendix G

Coaching Contract Example

Here is an example of a contracting letter from one of us as used in in our coaching practice.

Dear XXX,

Further to our meeting on Monday 31 August XXX, I am delighted to confirm how I might support you as an executive coach.

Your request
From our conversation, I have taken two main objectives for our collaboration:

1. For you to become more confident and more trusting of your talents and those of your colleagues. You have described yourself as very driven, goal-oriented and a high achiever – and you would like to regain the trust you have experienced before, to match your obvious talents and abilities. You described the movement that you intend to make with help of the coaching as "moving from private restlessness to confident collaboration", and "from a sense of uncertainty to greater self-confidence".
2. For you to become more comfortable and assured within yourself, and as a result to enhance the balance and integration between your strengths and vulnerabilities, and between your intellectual abilities and emotions. If we achieve this objective, we both expect more openness and more fulfilment in your relationships with colleagues.

These are themes that can very well be addressed coherently in coaching. Generally, I would like to propose to use every session both to think through the broader objectives above and also to talk through some of your current challenges: I expect simple everyday challenges to throw light on these broader themes as well.

I also suggest we take time to review every session, and that already after the third session we take stock and see whether we are on track for achieving the two outcomes above. If that seems appropriate and opportune, I would suggest considering your CEO and/or HR Director to participate in that review, either through e-mail or by inviting them to the first hour of a coaching session.

My approach to Executive Coaching

Executive Coaching is increasingly seen as a significant way of contributing to an organisation's change and management development agenda. In particular it is one of the key approaches through which leadership within complex organisations and networks can be developed.

By coaching I mean that the executive and the coach develop a relationship that encourages:

- Increasing awareness
- Reflecting on alternatives
- Finding new perspectives
- Reviewing outcomes and learning

I combine business and behavioural expertise although I rarely offer instant, readymade solutions. My approach to coaching is mainly 'person-centred' and 'psychoanalytic', which is jargon for keeping your own perspectives and evaluations central and striving for new insight by exploring what is going on, both in the 'material' you offer and in the conversation itself as it unfolds.

With this letter you receive my Coaching Bio-note for more background. You also receive our Ashridge Code of Conduct.

The coaching environment

In my experience coaching meetings are best held away from interruptions, telephone calls and the general day to day pressures. I suggest holding our next conversation(s) in peaceful Ashridge Business School, in the Ashridge Strategic Management Centre on Kingsway 71, Holborn, Central London, or in a neutral (rented) room in XXX

It would be good to set-up a series of five or six conversations to reach the objectives. I would also propose to start with a frequency of once every three or four weeks, and to take the last conversations at least a month apart. We have our first sessions booked:

- XXX
- XXX

I would like to ask you not to change session times close to the date, as it is common to charge for a session if it is cancelled within two weeks – see also our terms and conditions.

Information and confidentiality
I believe in maintaining strict client confidentiality in the coaching process. This client work or your organisation will not be mentioned in any referrals or publications. I only mention the organisations that I work for in a very general way, without touching on specific assignments, divisions, or clients.

Evaluation of outcomes and learning
My evaluation process usually involves an informal review at the end of each coaching conversation. Secondly, there will be a 'mid-term' review after 3 sessions, where we will discuss if the coaching is making a real difference on the stated objectives, and re-formulate longer-term outcomes and learning. Thirdly, at the end of the coaching journey there will be a questionnaire-based review and possibly a follow-up telephone conversation a few months after the last coaching meeting.

Terms and conditions
On the basis of my standard daily fee of £..., I expect to charge £ ... (¼ day) per session (including travel and preparation time), excluding VAT but including travel costs and other expenses. For the initial 5 coaching conversations the expected cost would be £ .... Invoicing will take place on a monthly basis.

Other terms and conditions can be found in the attachment to this letter.

If you agree with this proposal I would like to receive one signed copy for our administration.

If you have any questions please do not hesitate to contact me, my direct line number is ....

Yours sincerely,

Erik De Haan
Director
The Ashridge Centre for Coaching

Appendix H

A consultant in development

A coaching case history

The coachee is a 45-year-old woman. She married young, had children and then emigrated with her family. After a few years she looked for a job back in the Netherlands. Over time she has evolved from secretary to internal consultant for a large company. She has been in that line for a number of years now but for a while has been feeling a need for further development. She is keen to develop more self-confidence as a consultant and to have a greater impact on her clients, especially now that a challenging new task has been added to her duties. She cites these aims as her coaching objectives.

In our first session, I get the impression she is finding it a bit tense. She seems to have a need to make a 'good impression' on me, as if she is keen to be a good coachee. I take note of this: it might be a sign that this coachee sets high standards for herself, and possibly for others. I listen carefully and reflect back what I am hearing and feeling. Underneath, I sense a lot of tension and even anger. And I can see that from her face. She says she wants to be appreciated by her manager, but he doesn't show her any appreciation. She has high expectations of managers in general, and there are only a few within the company who meet her (exacting) standards and requirements. She is stern with herself as well: she seems to be avoiding her new set of responsibilities because she is afraid of failure. She looks tired. Next time, I resolve to run through a questionnaire with her to gauge the risk of burn-out.

In our second session, a few weeks after the first, I examine the risk of an imminent burn-out more closely and go through a questionnaire with her. Based on the results, I recommend taking a number of precautions. We also study her fear of making mistakes in more depth, and explore what would make it easier for her to carry out her new responsibilities. I listen as she recounts a distressing event in her personal life that she prefers not to share with colleagues. Sharing it with me brings her visible relief. At the same time, the fact of not discussing subjects like these with colleagues gives them the impression she is closed off and aloof. In a team session with an outside team coach, she was put under pressure to be more open about things that bother her. She didn't do so but stuck to her intention of keeping work and private life separate in this respect. She is proud to have guarded her personal boundaries. I offer her a piece of provocative advice concerning her perfectionism: to say 'absurd' things as much as possible in meetings, but still to stay sensitive as regards the process and other people's feelings. There is nothing wrong with her factual knowledge but, according to the coachee, there is room for development in terms of process. So I wonder if she is sometimes a perfectionist in this area too.

In the third session, we focus on her difficult relationship with a particular colleague. We examine the coachee's qualities, and the traps she tends to fall into, in relation to those of her colleague. The coachee discovers that perhaps she *can* learn a lot from her colleague's assertiveness, and the way in which he presents himself. We practise ways in which she might give her colleague effective feedback at times when she is disturbed by his behaviour. And how she can express its effect on her, how she feels about it. Then we look at the possible causes of her perfectionism, including the influence that her parents and upbringing had on her behaviour and presuppositions. I advise her to be a little gentler on herself.

In our fourth session she is very distressed. She is starting to realise that she sets high standards for herself, that she doesn't feel good enough and that she lets herself be easily dissuaded by criticism. She wants to like herself more. She is getting closer to her feelings, which is something she wants, and now plans to start communicating more about the way she feels. She resolves to start practising this with various people. We investigate the option of additional body-oriented therapy. The coachee has found her own form of therapy and practises it to become more aware of the signals from her body. I suggest that, next time, we evaluate how this and the coaching are progressing.

So, in our fifth session, we talk about the benefits of the coaching to this point. The coachee says that the coaching has helped her well so far. She comes across as more relaxed and self-assured. This strikes me as a good time to encourage her to take specific action, so that she can get over a number of barriers. So I opt for a more directive coaching style, rather than the counselling style I have mainly used until now. And I ask the coachee what specific benefits the coaching has brought up to this point. First of all, the coachee says she feels safe enough with me to be open about her feelings in the coaching. She is pleased about that, but finds it difficult to be more open outside the coaching context. So I challenge her, over the coming weeks, to initiate some conversations with people she knows in which she gives away more about herself than she usually does. Second, in this session the coachee says that she now adopts a more forceful stance in work situations. I challenge her to show more of that over the coming weeks. Third, the coachee says that the organisation can still paralyse her so that she finds it difficult to take on responsibilities. My advice, first and foremost, is to get behind the wheel anyway and so I invite her, over the coming weeks, to experiment with a number of specific initiatives that give her energy. We think through together how to tackle the initiatives. The last topic she broaches concerns the times when things don't go so well, when perfectionism and fear of failure gain the upper hand. We review the things that give her energy at times like these: music and sport help more than ideas and analysis, she says.

In this session I notice that a number of insights are becoming clearer, her self-confidence has increased and she is prepared to take new steps towards the learning objectives that were set previously, such as experimenting with new, specific behaviour that may make it easier to continue on her chosen course. The coaching objectives seem to be shifting slightly from self-confidence and impact towards openness in dealings with other people.

In the sixth session, the coachee brings up a number of times when she experimented specifically with new behaviour. She is unhappy about some confrontations she has had with colleagues, and doubts the effectiveness of her actions. She wants to work more on showing openness, both about her own feelings and about what she perceives in others. At the same time, she realises that her perfectionism might be an obstacle in the coaching as well. Then we move on to what she wants to achieve with her work. For some time now, she has wanted a more strategic assignment but is constantly distracted by other activities. She suspects that she is avoiding it, that she is allowing her 'perfectionism' to obstruct her. She resolves to draw up a specific project plan for our next session. However, after a while the coachee rings me to say that practising different behaviour has to take priority. She wants to take up the option of practising this with an actor during a coaching session.

During the seventh session, an actor is present. The coachee has identified certain situations she wants to practise: she wants to express her own feelings more, to be able to parry a colleague's dominance, to deal with someone else's anger without reacting to its content, and to maintain her bearing when the quality of her work is criticised. For the most part, we practise expressing what the coachee feels; this is often clear to see but she finds it difficult to put it into words. When she finally does say it, she comes across very naturally. She finds the session very enlightening. We don't schedule another meeting: the coachee says she will contact me later to arrange another session.

I don't hear from the coachee for two months and decide to send an e-mail to ask how things are going. The coachee was always very regular about making appointments and I am curious to know why I haven't heard anything for so long. I am also slightly concerned that the previous session may not have been rounded off properly, but I realise that this concern may be my identification with her fear of failure, that is, it may be that her perfectionism has stirred up my own. Or perhaps she wants to avoid any follow-up sessions? Out of concern for the coachee, I consider it important to check this. So, contrary to my usual practice, I initiate contact myself. The coachee e-mails back a week later:

> 'Things are fine with me. Though it's a pretty turbulent time. Despite all the changes going on in the organisation, I am managing (in spite of long days) to take pleasure in my work, to feel appreciated and to be optimistic about the future. I also have my not-so-good times of course, but in general things are going well. Unlike some colleagues who are finding everything difficult, lack motivation and in some cases are unable to work. On the one hand, this means that I try to help them where possible and feel a bit guilty sometimes. On the other hand, I have decided not to let myself be drawn into negativity, to do what I can do and want to do, and try to help influence the processes that are intended to lead to new clarity and direction. However, I am not responsible for their future and can only have a limited influence on it, so I don't need to feel guilty. But still, it's not always that easy.

As for the last coaching session, I found it quite exceptionally useful. I still think about it a lot. Especially in difficult situations with my team. I notice that I am managing to show more openness about my own feelings. Even in management teams and discussions with managers, I am able now and again to show more courage and to give people honest feedback, and to express my feelings and opinions. It's not always easy, but I'm doing it.

As part of our organisational development I have taken a role on the "change management team". As example, I have to work out new organisational principles. It's a good job, I enjoy doing it and people listen to me. Secretly, of course, I do sometimes think "who am I to do this, and to be allowed to do this?" But that usually passes quickly. Thank goodness!

Regarding our future coaching sessions, I thought I would come and see you again once my set of duties and responsibilities is clear. We expect to work that out more in the coming months. Then there is also a new director who will be taking charge. As soon as we have an idea of that, I will be glad to spar with you about what it means for me. What do think?

Thank you for showing an interest. See you soon.'

I reply as follows:

I am pleased to hear that things are fine with you despite these busy times. That you know what comes from you and what comes from others, and are able to show your feelings more (and bring other people's feelings into consideration as well?). I also understand that you now have the courage to take on an influential job, and I'm very pleased about that: it's exactly what you wanted, so that's great!

I look forward to discussing your new role with you when things are clearer. Just let me know when would be good for you, nearer the time.

I think it's terrific that you have already achieved so much. You can give yourself a big pat on the back: you have clearly made progress on all your learning objectives. Fantastic!

> But take care that you don't get tempted to get stressed again. Or in any case try to maintain your energy levels outside of and during your work, so you can keep going. But you had probably already thought of that yourself.
>
> Kind regards and best wishes.'

'Two months later, I have still heard nothing and it seems that the coaching sessions have come to a natural end. I suspect the coachee doesn't have so much need to talk any more, for whatever reason. It might be that her progress in the area of open communication is helping the coachee to achieve her pre-defined learning objectives: to develop more self-confidence and impact. Or again, it might be that she has other reasons for not wanting to come any more. I contact the coachee on my own initiative again, to check whether my suspicions are correct and in any case to invite her to a final meeting. 'Goodbye sessions' are often avoided in coaching – especially if saying goodbye is a difficult theme – but I have noticed that it is important to mark the completion of a series of sessions in a formal manner. The coachee says she would like two more sessions: one when her set of responsibilities in her new (senior) position is clearer, and one in order to say goodbye.

In our eighth session, which takes place around two months later, the coachee relates how difficult she finds it to let go of old patterns, especially where it is a question of being 'strict' with herself and with others. The coachee still finds it hard to make mistakes and to take a position independent of others, but she now notices this sooner and experiments more often with different behaviour, namely being more proactive, setting boundaries and standing up for herself. She tries to allow more of her feelings and to make them a subject of conversation. We observe that a 'relapse' is sometimes part of learning.

In the ninth and final session, we say our goodbyes. Based on a reflective report from the coachee, we discuss fear and anxieties in her organisation and look back at her coaching issues:

1. First, her perfectionism and fear of making mistakes, linked with a strictness towards herself and others, and her need to be more gentle.
2. Second, the difficulty she has with observing and discussing her own feelings and those of others, and her need to be more open.

3. Third, her desire to swing into action, to be proactive, without allowing herself to be impeded by the first two points for development.

The coachee says that she has gained a good understanding of her issues and that this was necessary in order to progress to action. She won't be dissuaded again in future, however difficult it may still be at times. That is part of her learning. Looking back over the series of coaching sessions, she says that the counselling approach in the first few sessions was necessary in order to promote insights in a safe setting. The directive approach in later sessions was useful in progressing to action, especially the practice session with the actor. And the confrontational session at the end, with the coach's 'chasing up' the coachee contrary to her usual practice, was helpful in moving from 'avoidance' to 'action'. Both partners look back at a series of sessions in which the coachee's self-confidence has grown, she knows what contribution she wants to make in her organisation and she claims her own place more, in order to actually deliver that contribution.

Some time later, I ask the coachee if I can describe her coaching sessions for the second edition of this book. I see it as an example of an integrative approach because, over the series of sessions, I moved consciously from a predominantly counselling style towards more provocative, directive and confronting interventions. I also ask her to write a reflective account of the sessions from her own perspective. That account is reproduced below.

The coachee's reflections on the coaching sessions
'As a consultant within a large organisation, I am familiar with coaching and regularly talk to colleagues who have an external coach. I'd been having a bad time for a while, partly influenced by upheaval in the organisation, and I knew it would be desirable and sensible to do something about it. So I decided to request a coach myself. I had given it reasoned and sensible consideration but I still found the first session quite radical. I was aware that complete openness on my part is necessary for success. But it is still pretty scary. In that initial stage, the coach created an atmosphere of acceptance and trust for me, so that giving openness, to the coach and to myself, came entirely naturally. This helped me to settle down and to rebuild my self-confidence. The result was space to think about how to proceed.

One of the traps I fall into seems to be "avoiding" awkward and difficult situations. By continuing to work hard, sorting out the daily routine in great detail, I avoid the things I would actually like to do and achieve. And that I am sure I am capable of.

We talked about this in the coaching, and that helped me to understand and accept it and then to think about how to break the pattern. There was a lot of focus on 'it's ok to make mistakes' and a more light-hearted approach to mistakes. A session with an actor to practise expressing feelings (my own and other people's) and bringing them up for discussion was hugely beneficial. It was a difficult exercise, but there was a feeling of relief when it finally 'worked'.

Now that I'm doing much better (and a measure of peace has returned to the organisation), I am keen to take further steps in my development and ambitions. But it seems that my old behaviour (burying myself in work) is sometimes still a pretext for avoiding 'difficult' situations. I was confronted with this various times during the coaching. Confrontations like these are painful at first, but with the coach's help the insights then come to the surface. That gives one the courage and energy to really convert one's plans into action. That's where the challenge lies for me now.

I can look back at a valuable relationship with a sincere coach who clearly understood at the various times what I needed in order to progress. I am glad to have had this experience."

This case study is reproduced with permission from the coachee.

Appendix I

Experiences of telephone coaching

With modern organisations stretching out more and more across the globe and making increasing use of internationally dispersed, 'virtual' teams, executive coaching has also gone increasingly *virtual*. This development has been facilitated by the growing reliability and versatility of digital telecommunications. There are various applications of 'virtual coaching', such as telephone, videophone and Skype, as well as E-coaching through email and other internet platforms.

We believe the simplest one of these, telephone coaching, holds the most promise. Telephone coaching retains the conversational aspects of coaching almost in full, whilst the loss of other perceptual channels, such as visual and kinaesthetic, is mostly experienced as freedom from distraction. Although this is initially counterintuitive for most coaches and clients, telephone coaching works as well as face-to-face coaching. In fact, many experienced coaches will tell you that in many ways it works *better* than face-to-face coaching.

So even though it is said that you might miss most of the proverbial 93% of communication that is non-verbal (remember Mehrabian, 1972), telephone coaching feels realistic and has an impact entirely compatible with face-to-face coaching, from the perspective of the coach as well as from that of the client.

Only during moments of sudden (strong) emotion a 'telephone coach' may not pick up the usual signals of for example a cynical smile or a tear welling up in the corner of the eye. The rest of the time you will, surprisingly, pick up as much – or as little as – you normally will in your coaching conversations.

Interestingly, telephone coaching harks back all the way to the very beginnings of helping conversations. It dates back to an early time, to when the telephone had barely been invented and had not come into mass use. The model Breuer and Freud developed in the 1880s (see Chapter 8) as they gradually moved away from hypnosis, introduced a very similar situation to telephone conversations. This format, with the patient lying on the couch not being able to see the psychoanalyst, has been preserved to the present day. Both client and psychoanalyst respond almost exclusively to information conveyed by the voice of the other person. Freud already remarked that for that reason they are freer to work and make associations, as they are less busy responding to or controlling their facial expressions. On the couch and the phone etiquette becomes less important and free expression reigns, together with focused and unhampered listening.

Similarly, we would argue that telephone coaching is more *inclusive* than face-to-face coaching, because size, shape, race, colour and dress differences between coach and client are less conspicuous, or even unknown. Coach and client become more equal in the relationship, and power differentials diminish. Moreover, it is well known that our capacity to recognise voices or infer physical characteristics from tone, pitch and pace of speaking is rather limited – so much of those are missed whilst the emotional content and message is preserved.

Another advantage of telephone coaching is that you as a coach will feel freer to make copious notes or a personal log during the session. By contrast you and your clients will always retain that slight feeling of 'being watched' when making notes during a face-to-face session.

Some argue that it is better for coach and client to have a few live sessions before they start their telephone coaching relationship. This certainly makes it easier and more comfortable to settle into the telephone relationship. Without having met your phone coaching client you will have questions and sometimes wild phantasies about how they look and who they are. In our experience such a 'proper meeting' is not actually necessary for telephone coaching to be effective. Even those (visual) associations we have with a client we have never met in the flesh can actually be used to further our understanding of the material of that client.

A few *rules of engagement* of telephone coaching, which we try to agree with telephone-coaching clients in advance:

1. Make sure you and your client will be undisturbed and alone in your respective study or office space,

2. Switch off all other telecommunications equipment during the
    sessions,
3. Ideally, make sure your desk is clean and you have only a white
    sheet of paper and a pen in front of you.

We hope with this you will delight in the joys of freer association by
phone coaching, as we do as well.

Bibliography

Allen, T.D., Eby, L.T., Poteet, M.L., Lentz, E. and Lima, L. (2004). Career benefits associated with mentoring for protégés: a meta-analysis. *Journal of Applied Psychology* 89, pp. 127–36.

Appiah, K.A. (2008). *Experiments in Ethics.* Cambridge (MA): Harvard University Press.

Argyris, C. (1990). *Overcoming Organizational Defenses: Facilitating Organizational Learning.* Englewood Cliffs, N.J.: Prentice-Hall.

Armstrong, D. (1997). The 'institution in the mind': reflections on the relation of psycho-analysis to work with institutions. *Free Associations* 7.41, pp. 1–14.

Arthur, M.B. (1994). The boundaryless career: a new perspective for organizational inquiry. *Journal of Organizational Behaviour* 15.4, pp. 295–306.

Baron, L. and Morin, L. (2009). The coach-coachee relationship in executive coaching: a field study. *Human Resource Development Quarterly* 20.1, pp. 85–106.

Baron, L. and Morin, L. (2012). The working alliance in executive coaching: its impact on outcomes and how coaches can influence it. In: *Coaching Relationships* (edited by E. de Haan and C. Sills), pp. 213–26. Libri: U.K.

Beutler, L.E., Crago, M. and Arizmendi, T.G. (1986). Therapist variables in psychotherapy process and outcome. In: *Handbook of Psychotherapy and Behavior Change*, 3rd edition (edited by S.L. Garfield and A.E. Bergin), pp. 257–310. New York: Wiley.

Beutler, L.E., Machado, P.P. and Allstetter Neufeldt, S. (1994). Therapist variables. In: *Handbook of Psychotherapy and Behavior Change*, 4th edition (edited by S.L. Garfield and A.E. Bergin), pp. 229–69. New York: Wiley.

Bion, W.F. (1959). Attacks on linking. *International Journal of Psycho-Analysis* 40 (5–6), p. 308.

Bion, W.R. (1961). *Experiences in Groups.* London: Tavistock.
Bion, W.R. (1962). *Learning from Experience.* London: William Heinemann.
Bion, W.R. (1963). *Elements of Psychoanalysis.* London: William Heinemann.
Bion, W.R. (1965). *Transformations.* London: William Heinemann.
Bion, W.R. (1970). *Attention and Interpretation.* London: Tavistock.
Bordin, H. (1979). The generalizability of the psychoanalytic concept of the working alliance. *Psychotherapy: Theory, Research and Practice* 16, pp. 252–60.
Bowles, S.V., Cunningham, C.J.L., De La Rosa, G.M. and Picano, J.J. (2007). Coaching leaders in middle and executive management: goals, performance, buy-in. *Leadership and Organization Development Journal* 28.5, pp. 388–408.
Boyce, L.A., Jackson, R.J. and Neal, L.J. (2010). Building successful leadership coaching relationships: examining impact of matching criteria in a leadership coaching program. *Journal of Management Development* [Special Issue on Coaching and the Relationship] 29.10, pp. 914–31.
Breuer, J. and Freud, S. (1895). *Studien über Hysterie.* Leipzig/Vienna: Verlag Franz Deuticke. Translated as *Studies on Hysteria* by James Strachey in collaboration with Anna Freud in *The Standard Edition of the Complete Psychological Works of Sigmund Freud,* Volume II.
Brown, D. and Pedder, J. (1979). *Introduction to Psychotherapy.* London: Tavistock.
Carroll, M. and Shaw, E. (2012). *Ethical Maturity in the Helping Professions.* Victoria (Australia): Psychoz.
Clutterbuck, D. (1965). *Everyone Needs a Mentor: Fostering Talent in Your Organisation.* London: IPM
Cooper, M. (2008). *Essential Research Findings in Counselling and Psychotherapy – the Facts Are Friendly.* London: Sage.
Cooperrider, D.L. and Srivastva, S. (1987). Appreciative inquiry in organizational life. In: *Research in Organizational Change and Development, Volume* 1 (edited by W.A. Pasmore and R.W. Woodman), pp. 129–69. Greenwich, Conn.: JAI Press.
Cooperrider, D.L. and Whitney, D.L. (2002). *Appreciative Inquiry: The Handbook.* Euclid, Ohio: Lakeshore.
Corsini, R.J. and Wedding, D. (1989). *Current Psychotherapies.* Ithasca, Ill.: Peacock.

Czander, W.M. (1993). *The Psychodynamics of Work and Organizations*. New York: Guilford Press.

De Board, R. (1978). *The Psychoanalysis of Organizations*. London: Routledge.

de Haan, E. (1994). *Contributions to Vision Research*. University of Utrecht, Ph.D. thesis.

de Haan, E. (1999). Weldadig spreken met dubbele tong: ironie als techniek van de helpende buitenstaander bij veranderingen [Speaking helpfully with a 'double tongue': irony as a technique of the helping outsider in change]. *Filosofie in Bedrijf* 34, pp. 54–64.

de Haan, E. (2004). *Learning with Colleagues: An Action Guide for Peer Consultation*. Basingstoke, UK: Palgrave Macmillan.

de Haan, E. (2008). *Relational Coaching – Journeys towards Mastering One-to-one Learning*. Chichester: Wiley.

de Haan, E., Culpin, V. and Curd, J., (2011). Executive coaching in practice: what determines helpfulness for clients of coaching? *Personnel Review* 40.1, pp. 24–44.

de Haan, E. and Duckworth, A. (2013). Signaling a new trend in coaching outcome research. *International Coaching Psychology Review* 8.1, pp. 6–20.

de Haan, E., Duckworth, A., Birch, D. and Jones, C. (2013). Executive coaching outcome research: the predictive value of common factors such as relationship, personality match and self-efficacy. *Consulting Psychology Journal: Practice and Research* 65.1, pp. 40–57.

De Jong, P. and Berg, I.K. (2001). *Interviewing for Solutions*. Florence, Ky.: Wadsworth.

De Shazer, S. (1985). *Keys to Solution in Brief Therapy*. New York: Norton.

Digman, J.M. (1990). Personality structure: emergence of the five factor model. *Annual Review of Psychology* 41, pp. 417–40.

Downey, M. (1999). *Effective Coaching*. New York: Thomson Texere.

Dumont, F. (1991). Expertise in psychotherapy: inherent liabilities of becoming experienced. *Psychotherapy* 28, pp. 422–8.

Eby, L.T., Allen, T.D., Evans, S.C., Ng, T. and DuBois, D.L. (2008). Does mentoring matter? A multidisciplinary meta-analysis comparing mentored and non-mentored individuals. *Journal of Vocation Behavior* 72, pp. 254–67.

Ellinger, A.D., Ellinger, A.E., Keller, S.B. (2003). Supervisory coaching behavior, employee satisfaction, and warehouse employee performance: a dyadic perspective in the distribution industry. *Human Resource Development Quarterly* 14.4, pp. 435–58.

Erickson, M.H. (1959). Further clinical techniques of hypnosis: utilization techniques. *American Journal of Clinical Hypnosis* 2, pp. 3–21.

Evers, W.J.G., Brouwers, A. and Tomic, W. (2006). A quasi-experimental study on management coaching effectiveness. *Consulting Psychology Journal: Practice and Research* 58, pp. 174–82.

Farrelly, F. and Brandsma, J. (1974). *Provocative Therapy*. Cupertino, Calif.: Meta.

Freud, A. (1936). *Das Ich und die Abwehrmechanismen*. Vienna: Internationaler Psychoanalytischer Verlag. Translated as *The Ego and the Mechanisms of Defence* by Cecil Baines. London: Hogarth.

Freud, S. (1894). Die Abwehr-Neuropsychosen. *Neurologisches Zentralblatt* 10 and 11. Translated as *The Neuro-Psychoses of Defence* by James Strachey in collaboration with Anna Freud in *The Standard Edition of the Complete Psychological Works of Sigmund Freud*, Volume III, pp. 45–61.

Freud, S. (1896). Weitere Bemerkungen über die Abwehr-Neuropsychosen. *Neurologisches Zentralblatt* 10. Translated as *Further Remarks on the Neuro-Psychoses of Defence* by James Strachey in collaboration with Anna Freud in *The Standard Edition of the Complete Psychological Works of Sigmund Freud*, Volume III, pp. 163–88.

Freud, S. (1900). *Die Traumdeutung*. Vienna: Verlag Franz Deuticke. Translated as *The Interpretation of Dreams* by James Strachey in collaboration with Anna Freud in *The Standard Edition of the Complete Psychological Works of Sigmund Freud*, Volumes IV and V.

Freud, S. (1904/1924). *Zur psychopathologie des Alltagslebens: 10. weiter vermehrte Auflage* (1924). Vienna: Internationale Psychoanalytische Verlag. Translated as *The Psychopathology of Everyday Life* by James Strachey in collaboration with Anna Freud in *The Standard Edition of the Complete Psychological Works of Sigmund Freud*, Volume VI.

Freud, S. (1905). *Der Witz und seine Beziehung zum Unbewußten*. Vienna: Verlag Franz Deuticke. Translated as *Jokes and Their Relation to the Unconscious* by James Strachey in collaboration with Anna Freud in *The Standard Edition of the Complete Psychological Works of Sigmund Freud*, Volume VIII.

Freud, S. (1912a). Die Handhabung der Traumdeutung in der Psychoanalyse. In: *Zentralblatt für Psychoanalyse*, Volume II. Translated as *The Handling of Dream-Interpretation in Psycho-Analysis* by James Strachey in collaboration with Anna Freud in *The Standard Edition of the Complete Psychological Works of Sigmund Freud*, Volume XII, pp. 89–96.

Freud, S. (1912b). Zur Dynamik der Übertragung. *Zentralblatt für Psychoanalyse*, Volume II. Translated as *The Dynamics of Transference* by James Strachey in collaboration with Anna Freud in *The Standard Edition of the Complete Psychological Works of Sigmund Freud*, Volume XII, pp. 97–108.

Freud, S. (1912c). Ratschläge für den Arzt bei der Psychoanalytischen Behandlung. *Zentralblatt für Psychoanalyse*, Volume II. Translated as *Recommendations to Physicians Practising Psycho-Analysis* by James Strachey in collaboration with Anna Freud in *The Standard Edition of the Complete Psychological Works of Sigmund Freud* , Volume XII, pp. 109–20.

Freud, S. (1913). Zur Einleitung der Behandlung. *Internationale Zeitschrift für ärztliche Psychoanalyse*, Volume I. Translated as *On Beginning the Treatment* by James Strachey in collaboration with Anna Freud in *The Standard Edition of the Complete Psychological Works of Sigmund Freud*, Volume XII, pp. 121–44.

Freud, S. (1914a). Erinnern, Wiederholen und Durcharbeiten. *Zeitschrift für Psychoanalyse*, Volume II. Translated as *Remembering, Repeating and Working Through* by James Strachey in collaboration with Anna Freud in *The Standard Edition of the Complete Psychological Works of Sigmund Freud*, Volume XII, pp. 145–56.

Freud, S. (1914b). Der Moses des Michelangelo. *Imago*, Vol. III. Translated as *The Moses of Michelangelo* by James Strachey in collaboration with Anna Freud in *The Standard Edition of the Complete Psychological Works of Sigmund Freud*, Volume III, pp. 43–61.

Freud, S. (1915). Bemerkungen über die Übertragungsliebe. *Zeitschrift für Psychoanalyse*, Vol. III. Translated as *Observations on Transference-Love* by James Strachey in collaboration with Anna Freud in *The Standard Edition of the Complete Psychological Works of Sigmund Freud*, Volume XIII, pp. 211–40.

Freud, S. (1923). *Das Ich und das Es*. Leipzig/Vienna/Zürich: Internationaler psychoanalytischer Verlag. Translated as *The Ego and the Id* by James Strachey in collaboration with Anna Freud in *The Standard Edition of the Complete Psychological Works of Sigmund Freud*, Volume XIX, pp. 12–68.

Freud, S. (1925). Die Verneinung. *Imago*, Volume XI. Translated as *Negation* by James Strachey in collaboration with Anna Freud in *The Standard Edition of the Complete Psychological Works of Sigmund Freud*, Volume XIX, pp. 235–42.

Freud, S. (1926). *Hemmung, Symptom und Angst*. Leipzig/Vienna/Zürich: Psychoanalytischer Verlag. Translated as *Inhibitions, Symptoms and Anxiety* by James Strachey in collaboration with Anna Freud in *The Standard Edition of the Complete Psychological Works of Sigmund Freud*, Volume XX, pp. 87–178.

Freud, S. (1928). Der Humor. *Imago*, Volume XIV. Translated as *Humour* by James Strachey in collaboration with Anna Freud in *The Standard Edition of the Complete Psychological Works of Sigmund Freud*, Volume XXI, pp. 159–66.

Frisch, M.H. (2001). The emerging role of the internal coach. *Consulting Psychology Journal: practice and research* 53.4, pp. 240–50.

Gallwey, T. (1974). *The Inner Game of Tennis*. London: Jonathan Cape.

Gergen, K.J. (1999). *An Invitation to Social Construction*. London: Sage.

Goldfried, M.R., Greenberg, L.S. and Marmar, C. (1990). Individual psychotherapy: process and outcome. *Annual Review of Psychology* 41, pp. 659–88.

Grant, A.M. and Cavanagh, M.J. (2007). The goal-focused coaching skills questionnaire: preliminary findings. *Social Behaviour and Personality* 35.6, pp. 751–60.

Grencavage, L.M. and Norcross, J.C. (1990). Where are the commonalities among the therapeutic common factors? *Professional Psychology: Research and Practice* 21, pp. 372–378.

Haley, J. (1963). *Strategies of Psychotherapy*. New York: Grune and Stratton.

Horvath, A.O. and Greenberg, L. (1986). The development of the working alliance inventory: a research handbook. In: *Psychotherapeutic Processes: A Research Handbook (edited by L. Greenberg and W. Pinsoff)*. New York: Guilford Press.

Hawkins, P. and Shohet, R. (2000). *Supervision in the Helping Professions – an Individual, Group and Organizational Approach*. Buckingham: Open University Press.

Hawton, K., Salkovskis, P.M., Kirk, J. and Clark, D.M. (1989). *Cognitive Behaviour Therapy for Psychiatric Problems: A Practical Guide*. Oxford: Oxford University Press.

Heimann, P. (1950). On counter-transference. *International Journal of Psychoanalysis* 31, pp. 81–4.

Heron, J. (1975). *Helping the Client*. London: Sage.

Homer (8th century BC). *The Odyssey*. Translated by E.V. Rieu. London: Penguin Classics (1946).

Ianiro, P.M., Schermuly, C.C. and Kauffeld, S. (2012). Why interpersonal dominance and affiliation matter: an interaction analysis of the coach-client relationship. *Coaching: An International Journal of Theory, Research and Practice* 6.1, pp. 1–22.

Kampa-Kokesch, S. and Anderson, M.Z. (2001). Executive coaching: a comprehensive review of the literature. *Consulting Psychology Journal: Practice and Research* 53.4, pp. 205–28.

Kanter, R.M. (1989). Careers and the wealth of nations: a macro-perspective on the structure and implications of career forms. In: *Handbook of Career Theory* (edited by M.B. Arthur, D. Hall and B. Lawrence), pp. 506–21. New York: Cambridge University Press.

Klein, M. (1946) Notes on some schizoid mechanisms. *International Journal of Psychoanalysis* 27 pp. 99–109.

Kolb, D.A. (1984). *Experiential Learning: Experience as the Source of Learning and Development*. Englewood Cliffs, N.J.: Prentice-Hall.

Kombarakaran, F.A., Yang, J.A., Baker, M.N. and Fernandes, P.B. (2008). Executive coaching: it works! *Consulting Psychology Journal: Practice and Research* 60, pp. 78–90.

Lambert, M.J. (1989). The individual therapist's contribution to psycho-therapy process and outcome. *Clinical Psychology Review* 9, pp. 469–85.

Lambert, M.J. and Bergin, A.E. (1994). The effectiveness of psychotherapy. In: *Handbook of Psychotherapy and Behaviour Change*, 4th edition (edited by S.L. Garfield and A.E. Bergin), pp. 143–89. New York: Wiley.

Lapworth, P., Sills, C. and Fish, S. (2001). *Integration in Counselling and Psychotherapy: Developing a Personal Approach*. London: Sage.

Lear, J. (2003). *Therapeutic Action: An Earnest Plea for Irony*. London: Karnac.

Levenson, A. (2009). Measuring and maximizing the business impact of executive coaching. *Consulting Psychology Journal: Practice and Research* 61, pp. 103–121.

Luft, J. (1969). *Of Human Interaction*. Palo Alto, Calif.: Mayfield.

Malan, D.H. (1995). *Individual Psychotherapy and the Science of Psychodynamics*. London: Butterworth Heinemann.

Maslow, A.H. (1962). *Towards a Psychology of Being*. Princeton, N.J.: Van Nostrand.

McGovern, J., Lindemann, M., Vergara, M., Murphy, S., Barker, L. and Warrenfeltz, R. (2001). Maximizing the impact of executive coaching: behavioural change, organizational outcomes, and return on investment. *Manchester Review* 6.1, pp. 1–9.

McKenna, D.D. and Davis, S.L. (2009). Hidden in plain sight: the active ingredients of executive coaching. *Industrial and Organizational Psychology* 2, pp. 244–260.

McNeal, B.W., May, R.J. and Lee, V.E. (1987). Perceptions of counsellor source characteristics by premature and successful terminators. *Journal of Counselling Psychology* 34, pp. 86–9.

Mehrabian, A. (1972). *Nonverbal Communication*. Chicago: Aldine-Atherton.

Norcross, J.C. (ed.) (2011). *Psychotherapy Relationships That Work: Evidence-based Responsiveness*. New York: Oxford University Press.

Olivero, G., Bane, K.D. and Kopelman, R.E. (1997). Executive coaching as a transfer of training tool: effects on productivity in a public agency. *Public Personnel Management* 26.4, pp. 461–9.

Patterson, C.H. (1987). Comments. *Person-Centered Review* 1, pp. 246–8.

Peltier, B. (2001) *The Psychology of Executive Coaching: Theory and Application*. New York: Brunner and Routledge.

Perkins, R.D. (2009). How executive coaching can change leader behaviour and improve meeting effectiveness: an exploratory study. *Consulting Psychology Journal: Practice and Research* 61.4, pp. 298–318.

Peterson, D. B. (1993). *Measuring Change: A Psychometric Approach to Evaluating Individual Coaching Outcomes*. Presented at the annual conference of the Society for Industrial and Organizational Psychology, San Francisco.

Ragins, B.R., Cotton, J.L. and Miller, J.S. (2000). Marginal mentoring: the effects of type of mentor, quality of relationship, and program design on work and career attitudes. *Academy of Management Journal* 43.6, pp. 1177–94.

Raskin, N.J. (1952). An objective study of the locus-of-evaluation factor in psychotherapy. In: *Success in Psychotherapy* (edited by W. Wolff and J.A. Precker), pp. 143–62. New York: Grune and Stratton.

Reed, B.D. (2000). *An Exploration of Role.* London: Grubb Institute.

Rogers, C.R. (1957). The necessary and sufficient conditions of therapeutic personality change. *Journal of Consulting Psychology* 21, pp. 95–103.

Rogers, C.R. (1961). *On Becoming a Person: a therapist's view of psychotherapy.* London: Constable.

Rogers, C.R. (1970). *Carl Rogers on Encounter Groups.* New York: Harper and Row.

Rosenzweig, S. (1936). Some implicit common factors in diverse methods of psychotherapy: 'At last the Dodo said, "Everybody has won and all must have prizes."' *American Journal of Orthopsychiatry* 6, pp. 412–415.

Roth, A. and Fonagy, P. (1996). *What Works for Whom? A Critical Review of Psychotherapy Research.* London: Guildford.

Schlosser, B., Steinbrenner, D., Kumata, E. and Hunt, J. (2006). The coaching impact study: measuring the value of executive leader coaching. *The International Journal of Coaching in Organizations,* 3, pp. 8–24.

Schutz, W.C. (1958). *FIRO: A Three-Dimensional Theory of Interpersonal Behaviour.* New York: Rinehart.

Schulz von Thun, F. (1982). *Miteinander reden* [Talking together]. Reinbek bei Hamburg: Rowohlt.

Schwarzer, R., Mueller, J. and Greenglass, E. (1999). Assessment of perceived self-efficacy on the internet: data collection in cyberspace. *Anxiety, Stress and Coping* 12, pp. 145–61.

Scoular, A. and Linley, P.A. (2006). Coaching, goal-setting and personality type: what matters? *The Coaching Psychologist* 2, pp. 9–11.

Senge, P.M., Kleiner, A., Roberts, C., Ross, R.B. and Smith, B.J. (1994). *The Fifth Discipline Fieldbook: Strategies and Tools for Building a Learning Organization.* London: Nicholas Brealey.

Smith, M.L. and Glass, G.V. (1977). Meta-analysis of psychotherapy outcome studies. *American Psychologist* 32, pp. 752–760.

Smither, J.W., London, M., Flautt, R., Vargas, Y. and Kucine, I. (2003). Can working with an executive coach improve multisource feedback ratings over time? A quasi-experimental field study. *Personnel Psychology* 56, pp. 23–44.

Stewart, L.J., Palmer, S., Wilkin, H. and Kerrin, M. (2008). The influence of character: does personality impact coaching success? *International Journal of Evidence Based Coaching and Mentoring* 6.1, pp. 32–42.

Sue-Chan, C. and Latham, G.P. (2004). The relative effectiveness of external, peer and self-coaches. *Applied Psychology* 53.2, pp. 260–78.

Symington, N. (1986). *The Analytic Experience.* London: Free Association Books.

Thach, E. C. (2002). The impact of executive coaching and 360 feedback on leadership effectiveness. *Leadership and Organization Development Journal* 23, pp. 205–214.

Twijnstra, A. and Keuning, D. (1988). *Organisatieadvieswerk* [The practice of organisation consulting]. Leiden, the Netherlands: Stenfert Kroese.

Vaillant, G.E. (1992). *Ego Mechanisms of Defense: A Guide for Clinicians and Researchers.* Washington D.C.: American Psychiatric Press.

Wampold, B.E. (2001). *The Great Psychotherapy Debate: Models, Methods and Findings.* Mahwah, NJ: Lawrence Erlbaum Associates.

Wasylyshyn, K.M. (2003). Executive coaching: an outcome study. *Consulting Psychology Journal: Practice and Research* 55.2, pp. 94–106.

Wasylyshyn, K.M., Gronsky, B. and Haas, W. (2006). Tigers, stripes, and behavior change: Survey results of a commissioned coaching program. *Consulting Psychology Journal: Practice and Research* 58, pp. 65–81.

Watzlawick, P., Beavin, J. and Jackson, D.D. (1967). *Pragmatics of Human Communication.* New York: W.W. Norton.

Weick, K.E. (1995). *Sensemaking in Organizations.* London: Sage.

Whitmore, J. (1992). *Coaching for Performance: Growing People, Performance and Purpose.* London: Nicholas Brealey Publishing.

Yalom, I.D. (1992). *When Nietzsche Wept.* New York: HarperCollins.

Index

of coachee 32, 36, 120,
145, 180
Rogers, C. 55fn2, 77, 78ff82,
132, 160, 134
role behaviour 170, 175

S
self-actualisation 79
self-confidence 67, 77, 133,
136, 140
sensemaking 170
sensitivity 137, 139, 161, 167
splitting 92
super-ego 23
supervision 7f, 12, 132, 135,
137, 187
symptom 103, 174

T
telephone coaching 231ff
rules of engagement 232
transference 46, 87, 90,
137, 150

counter-transference 87f,
177fn3
positive 43
transparency 79, 82, 137
Trolleyology 192
trust 36, 128

U
unconditional positive
regard 84, 207
unconscious 23, 87, 97,
111, 173
utilisation technique 103, 107

V
valency 177
vulnerability 219

W
warmth 26, 78, 131, 147
Whitmore, J. 65, 112
working alliance 27, 38,
43, 128

Printed and bound in Great Britain by
CPI Group (UK) Ltd, Croydon, CR0 4YY